Headquartered

A Timeline of
The Monkees Solo Years

Michael A. Ventrella
and Mark Arnold

BearManor
Media

Orlando, Florida

For information, address:
BearManor Media
1317 Edgewater Dr. #110
Orlando, FL 32804
bearmanormedia.com

Cover artwork by Scott Shaw!
Layout by Michael A. Ventrella

Photos used by permission. Thanks to Gina Detate, Stephanie Fine and Fred Velez for some of the pictures.

Published in the USA by BearManor Media.

Library of Congress Cataloging-in-Publication Data
Ventrella, Michael A., and Mark Arnold
HEADQUARTERED: A Timeline of The Monkees Solo Years / by Michael A. Ventrella and Mark Arnold
Includes index.
ISBN 978-1-62933-534-6   Headquartered paperback
ISBN 978-1-62933-535-3   Headquartered hard cover

Dedicated to the memory of
Davy Jones and Peter Tork

Table of Contents

Foreword

by Peter Noone of Herman's Hermits

I missed *The Monkees* when they were on TV, but was fortunate to work with three of them outside of The Monkees.

Of course, Davy was a fellow Manchunian with a very similar background to my own, so we, as they say in Manchester, "We got on like a house on fire!"

Micky Dolenz is a brilliant man, and like everyone else in the world there is more to him than meets the eye. I am sure there will be more brilliant stuff from Micky.

I last saw Peter when he invited me onstage to sing a Monkees song at Westbury Music Fair in New York City, and nothing I saw or heard gave me a clue that he was unwell. A truly brilliant talent.

I don't know Mike Nesmith. I met him at *Top of the Pops* with The Beatles, and I know he is the one with the hat!

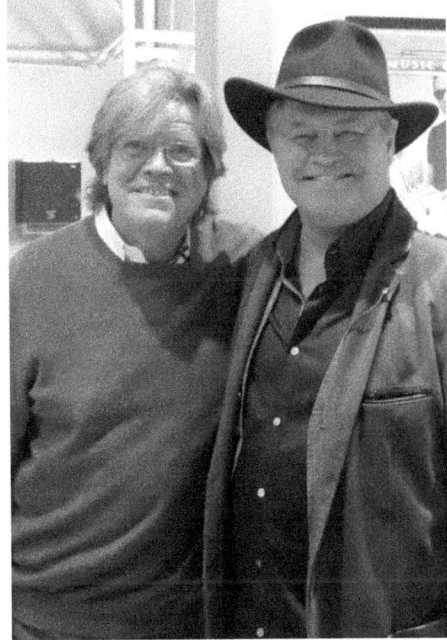

HEADQUARTERED: A TIMELINE OF THE MONKEES SOLO YEARS

Introduction

by Eddie Deezen, Actor and Fan

The Monkees were one of the strangest stories in both musical and television history.

The story's genesis was actually in July of 1964, when the Beatles first movie, *A Hard Day's Night* was released. The film's smash hit success inspired producers Bert Schneider and Bob Rafelson to cook up a very interesting idea for a new TV series.

The two had the idea of a musical group, sort of like The Beatles, long-haired—yes, but not successful, rich or famous like the Fab Four. The original idea was to cast either the Dave Clark Five or the Lovin' Spoonful as the series leads, but the concept was soon changed to assembling a cast of four unknowns. The fictional rock band, and their TV series, were to be called *The Monkees*.

The name "Monkees" was derived from a 1957 Elvis Presley movie called *Loving You*, a movie whose plot featured Elvis as a singer being exploited by an unscrupulous manager. In one overly dramatic scene in *Loving You*, Elvis confronts his manager and says, "That's what you want, isn't it? A monkey in a zoo!" (The double e's in "Monkees" was a semi-pun, like the "beat" in "Beatles.")

On September 8, 1965, open ads appeared in the two show biz bibles, *Daily Variety* and *The Hollywood Reporter*, seeking "folk and musicians-singers for acting roles in a new TV series." The ad stated that they were looking for "insane boys."

A total of 437 applicants answered the ad, including later-to-become-famous musicians Paul Williams, Stephen Stills, and Harry Nilsson. (There is no truth to the later urban legend that Charles Manson was one of the applicants, as Manson was incarcerated in federal prison at the time.) Four young men, two musicians and two actors, were finally chosen.

The first one cast was Davy Jones, a good-looking British actor, already under contract to Screen Gems. Jones, a former jockey, had recently been touring in the musical *Oliver!* and, by an amazing coincidence, had actually appeared on *The Ed Sullivan Show* on February 9, 1964, the night of the Beatles legendary appearance.

3

George Michael "Micky" Dolenz was an actor who had starred as a child in the TV show *Circus Boy* in the fifties. Micky was making the rounds at local auditions and had played guitar in a band called the Missing Links.

Robert Michael "Mike" Nesmith, having served briefly in the U.S. Air Force, was a musician/composer/singer who had made a handful of recordings under the alias "Michael Blessing." (Mike was the only member of the Monkees who actually saw the ad in the trades.)

Peter Tork, the last Monkee to be cast, was suggested for the audition by Stephen Stills, his roommate, and was currently a musician playing gigs in the Greenwich Village area.

The four young men took a six-week course in improvisational comedy (taught by director James Frawley) and it was soon discovered that all four displayed real humor, talent and chemistry in front of the camera. On the show, the four would be playing a rock band and, in an unprecedented move, would actually be recording songs, which would be released as records and albums. The songs would be premiered and promoted in videos that would be featured every week on the show.

The Monkees television series debuted on September 12, 1966, and was an immediate hit with the younger viewers.

Each Monkee, almost naturally, assumed his own character, paralleling the Beatles. Mike was the John Lennon of the group, their intellectual leader; Davy was the Paul McCartney heartthrob the little girls swooned over; Peter was Ringo Starr, dumb but lovable; the Micky-George Harrison match-up didn't quite mesh, as Micky was the group's resident joker and wackiest member, unlike George—the "quiet Beatle."

The show was funny, clever and original, especially for the times.

After season one, *The Monkees* TV series won two Emmys—one for Outstanding Comedy Series—at the 1967 Emmy Awards. As frosting on the cake, the boys' records and albums started racking up huge sales numbers.

Each Monkee was paid a near-stipend salary of $450.00 a week as actors (increased to $750.00 in the show's second season). It was the record and album royalties, plus composer's fees, that brought the boys their initial "real money," not, ironically, the show.

Monkee records, including "Last Train to Clarksville," "I'm a Believer," "(I'm Not Your) Stepping Stone," "Pleasant Valley Sunday," and others both charted and garnered huge sales figures. Incredibly, in a never-to-be-duplicated feat, four Monkees albums hit the number one spot on the Billboard Hot 100 charts in one year (1967).

A threat to the Monkees' amazing success came after season one, when Davy Jones became eligible for the U.S. military draft. Davy disappeared for three weeks and literally starved himself, dropping several pounds from his already small frame. His plan worked and Davy dodged the bullet of serving Uncle Sam.

But trouble was brewing and the Monkees' biggest controversy occurred when the news broke out that the Monkees did not play their own instruments. Sadly, this controversy was the first big chink in the armor of the Monkees' huge success, and to this day many fans and "real" rock bands still somewhat "look down" on the Monkees as "impostors" or "fakes."

As if to answer their accusers, the Monkees actually developed a live stage act and were to play over 200 live concerts together over the years, starting in December of 1966. In 1967, the Monkees toured the U.S. and the U.K.; in '68 they toured Australia and Japan. On the '67 tour, a young guitarist named Jimi Hendrix was actually booed off the stage, as a warm-up act for the Monkees, and left the tour in frustration after a handful of embarrassing gigs.

The show's 1967-68 second season had a few changes that were to prove both unpopular and unsuccessful, as they diverged too greatly from the magic formula of season one. A laugh track had been featured in season one and it was scrapped for season two.

Musical guests were featured at the end of the show's last three episodes. Mike chatted with Frank Zappa, Micky introduced Tim Buckley and Davy talked to Charlie Smalls about soul. (Peter had planned to bring on Janis Joplin to make an appearance, but the idea was never used.)

But worst of all, the Monkees themselves had changed—too quickly. Like the Beatles, success and fame changed the band, but the Beatles had changed slowly and gradually. By season two, the Monkees had already changed from their previous season of just a few months ago.

Micky Dolenz now sported a Harpo Marx-like afro haircut, switching from his Beatle-like coif. Mike had ditched his trademark wool hat. The boys seemed somewhat blasé, somehow world-weary.

Instead of the "safe" Monkee image that appealed to the young girls and teenyboppers, the Monkees tried to go more "psychedelic," more hip. The ratings soon plunged and after just 58 episodes, *The Monkees* was pulled from the NBC schedule.

The boys made a bizarre film called *Head*, with the help of then-little-known actor Jack Nicholson and filmed a TV special called *33 1/3 Revolutions Per Monkee*.

By December of 1968, Peter Tork bought out his four-year Monkee contract. Mike left the group in 1970. (The final gig for Mike, Micky and Davy was a Kool-Aid commercial.) Davy and Micky played gigs and made a few recordings as a twosome and in various incarnations with others, but the magic was gone.

Over the years, the four would periodically join up and tour and record together. But Mike Nesmith had pretty much moved on, having inherited millions from his mother, who invented a new product called Liquid Paper. Davy Jones died unexpectedly in 2012, and with his passing, the strange, incredible saga of Monkees officially ended.

Their legacy? Four #1 albums, three #1 records, 5 gold albums, and total record sales (reputedly) of over 65,000,000. Plus a cult film and a pretty funny and very enjoyable television series.

Not a bad legacy, I'd say.

Eddie Deezen

© 2014 *Eddie Deezen for Neatorama.*

Used with permission.

Call Me Crazy

by Jeffrey Morgan

"I hate to pop your balloon about 'Pleasant Valley Sunday.'
That song was actually written about a mental institution."

— Michael Nesmith, 1978

As parole hearings for the critically insane go, I imagine that it was a relatively short affair compared to other similar proceedings; at least mine always is, if only because the sheer repetition tends to speed things up. Every four years the same three member board of bluenoses sits me down opposite them on the same barely padded metal folding chair at the same severely scarred wooden table and the first bluenose asks me the same inane starting question: "Do you still persist in believing that The Monkees are the all-time greatest American rock 'n' roll band?"

I glance at my mouthpiece who gives me a surreptitious nod of support. This would be the same shyster who said "The plea is self-defense" at my arraignment. A lot she knew. Anyway, everyone in the room already knows what my rejoinder is going to be, so all I do is give them the lunatic leer that Nappy taught me. The same smirk I've been dishing out ever since this quadrennial charade began who knows how many decades ago.

Then the second bluenose pipes up with the next repetitive query: "Do you still persist in believing that The Monkees' *Head* is the all-time greatest American rock 'n' roll movie?"

Smirk.

Finally they get right down to the meat of the matter and slide a sheet of paper across the table to me. Judging from the curled edges and faded thermal printing, it's the same one they showed me four years ago. But since I always dig reading my own work, I look down and give it the once over.

The Monkees—*Pisces, Aquarius, Capricorn & Jones Ltd.* (RCA)... While the Beatles and Stones spent 1967 getting doped up and recording their hippy-dippy stoner albums *Lonely Hearts Club Band* and *Majesties*

7

Request, these hardcore radical Yankee outlaws were singing about drug pushers ("Salesman"); horny teenage sluts ("She Hangs Out"); a naïve girl getting brutally gangbanged by the Hells Angels ("Cuddly Toy"); promiscuous groupies on the prowl ("Star Collector"); and suburban surreal estate ("Pleasant Valley Sunday"). That's right, a Hells Angels gangbang. Who you gonna believe: me or your own ears?

If my arms weren't bound, I'd flip it back across the table as the third bluenose hits me with the trifecta: "Are those your words? Did you write that for CREEM: America's Only Rock 'n' Roll Magazine? Do you still persist in believing that The Monkees' *Pisces, Aquarius, Capricorn & Jones Ltd.* is the all-time greatest American rock 'n' roll album? Furthermore…"

"Never mind the furthermore," I interrupt as I nod for the turnkey to come and take me away back to my padded cell. "And stop wasting my time trying to get me to recant because there *isn't* a better American rock 'n' roll band, there *isn't* a better American rock 'n' roll movie, and there *isn't* a better American rock 'n' roll record. Nobody beats The Monkees at their own game because they *own* the game of American rock 'n' roll. Always have, always will."

It's at this point in the proceedings that two nice young men in their clean white coats hoist me up, cinch the straps tighter on my jacket, and start to hustle me out of the room, one on each side. But before they get me through the door I have just enough time to twist my head around. "You can investigate and you can obfuscate and you can obliterate. You can even call me crazy. Just don't call on me because all you got is zilch."

Halfway down the hall I can still hear the three bluenoses express bafflement at my belief. There might even be a slight tinge of doubt in their voices. I'm not worried. They'll come around. Eventually they all will. And then I'll be back upon my feet.

They throw me into the slammer and I roll up to my cellmate Nappy. Like me, Nappy's also a Monkee Man who understands. He's even writing a book about the solo recordings made by the four members of the all-time greatest American rock 'n' roll band. At least he manages to jot down a few words every time they unbuckle him so he can eat.

Nappy looks down at me and I know what's coming. It's an old routine of ours which is why he says the same thing to me every four years after my hearing. "You lose?"

"No," I say, looking up and giving him that lunatic leer. "I usually win."

JEFFREY MORGAN is the authorized biographer of both Alice Cooper and Iggy Pop & The Stooges. Isn't that enough?

Never Mind the Furthermore

by Ken Mills

If you are reading this book, I want you to know that I appreciate your curiosity and respect the level of Monkees fan that you are today. You care about them and the music that they made far beyond the TV show, far beyond the hits. I'm glad you are here and with us.

One of the things that bothers me about some Monkees fans is that their love and fandom often just stops at some point. It is frustrating when you find people who claim to love The Monkees. You know the ones— the people who love the television show, the pin-ups, the hits, and can recite the same two or three bits of trivia. (Liquid Paper? Really! Who knew!!) But for some odd reason, for many, the Monkees discography stops after the first five albums.

But *you*, dear reader, know the albums that are harder to find: *Head, Instant Replay, The Monkees Present* and *Changes*.

Once upon a time, I was in the same boat—long before there was a Wikipedia page or great resource books from people like Andrew Sandoval. Information was harder to come by.

I remember being eleven or twelve (1974 or so) and reading a book about rock history (forgive me, I cannot remember the name of it). There was a paragraph and a half with a photo of the guys from the TV show. That paragraph, which was gold to me, talked about how the band The Monkees were created for television, and they toured, and did the TV show until it was cancelled, and they made one movie. The discography listed only covered up through the *Head* soundtrack (which I never could find at a garage sale or Goodwill). Oh, sure, there were plenty of copies of *The Monkees* or *More of The Monkees*, but no copies of *Changes* were to be found.

I actually did not find out that the Monkees discography went far beyond those first five or six albums until I went to a record store in 1981, where a clerk showed me a mighty, wondrous book that listed every album that was available to purchase. You could look up The Monkees and it would cross-reference "see Micky Dolenz" or "see Dolenz, Jones, Boyce and Hart." The revelation of the truth found on these beautiful, golden pages led me on a chase of releases from Davy, Micky, Mike and Peter (some only available in other countries). Sure, we had seen Davy on *The Brady Bunch* and *Scooby-Doo*, and we

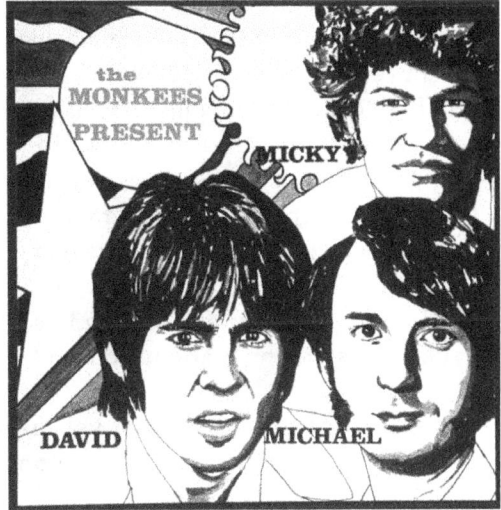

would hear "Joanne" and eventually "Rio" and "Cruisin'" (which was, ironically, featured on *Don Kirshner's Rock Concert*).

Every so often I would find a Nez album, or a Micky or Davy 45. It was always something that fascinated me. Not necessarily because of the quality of the music, but because the music simply existed.

Most of the best-known music journalists—chief among them, the writers at *Rolling Stone* magazine (who seem to have come around a bit in recent years)—had pretty much written off The Monkees, or the individuals as solo acts, as anything worth listening to. Some Monkees fans are doing themselves a great disservice by not investigating the solo/group efforts that came after the show went off the air.

The fact that you are holding this book says something about you and your fandom.

Long Title: Looking For
The Good Times
Examining the Monkees' Songs, One By One

by Michael A. Ventrella and Mark Arnold

Your journey may have not yet taken you to First National Band or to a *Cambria Hotel* or you may not yet *Remember* on your way to *Davy Live In Japan*, but you should!

I have said many times, that "As We Go Along," we, the fans, will have to carry the load and kind of become The Monkees. What I mean by that is—any band, phenomenon or pop culture *thing* counts on its audience to be part of the crucial chemistry that defines it. Fans are as an important part of a Band as who played bass on a track.

Those four young men—Davy, Micky, Mike and Peter—went far beyond anything that any critic or fan could have imagined. Far beyond anything that television producers Bob Rafelson and Bert Schneider or record producer Don Kirshner could have imagined.

The television show is a piece of the puzzle. The albums are another piece of the puzzle. And what the guys did on their own under the banner of the famous Monkees logo is yet another piece of that same puzzle. As you find these other albums, the image becomes clearer.

I challenge Monkees fans to step beyond those first four or five albums. Take a trip with Peter Tork and Shoe Suede Blues; follow Michael as he questions the "Grand Ennui"; let Micky Dolenz "Put You to Sleep"; and gallop along with David Jones as he sings about being a "Manchester Boy."

Earlier, I mentioned how the fans are the other part of the story. So many fans got us where we find ourselves today. Starting with the people who kept the fan clubs and fanzines going (Thanks, Maggie and gang) to the folks doing Monkees-dedicated podcasts, to the folks at Rhino, to Andrew Sandoval, to Glenn Gretlund and Iain Lee over at 7a Records. Because of all of them—and all of US—today, it is 50-plus years after The Monkees debuted, and new products, tours, and information are coming at a rate we could have only dreamed of back in the 60s, 70s, or 80s!

Who could have imagined that we would have a *Good Times* or a *Christmas Party*? And to top it off we have *The MGM Singles Collection*; *Live at the Troubadour*, with more coming. The guys are getting more respect among their peers and journalists, now more than ever. I'm glad to see that folks are not as worried about being "cool" as they are maybe interested in great pop music.

I am glad that Michael A. Ventrella and Mark Arnold wrote *HEADQUARTERED: A Timeline of The Monkees Solo Years*, because it may be the start for someone today to investigate the work of the Monkees' solo material, to go beyond a belt buckle worn on the hip, wool hats and the eight button shirts, red maracas and a tablecloth poncho worn on any given "Pleasant Valley Sunday." Maybe they will check out the work of the men—David, Micky, Michael and Peter.

Check out the previous book on the Monkees from Michael A. Ventrella and Mark Arnold entitled *Long Title: Good Clean Fun; Examining the Monkees Songs, One By One*.

I dedicate this introduction to Peter Tork, a loving soul whose love of peace and the blues shined on always. He would not allow himself to ever be "Kirshnered" again.

In closing, may you keep the love of music that you had as a teen, never let anyone take that away from you.

Explore music.

Peace and Love,
Ken Mills
Artist/Podcaster/Monkeesfan
Creator and owner of *Zilch!: A Monkees Podcast*

Headquartered:
A Timeline of The Monkees Solo Years

February 9, 1964...

David Jones watched from behind the curtain at the Ed Sullivan theater, mesmerized not by the performance of the four moptops from Liverpool, but by the girls in the audience screaming "Beatles!" over and over again.

He had come a long way from his youth in Manchester, and his acting and singing ability had even gotten him a job on Broadway, playing the Artful Dodger in *Oliver!* to acclaim. The cast had walked a few blocks to perform on *The Ed Sullivan Show* on the very night that the Beatles made their debut, earning the largest audience ever for a television show in those days.

Davy, being a theater kid, wasn't really interested in pop music and didn't know much about the Beatles, but watching them that night, he knew one thing for sure: He wasn't going to be the one the girls would remember the next day.

A fellow actor named Micky Dolenz watched the show like all the teenagers of the day. "I want to be in a rock band, too!" he said, and soon started a group he led called the Missing Links. "Wouldn't it be great to get a contract and make records for a living?" he thought.

Peter Tork was still hanging out with his folkie friends in Greenwich Village when the Beatles appeared on his black-and-white television. It may have been the catalyst that encouraged him to move to LA to seek better things.

Michael Nesmith was sitting with his wife Phyllis watching the television in awe. "It was shattering—an indescribable experience," he said in his book *Infinite Tuesday*. "Not unique in the times of man, certainly, but unique in ours. The Beatles' appearance on *Sullivan* was media curiosity as tectonic shift." He saw the future of music, and he wanted to be part of it.

Also watching were a couple of Hollywood soon-to-be producers...

There are numerous books about the Monkees, and each Monkee except Peter has published autobiographies that discuss their lives both with and without the Monkees.

This book is *not* a detailed biography, nor is it trying to be. Instead, it is primarily a timeline of every performance and record they created in their "solo" years (as well as mentioning the various Monkees reunions). We try to keep this mostly in chronological order, but sometimes it's easier to stick with one person through the year before moving on to the next person.

Peter Halsten Thorkelson was born on February 13, 1942, in Washington, DC;
Robert Michael Nesmith was born on December 30, 1942, in Houston;
George Michael Dolenz, Jr. was born on March 8, 1945, in Los Angeles; and
David Thomas Jones was born on December 30, 1945, in Openshaw, Manchester

1956

Young Micky Dolenz, the Hollywood kid whose father George Dolenz had been the star of the TV series *The Count of Monte Cristo*, had landed the job as Corky on the TV show *Circus Boy*. He dyed his hair blonde and was re-christened "Mickey Braddock" perhaps to downplay the connection to his father and also to make him sound more "American."

His parents had been sending him to auditions constantly as a child. "I was even up for Lassie," he says in his book *I'm a Believer*, "but they cast a collie instead."

For 11-year-old Micky, it was a marvelous adventure. The studio had purchased an old abandoned circus' props and tents, which gave the show a very real feeling not just for the audience but also for a young boy.

The series ran for three years and fifty-two episodes through September 11, 1958. During the series, Micky sang three songs: "Camptown Races," "The *Circus Boy* Theme" and "Alouette."

The studio didn't care about child labor issues, and pushed Micky all over the place to promote the show—not that he minded it. He appeared as a guest on *The Steve Allen Plymouth Show*, which aired on September 16, and on *The Today Show* on September 17, to announce the show's start, and later they suggested a personal appearance tour. "The stage act was very simple, but effective," Micky said. "I would come out on stage and sing a few songs with a band. At the time, my repertoire consisted of the theme song from the *Circus Boy* TV show, and a couple of contemporary hits like 'The Purple People Eater' and 'Witch Doctor.'"

1957

Micky appeared in a Kellogg's Sugar Corn Pops a full decade before he would shill for Kellogg's again with Rice Krispies. The final first run episode of *Circus Boy* on NBC ran on June 23 with the final repeat NBC broadcast on September 8.

The series resumed on ABC on September 19 with the final first-run episode on December 12.

1958

The final repeat broadcast of *Circus Boy* aired on ABC on September 11. Micky discussed the end of the series in *I'm a Believer*: "One day in 1958, the inevitable happened. *Circus Boy* was canceled. My parents told me that the producers had said I was growing up too fast and changing from a cute little kid into a gawky teenager. I was out of a job, and strangely enough, it didn't bother me in the slightest."

Micky also appeared on *Zane Grey Theatre* in an episode called "The Vaunted" that aired on November 27. He was again billed as Mickey Braddock.

1959

Micky appeared on *Playhouse 90* in an episode called "The Velvet Alley" that aired on January 22. He was billed as Micky Braddock, losing the "e." Micky would not appear again on TV until 1962, presumably to finish up schooling.

Micky explained in *I'm a Believer*: "My parents decided to send me to a child psychologist. They wanted to find out where I was at with my emotional and intellectual levels. It was one of the smartest things they ever did. After my parents got the psychiatrist's report, they made another very important decision. They took me out of show business altogether. Immediately. Years later, they told me that I had been offered another series by the same producers called *Cabin Boy*, but they had turned it down. That was the second smartest thing they ever did."

1960

"My dad thought I could be a jockey 'cos of my size," Davy said in his book *They Made a Monkee Out of Me*. "I wasn't going to grow. I was 14 and still only 4'5". I worked there for six weeks during my summer holidays and I really got to like it. So at the end of 1960, I said goodbye to school and started working at Basil Foster's Holland House as a stable boy."

He then met someone who saw talent in him and recommended that he audition for a new play that was opening in London called *Oliver!* Davy went ahead and sang his heart out but didn't think much of it, but the producers were impressed. The first performance was on June 30 at the New Theatre in the West End in London. Davy, as the Artful Dodger, found himself crooning "Consider Yourself" night after night.

This even led to his first TV appearance on *BBC Sunday Night Play*: "Summer Theatre: June Evening," which aired on the BBC on July 10.

1961

Davy's career was building. He performed his first solo show in The California Ballroom in Dunstable, England on November 10. He also appeared on the March 6 episode of the long-running British soap opera *Coronation Street*, which aired on ITV, and he appeared on another long-running British soap opera *Magnolia Street*, which aired on BBC on June 23.

1962

Davy appeared three times this year on the British drama series *Z Cars*, which aired on BBC, each time as a different character. These aired on January 2, April 10, and September 19.

Davy performed another live show at the California Ballroom in Dunstable, England on March 23, unaware that America's California loomed in his future.

Oliver! had caught the attention of the American producer David Merrick, who brought the cast over to the States with the ultimate goal of bringing it to Broadway. Davy remembered going with *Oliver!* to Broadway in New York in 1961 in his autobiography, but *Oliver!* didn't premiere in America until 1962, with a national tour beginning in Los Angeles with Edwin Lester's LA and San Francisco Civic Light Opera Association.

"Seeing my name in a real programme for the first time was fantastic," Davy said. "I'd seen it flash by on *Coronation Street* and other TV shows, but now on posters outside the theatre, it felt different. I was impressed."

It had been three years since he was seen on TV, but Micky appeared as a guest on *The Steve Allen Playhouse*, airing October 10.

1963

After touring America, *Oliver!* premiered on Broadway on January 6. On arriving in New York City, Davy jumped for joy. This was the Big Time! "Nothing can compare with the magic of an opening night on Broadway," he said in his autobiography, and in many ways, he meant it—Broadway was his real love.

Micky's father George Dolenz (born Dolentz) passed away on February 8 at the young age of 55. Despite the fact that he had grown apart from his father, as many teenagers do, the loss threw Micky's life into a tailspin. "I was not very close to my father when he died. I was off into my world of drag-racing and rock & roll, and he was firmly anchored in his world of veal scallopini and opera."
Micky quit school and found himself aimless.

Michael, meanwhile, had been playing music for quite some time in local places in Dallas, Texas, but was going nowhere. He was twenty years old and concentrating on his music instead of finding a good job, and this did not sit well with his parents.

He had appeared on radio in San Antonio, singing "Pastures of Plenty" by Woody Guthrie, as well as "It Sure Looks Like Rain," "Wynken, Blynken and Nod" and "Don't Let the Deal Go Down" among others. Between songs, Michael engaged in some onstage patter with the audience which showed how comfortable and funny he could be, even at this early stage.

Los Angeles provided him with the connections he needed. He performed in many local nightclubs, meeting the local folkie crowd, and even becoming the host at the Troubadour, which at the time was the "hot spot" for the west coast folkies.

It was through these connections that he met Randy Sparks from the New Christy Minstrels who encouraged him and got him into the studio. He recorded a few songs as a demo but nothing happened.

Wanderin' (Michael Nesmith) / **Well, Well** (Michael Nesmith) (Highness 13) (Exact release date unknown; only one known copy exists)

Davy's career was going in the exact opposite direction as Michael's. He appeared on *The 17th Annual Tony Awards* airing April 28 and on *Merv Griffin's Talent Scouts* on July 16 while he was performing with *Oliver!* He sang "Where is Love?" and "Consider Yourself."

This attracted the attention of Hollywood. A cute non-threatening guy who could sing *and* had a wonderful British accent? What's not to like? Ward Sylvester, a Screen Gems executive, had seen *Oliver!* and approached Davy about doing some screen tests. Who wouldn't say yes?

Davy flew to LA and over time, tried out for bits like *The Wackiest Ship in the Army* and *Hogan's Heroes*. Although he didn't get cast, he was remembered ...

1964

And on February 9, everything changed, as the soon-to-be Monkees watched the Beatles perform on *The Ed Sullivan show*— Davy from backstage.

Michael traveled back to Texas to do some small-town shows with a few other musicians, and immediately saw a change in the way he was received by audiences. "The shows consisted of a set of old folk tunes and some children's songs, and one song I had written: 'Pretty Little Princess.' It was a simple ballad and not a very good song. I can't remember it well, but the effect was bewildering. After a verse or two, the girls would start screaming like the girls who chased The Beatles."

Michael saw the future. If the Beatles could write their own songs, so could he. From this time came "Different Drum," "Nine Times Blue," "Propinquity," and "Papa Gene's Blues." He was astounded at the positive reaction. The fact that these are all very good songs may have had something to do with that...

Upon finding his girlfriend Phyllis Barbour pregnant, he knew his conservative southern family would not approve. On March 16, Michael and Phyllis quickly married, packed their meager belongings, and headed for sunny California.

"The pressure of my new circumstances threw me into a well of woe I did not understand as a young man," he explained in his book *Infinite Tuesday*. "I wanted to make a living playing and singing. I started writing songs to explain the pain away. Those early songs were crude, but they provided a way to turn melancholy to grief."

Peter had been playing the Greenwich Village folkie scene along with his friend Stephen Stills, but was seriously considering moving to California, where more opportunities could present themselves. He continued to hone his "loveable dummy" persona that had worked for him onstage in New York.

Oliver! ran on Broadway until November 14 after 774 performances. The movie version would not be made for another few years, and by that time, Davy was rather occupied (and too old to play the Artful Dodger).

Micky resurfaced once again and appeared on the *Mr. Novak* episode called "Born of Kings and Angels," airing on December 1. He was still billed as Micky Braddock.

1965

Michael and Phyllis had a son named Christian DuVal Nesmith on January 31.

1965 found Micky rebuilding his professional career as he appeared in an uncredited role on three episodes of the soap opera *Peyton Place*, airing March 16, 18 and 25.

However, he was in love with music and had been greatly influenced by the Beatles, like many young men at the time. He'd show up at amateur nights at the Red Velvet Nightclub on the Sunset Strip. "I would get up there in my shiny sharkskin suit, razor-cut hairdo, pointy shoes and do my thing," he explained.

This eventually led to him starting a group called Micky and the One-Nighters. Micky commonly tells this story on stage by adding, "And that's how long we lasted: one night."

The band evolved and later called itself "The Missing Links" (Foreshadowing!). Micky eventually left and it appeared that his career in music was over. *Or was it?* (More foreshadowing!)

Oliver! made it to Chicago in early 1965. Davy was getting a bit too old to continue to play the Artful Dodger, and left the show. In perhaps a bit of stereotyping, he was cast in another play based on a Charles Dickens novel: *Pickwick*. This one featured the great British comedian Harry Secombe, and although it was not a huge success and only lasted a few months, it grabbed some major attention for Davy. All the industry insiders came to see it, and Davy's manager Ward Sylvester made sure they noticed the young rising talent.

Paul Mazursky and Larry Tucker were two young Screen Gems staff writers who saw the show and remembered Davy well. And they had an idea for a new television show...

Once *Pickwick* ended its run, Davy returned to Hollywood to stay in a house rented by Sylvester, who also arranged a deal with Colpix records. Soon Davy had recorded an album of traditional pop tunes of the time, primarily from Don Kirshner's group of songwriters—but with one Bob Dylan tune stuck in there to show he was "hip."

The Monkees concept was just in its embryonic stages at the time the *David Jones* album came out. Davy was being marketed as a new teen idol and no thought was being made to make it anything like a Beatles or Stones album. Rather, it was modeled closer to that of Frankie Avalon or Fabian or at the most progressive, Tom Jones. The fact that they used the name David rather than Davy speaks volumes as to how they were trying to get their audience to treat him as an all-around showman, and not so much a moptop ripoff.

DAVID JONES
Release: Colpix CP-493 (mono) / Colpix SCP-493 (stereo), February 1965

What Are We Going To Do? (Henry Levine, Murray MacLeod, Smokey Roberds)
Maybe It's Because I'm A Londoner (Hubert Gregg)
Put Me Amongst The Girls (Clarence Wainwright Murphy, Dan Lipton)
Any Old Iron (Charles Collins, E.A. Sheppard, Fred E. Terry)
Theme For A New Love (Berdie Abrams, Hank Levine)
It Ain't Me Babe (Bob Dylan)
Face Up To It (Roger Atkins, Gerry Robinson)
Dream Girl (Van McCoy)
Baby It's Me (Mark Anthony)
My Dad (Barry Mann, Cynthia Weil)
This Bouquet (Henry Levine, Murray MacLeod, Smokey Roberds)

2011 Friday Music reissue CD bonus tracks:
Take Me To Paradise (Wine, Venet)
The Girl From Chelsea (Gerry Goffin, Carole King)

Singles released from or at the time of this album:

Dream Girl (Van McCoy) / **Take Me to Paradise** (Wine, Venet) (Colpix 764, February 1965)

There were two pressings of the album cover. The original had a full head, shoulders and chest shot. After Monkeemania hit, the album was reissued with the same cover photo enlarged to emphasize Davy's face and head.

The Monkees Super Deluxe Edition (November 11, 2014) features 23 tracks from these sessions on disc 3: 11 album tracks in mono, the two CD bonus tracks listed above in mono, and the 11 album tracks in stereo. The majority of these tracks were recorded on July 26, 1965. More tracks were recorded on September 25 including the unreleased "I'll Be Here" and "Show Me Girl."

The album itself is standard pop music that would have been hits in 1963 or 1964, but by 1965 the Beatles were already moving pop music forward. These songs offered nothing special or memorable, although Davy's voice is distinctive and recognizable even under all the echo and mono mix.

A few songs were the kind of thing Herman's Hermits would have had a hit with—the kind of British Music Hall popular in Davy's home country. "What are We Going to Do?" even led the album off to set the mood, and was released as a single that hit the charts for three weeks, although never getting any higher than #93.

What Are We Going to Do? (Henry Levine, Murray MacLeod, Smokey Roberds) / **This Bouquet** (Henry Levine, Murray MacLeod, Smokey Roberds (Colpix 784, July 1965, #93)

The Girl From Chelsea (Gerry Goffin, Carole King) / **Theme For a New Love (I Only Saw You Once)** (Berdie Abrams, Hank Levine) (Colpix 789, November 1965)

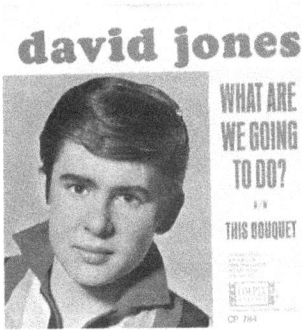

Davy appeared on *Shindig!* on November 13 to promote this album by singing "What Are We Going To Do?" It is likely that the *David Jones* album was released at this time since the album was still being recorded as late as September 25 but no official release date is revealed, even on the album's 2011 CD issue.

He also appeared on the episode of the US medical drama *Ben Casey* called "If You Play Your Cards Right, You Too Can Be a Loser," which aired on December 27 on ABC.

Davy appeared as himself on the UK music series *Thank Your Lucky Stars* on September 18 on ITV, and on *Where the Action is* on December 7, where he sang "The Girl From Chelsea" and "Theme For A New Love (I Saw You Only Once)."

Meanwhile, in August, *Variety* had posted the ad looking for young men to star in a new TV show to eventually be called *The Monkees*. Davy already had a leg up. Thanks to his connections, it was pretty much assumed from the start that if the show was sold, Davy would be there. Micky had connections as well, but, like Davy, still had to go through an official audition. Micky later joked that everyone in LA had auditioned, even Charles Manson. Micky remains astounded to see that even today, some people still believe it.

Peter and Michael were complete unknowns, however, and their stories fall into the traditional Hollywood "discovered" story that studios tend to dish out, except in this case it was true.

Peter discussed this in an interview on September 6, 1995, with Eliot Stein that was reprinted in *Monkee Business Fanzine* #75. "Stephen Stills told me about the auditions. We were friends. We were not living together as a rumor exists. We knew each other from Greenwich Village. Stephen knew Bob Rafelson socially, and was told that he was not videogenic, that his hair and teeth were wrong. Did he know anybody whose hair and teeth were right? And that was me! The main reasons I was selected: I did my screen test perfectly on the first try; the 'dummy' character I created on the screen was created by me. They said, 'We will give you the part if you don't mind playing the character!'"

Even still, Hollywood can move slowly. You pass the audition, they do a pilot episode, and there is no guarantee at all that anyone will pick it up. Even after the audition, Michael was still trying to gain a little success, and released various singles under his own name as well as his Michael Blessing pseudonym.

How Can You Kiss Me (Michael Nesmith) / **Just a Little Love** (Michael Nesmith) (Omnibus 239) (MN as Mike & John & Bill)

The New Recruit (Bob Krasnow, Sam Ashe) / **A Journey With Michael Blessing** (Bob Krasnow, Sam Ashe, Nields) (Colpix 787, September 1965) (MN as Michael Blessing)

Until It's Time For You To Go (Buffy Sainte-Marie) / **What Seems to Be the Trouble, Officer** (Bob Krasnow, Michael Blessing) (Colpix 792, November 9, 1965) (MN as Michael Blessing)

The Monkees Super Deluxe Edition (November 11, 2014) features the above four Michael Blessing tracks from these singles on disc 3, plus two never before released Michael Blessing tracks: "Who Do You Love" and "Get Out of My Life Woman." All are in mono. Strangely, the box set does not include the two above Mike & John & Bill single tracks, nor does it contain the two Nesmith tracks released on Highness Records in 1963.

"How Can You Kiss Me" is an echo-laden bit that kind of drags but is instantly recognizable as a Nesmith tune, and, as always, with more insightful lyrics than most pop songs of the time.

"The New Recruit" is an interesting protest song written by Tom Paxton where Michael sings in a weird way—almost as if he's trying specifically trying to emphasize the twang. It's an anti-war song where he asks for advice from his sergeant because "I've never killed before..."

Michael appeared on national television for the very first time as Michael Blessing on *The Lloyd Thaxton Show* on November 12 singing "Until It's Time For You To Go," and giving the briefest of interviews. He would later re-record this song for the Monkees, but it was never released on any of the official albums.

1966

Davy appeared on the episode of the US sitcom *The Farmer's Daughter* called "Moe Hill and the Mountains," which aired on January 7 on ABC. This is the show where Davy sings "I'm Gonna Buy Me a Dog," which was later recorded by The Monkees.

Peter played two solo concerts pre-Monkees on April 1 and April 10 at The Troubadour in Los Angeles.

Then *The Monkees* TV show aired. And this is where The Monkees story began. There are many books detailing this time, and that's not the goal of this book, so we're going to only discuss the solo projects they did outside of the Monkees here.

For a detailed account of the music being produced during these years and the various reunions, please refer to the companion volume to this book, *Long Title: Looking for the Good Times; Examining the Monkees' Songs, One By One.* However, we will list the releases here in the briefest form so that you can better keep the history coherent and complete.

"Last Train to Clarksville" was released in August, prior to the TV show, and did well, but once the show started, it zoomed to #1. *The Monkees* album came out in October and also hit number one, where it stayed until it was knocked off the top of the charts by *More of the Monkees*.

Having a half-hour weekly commercial for your music helped with sales, but the fact is that the music really did deserve it, which is why people are still listening to the music to this day and people are still writing books about it.

"I'm a Believer" was released in November and became The Monkees' biggest hit.

Due to the great success of *The Monkees* TV show and records, two more singles were pulled from the 1965 *David Jones* album in December, but not in the US.

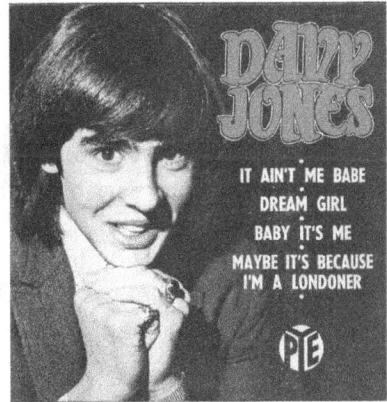

It Ain't Me Babe (Bob Dylan) / **Baby It's Me** (Mark Anthony) (DJ)

Maybe It's Because I'm A Londoner (Hubert Gregg) / **Put Me Amongst The Girls** (Clarence Wainwright Murphy, Dan Lipton) (DJ)

Let's point out just how weird it is to have *It Ain't Me Babe* paired with *Baby It's Me*. It's like Davy can't make up his mind or something!

1967

More of the Monkees was released in January, containing some of their most well-known songs ("I'm a Believer," "I'm Not Your Steppin' Stone," "Sometime in the Morning," "She," "Mary Mary"...)

Micky also had an old recording surface around this time, and it even made the charts, reaching #75. The B-side is an instrumental that has no Micky involvement.

Don't Do It (Micky Dolenz) / **Plastic Symphony III** (Romans, Fink, Richardson) (MD) (February 1967) (Challenge 59353) #75

"Don't do it, why don't you do it?" Micky says in a kind of monotone predictable rock and roll song that appears to have been recorded in one take, mistakes and all. "Why won't you dance with me?" Micky's first recorded composition has a few surprises but mostly sounds like a thousand other garage band songs of the time. But hey, Micky can indeed sing.

During a break in the show, Micky flew to England on February 6, and met up with Paul McCartney on February 7 at his home in St. John's Wood, London.

The next day he was invited to visit the Beatles as they worked on their new album, which was to become *Sgt. Pepper's Lonely Hearts Club Band.* He dressed in his finest hippie wear, ready for a recording freak-out, but instead found four very talented and serious musicians working on their latest tune "Good Morning, Good Morning" while taking a traditional break for tea time. (Sometimes Micky will tell this story and change the song to "Oh! Darling" so he can do his wonderful rendition of that song, but Beatles fans know that "Oh! Darling" wasn't even written until 1969's *Abbey Road.*)

But perhaps more important to Micky was his appearance on Britain's #1 music show, *Top of the Pops*, where he instantly fell in love with the co-host Samantha Juste, who would later become his wife.

The entire trip was the inspiration for his song "Randy Scouse Git."

Michael arrived in London soon after and he and Micky made the promotional stops, including an appearance on Britain's #1 music show, *Top of the Pops*.

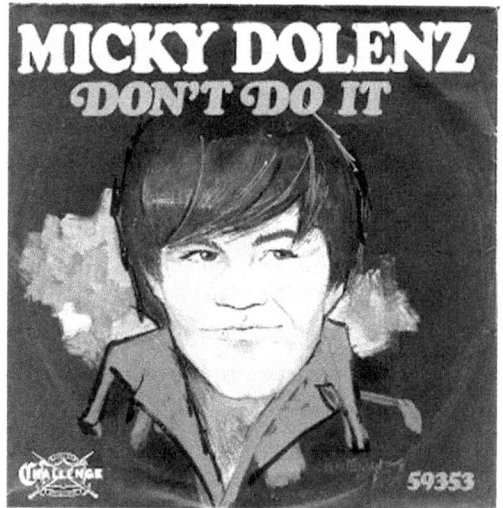

Then, on February 10, Michael attended The Beatles' recording sessions for "A Day in the Life" and appeared in film footage of the event. He commented on his London experience in *Infinite Tuesday* and mentioned how thrilled he was when he was invited to John Lennon's house. "When we arrived, John was in a kind of breakfast den next to the kitchen. John asked me if I wanted a drink, and without thinking, I said I would love a glass of milk. There was a breath of pause as he looked at Cynthia and said, 'Well, *we're* in for a good time, aren't we?' ... The manic scene of LA had not prepared me for a laid-back have-dinner, socialize, make wisecracks atmosphere. This was the way it was in Lennon's home."

A TV show called *Dream Girl of '67*, a *Dating Game*-type show, featured all of the Monkees at various times during 1967: Davy appeared on February 13-17 and July 24-28. Micky appeared five times from June 26-30. Michael also appeared five times from October 30-November 3, and Peter from November 20-24.

In March, the Monkees single "A Little Bit Me, A Little Bit You" was released.

Davy appeared alone on the *Miss Teen International Pageant,* airing March 25.

Michael's B-side "Just a Little Love" from the pre-Monkees days was re-released under a new label, but despite the Monkees' fame, it never charted.

Just a Little Love (Mike Nesmith) / **Curson Terrace** (C.H. Whitman) (Edan 1001, April 1967) (MN) (B-side by Mike & Tony)

This is a simple little song but the Michael songwriting is clear and obvious. A harmonica fills the lead, just like Bob Dylan would do, because it goes absolutely nowhere. It is, however, poorly recorded though as if it was done in someone's garage with one microphone and the bass echoing off the cement walls.

The B-Side is a kind of "I Want Candy" or "Bo Diddley" instrumental that is even more poorly recorded than the A-side. It's basically two notes, over and over again, going nowhere. How someone could give themselves songwriting credit for a basic jam like this is a mystery.

Micky appeared in an unbilled cameo as "Jungle Gino" in Sonny and Cher's movie *Good Times*, released in May. This movie was definitely not the inspiration for the Nilsson song "Good Times" nor the Monkees' recording of it and album named *Good Times*, nor the Monkees' song "Looking for the Good Times," nor the Monkees book of the same name. In fact, the movie itself provides no good times at all.

The *Headquarters* album was released in May. It was the first album produced by Chip Douglas and the first where all of the Monkees actually appeared on every song.

Micky and Peter both attended the *Monterey Pop Festival* in June. Micky is seen wearing a full Native American buckskins and headdress.

Peter introduced Buffalo Springfield and Lou Rawls, and informed the crowd that The Beatles were not there in disguise during The Grateful Dead set. The Monkees were considered, but ultimately were not invited to perform at these shows.

It was there that they saw Jimi Hendrix perform for the first time with his new band The Experience. They were immediately impressed. Micky invited Jimi to open for the Monkees' next tour, and Jimi agreed.

Michael thought it was a bit weird when he was told of it. "This conjunction of Hendrix and The Monkees was staggeringly weird in my eyes, but the idea that I would get to see him playing live night after night was electrifying."

The audience of young girls screaming "We want Davy" disagreed.

Micky went back to England later and appeared on *Top of the Pops* on June 29. Davy too traveled back to England and, on July 6, also appeared on *Top of the Pops*.

For some reason, no singles were released from *Headquarters* in America ("Randy Scouse Git" was renamed "Alternate Title" and was a hit in England). But in July in America, "Pleasant Valley Sunday" hit the charts.

Another old Micky recording was released in August, but this one failed to chart.

Huff Puff (Gary Pipkin) (MD) / **Fate** (Romans, Fink, Richardson) (The Obvious) (August 1967) (Challenge 59372)

Micky sings this as the Big Bad Wolf, complete with maniacal laughter and a voice that is hardly recognizable as Micky Dolenz. "I'm gonna huff and puff and blow your house down." Predictable music, written by Gary Pipkin (no relation to "The Pipkins" whose weird hit "Gimme Dat Ding" came out soon after).

CHALLENGE

4-Star Music-
Popcorn Music-
Cord Music (BMI)
(45-1436)

**PROMOTIONAL
COPY**

59372

Time: 2:07

NOT FOR SALE

HUFF PUFF
(Gary Pipkin)
MICKY DOLENZ
Prod. by Sape./Brooks Production

Micky's tenure with The Monkees could have ended prematurely around this time when he received his draft notice. Micky tells the story in *I'm a Believer*. "One day I received this very official-looking letter in the mail. It was from the Selective Service. I was being drafted!" As it turned out, he was turned down for "being too skinny." The producers of the Monkees sighed in relief almost as big as Micky did.

In November, what many consider the Monkees' best album was released: *Pisces, Aquarius, Capricorn and Jones, Ltd.* zoomed up the charts. At the same time, the single "Daydream Believer" hit the airwaves even though it was not on the album.

In December, Peter played banjo for some music that didn't make the final cut for George Harrison's *Wonderwall Music* album, but did appear in the film *Wonderwall*. Peter's contribution didn't really have a title, but is now referred to as "Banjo Solo."

Peter borrowed McCartney's five-string banjo for the session. "Paul couldn't play," Peter explained, "because the folk five-string banjo can't be restrung in reverse order for left-handers; it must be custom made. I played for 45 minutes. George said, 'Thanks very much,' and we went our separate ways."

Peter didn't get paid, but said that he considered just being a part of this as an honor.

1968

Peter co-hosted the January 4 edition of *Top of the Pops* with Jimmy Savile, which aired on BBC in the UK.

Next, Peter played a solo concert on February 2 at the Los Angeles Sports Arena. He directed *The Monkees* episode "Monkees Mind Their Manor," which aired on February 26. He also had a brief cameo as a ticket buyer in the movie *Wild in the Streets*, released May 29. Peter also appeared solo on *Top of the Pops* on May 23.

The Monkees' last single while the TV show was fresh was the old Boyce/Hart song "Valleri" which had been re-recorded. It came out in February and did not do as well as previous singles.

Micky made his directorial debut directing "Mijacogeo," the final original episode of *The Monkees*, which aired on March 25. He also wrote the story and co-wrote the teleplay. "I didn't have any formal training as a director," Micky later said, "but just being around a set all my life had taught me a lot. Little did I know at the time that this directing exercise would set me up for a very successful future in film and television production."

In April, the album *The Birds, The Bees, and the Monkees* was released, containing both "Valleri" and "Daydream Believer." Unlike the previous two albums, this one hardly had any Monkees performing together, and Peter only appears on the album as the keyboard player for "Daydream Believer," recorded during the *Pisces* sessions.

Michael became a dad again twice in 1968. Michael and his wife Phyllis had a son named Jonathan Darby on February 4. A few months later, on August 24, he had a son with Nurit Wilde, named Jason. This did not help his relationship with his wife.

And in the meantime, he released a strange little record.

THE WICHITA TRAIN WHISTLE SINGS (MN)
Released: June 1968
Highest Chart Position: #144

Nine Times Blue (Michael Nesmith)
Carlisle Wheeling (Michael Nesmith)
Tapioca Tundra (Michael Nesmith)
Don't Call on Me (Michael Nesmith)
Don't Cry Now (Michael Nesmith)

While I Cried (Michael Nesmith)
Papa Gene's Blues (Michael Nesmith)

You Just May Be the One (Michael Nesmith)
Sweet Young Thing (Nesmith, Gerry Goffin, Carole King)
You Told Me (Michael Nesmith)

Don't Cry Now (Michael Nesmith) / **Tapioca Tundra** (Michael Nesmith) (MN as The Wichita Train Whistle) (July 1968)

Everyone rushed out to buy Michael's first solo album, only to discover a completely instrumental album played by a big band in a huge room where it sounded like the recording was done by placing one microphone in the back of the hall. Ironically, it sold better than many of his later solo albums, since this was still when the TV show was airing. Having a half-hour commercial each week in prime time certainly helps sales.

The TV show was now in Saturday morning reruns, and without that extra publicity (and with a poor choice for a single), "D.W. Washburn," released in June, inched up the charts to stall at #19. The Monkees continued to work on their film "Head," unaware that their prime audience had moved on.

Micky married Samantha Juste on July 12.

Around this time, Davy released a special flexi-disc record to his Japanese fan club members. The disc was a message to let them know what the guys were doing and included news about the movie they were filming. The special disc was issued with a picture sleeve.

Davy appeared alone on the German show *Baff - Fast eine Sendung*, a music show, on May 1, and in the UK on *Dee Time*, airing June 1 and once again on *Top of the Pops* on June 6.

Soon he became a husband and father. "I thought that having a baby and getting married would be a good responsibility. I thought it would make me take the initiative, be decisive, but when you've never done it before, it's not so easy," commented Davy in his book *They Made a Monkee Out of Me*.

"Linda traveled to England to have the baby at the London Clinic. Meanwhile I was halfway around the world touring Australia and Japan, September / October 1968." Daughter Talia Elizabeth was born on October 2. Davy flew to London to be with Linda and the baby when he discovered that his father Harry was seriously ill and in the hospital. Then, he seemed to be improving, so Davy, Linda and Talia went to Hollywood, and Davy's father passed away on October 24. Davy immediately turned around and flew back for the funeral alone.

"I was so angry at myself. Sure, I had commitments back in Hollywood, but were they more important than my dad, ill in a hospital? If that happened today I'd say, 'Screw the shows, I'm stayin' with me dad!', but I was a kid being led around."

After the funeral, Davy flew back to California and he and Linda went over the Mexican border to get married in Tijuana on October 31.

Next, Davy was threatened to be drafted into the Vietnam War. He hired Hollywood lawyer Harry Schtumm, who was well-known for fixing things like this. Davy paid Schtumm a lot of money only to later discover that Schtumm's great legal plan to save Davy was to hire people to break into the draft building and steal Davy's records. The records were eventually recovered but Davy was fortunately denied for being such a "99-pound weakling." (No, this was not the inspiration for the Monkees song "99 Pounds.")

The TV show was no longer on the air, and most of the albums had dropped off the charts when one of the Monkees' greatest songs was released in October. "Porpoise Song" was subtitled "Theme from Head" to promote the upcoming film, but the single bombed, never getting any higher than #62. Was it because there was no show promoting it? Was it because it was just too psychedelic for the teenybopper fans? Or was it because the radio stations had decided the Monkees fad was over?

The *Head* album came out in December and also performed very poorly, as did, of course, the film itself.

The Monkees, unaware that the film, single and album would flop, had been working on a TV special called *33 1/3 Revolutions Per Monkee* which shared many of the same themes as the Head movie ("We know we're manufactured, but we'd like you to take us seriously.")

Peter left The Monkees at the end of filming the *33 1/3 Revolutions Per Monkee* special. He paid his way out of his contract and soon was setting up his own band, Release, which didn't. Micky remembered in *I'm a Believer*: "The day Peter quit was probably the happiest day in Mike's life. They'd never really gotten along, right from day one. Finally, he was out of the way. Now, Mike could get on with doing what he had always wanted to do, make The Monkees *his* group."

The film of the *Monterey Pop Festival* was released on December 26, and Micky can be seen wearing his American Indian regalia.

1969

Micky's daughter with Samantha, Ami Bluebell Dolenz, was born on January 8. Micky was thrilled, and Ami later grew up to be quite a famous actor on her own.

In February, the Monkees tried again with an old Boyce/Hart song "Tear Drop City" which, like "Valleri," had been written and recorded years earlier and thus sounded out of date to the 1969 hippie crowd. It did not do well on the charts. The album *Instant Replay* was quickly released, featuring mostly left-over songs from previous sessions. The cover showed only three Monkees. It reached #32 on the charts, which was much better than *Head*'s chart performance, but disappointing for a group that had easily hit #1 with their first four albums.

Davy appeared alone on the February 10 edition of the comedy variety series *Rowan and Martin's Laugh-In*, which aired on NBC. He also appeared on *This is Tom Jones* on February 14, *The Andy Williams Show* on October 25, the game show *Letters to Laugh-In* from December 8-12, and on *Music Scene* on December 22, where he sang "Together."

Michael rode his Triumph motorcycle in the 1969 Mexican Baja 1000 Off-Road race during October 31-November 1 from Ensenada to La Paz. Other participants included James Garner and Steve McQueen driving automobiles. There was a documentary made about this race that was released in 2018.

Michael was determined to make the Monkees his band, and the three Monkees went into the studio to make their next album ... but they didn't go together. Micky wrote and recorded a bunch of songs, Davy did his own, and Michael did his own and then each got to pick four songs each.

In April, the single "Someday Man" was released and bombed. The single was then turned over and the B-side "Listen to the Band," written by Michael, was promoted instead and did better, but still never hit the top 40.

Peter played a solo concert on June 19 at the Fond du Lac County Fairgrounds, in Fond du Lac, Wisconsin. He also appeared as a band contest judge on three episodes of *It's Happening*, that aired consecutive weeks on July 5, 12, and 19.

According to Eric Lefkowitz's *Monkee Business*, Peter was having a harder time than Michael at being taken seriously. "After I left The Monkees, I went through an identity crisis right away," Peter said. "I called up Dick Clark and said, 'Put me on the road,' He said, 'Get a hit record. Nobody will recognize you.' I went, '*What?* That was so staggering to me that it completely stopped me cold. I thought 37 promoters would be dying to have me perform."

Peter didn't know how to handle this, and his life starting spiraling out of control. He had not known how to manage his money and soon found his house foreclosed. He disappeared from public life, trying different avenues to start his own music career.

In September, the first (and last) Monkees single written entirely by Monkees was released. Michael's "Good Clean Fun" was backed with Micky's "Mommy and Daddy." It was not a success, reaching only #82. The album *Present* came out a month later and never got any higher than #100—the worst a Monkees album had ever performed, despite a promotional push and a nationwide tour.

This was a turning point for Michael. He knew the time was right to go his own way. He would be able to record what he wanted without being told that it didn't sound "Monkees" enough. And he could use the session musicians who had played on all his songs for the past year (since by this time, the Monkees were essentially three solo acts sharing vinyl).

"The IRS, which I had ignored for several years, showed up with a huge bill for unpaid taxes and started seizing property," Michael said. "I ran away from the few assets I had, and left money at Screen Gems in return for being let out of my contract."

What made it worse, and what only added to the anger between Michael and Peter, was that the Monkees were deeply in debt to the record label. "The royalties that were due to us were held up by the recording of Peter's 'Lady's Baby,'" Michael told *Rolling Stone* magazine late in 2019. "He stayed in [the studio for] 24 hours a day for months and he wound up with a $200,000 or $300,000 recording bill. That had the net effect of wiping out everyone's royalties, including mine."

Michael signed on with RCA Nashville and was shocked when famous session musician Red Rhodes agreed to join his new project: The First National Band. They quickly recorded a number of songs and a trio of albums were released just months apart.

1970

Davy appeared on the music show *Get it Together*, which aired on January 3 on ABC.

In late February and early March, Davy and Micky traveled to the studio separately to quickly record their Contractual Obligation album (*Changes*), which completely failed to chart upon its release a few months later. The single from that album ("Oh My My") was released in May and never got any higher than #98. The cover showed the two of them in tuxedos playing percussion instruments, which did not exactly garnish a rock-and-roll image. The idea of "take us seriously" had died when Michael had left, and the joke was that one of them would record another album which would be billed as "The Monkee."

Michael's First National Band album debuted right about the same time as Davy and Micky's swan song *Changes*. "When *Magnetic South* was released, it was the first time I stared into the abyss," Michael said. Fortunately, it grabbed some attention, and specifically from a radio station in Philadelphia which played "Joanne" despite the station mostly playing only pop records. (This was back in the old days when DJs on radio stations actually were able to decide what to play instead of the corporations owning the station.) This led to "Joanne" being released as a single and becoming a mild hit across the country.

MAGNETIC SOUTH (MN)
Released: June 1970
Highest Chart Position: #143

Calico Girlfriend (Michael Nesmith)
Nine Times Blue (Michael Nesmith)
Little Red Rider (Michael Nesmith)
The Crippled Lion (Michael Nesmith)
Joanne (Michael Nesmith)
First National Rag (Red Rhodes)

Mama Nantucket (Michael Nesmith)
Keys to the Car (Michael Nesmith)
Hollywood (Michael Nesmith)
One Rose (D. Lyon, L. McIntyre)
Beyond the Blue Horizon (Richard A. Whiting, W. Franke Harling, Leo Robin)

Bonus tracks on 16 Original Classics re-release:
Silver Moon (Michael Nesmith)
Lady of the Valley (Michael Nesmith)

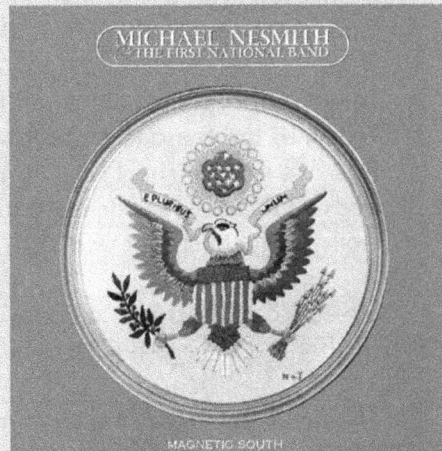

Here I Am (Michael Nesmith)
Nevada Fighter (Michael Nesmith)
Tumbling Tumbleweeds (Bob Nolan)

Little Red Rider (Michael Nesmith) / Rose City Chimes (J. Robert Garrett) (MN) (July 1970)

When this single failed to chart, RCA wisely and quickly released "Joanne."

Joanne (Michael Nesmith) / One Rose (D. Lyon, L. McIntyre) (MN) (August 1970)
Highest Chart Position: #21

Michael kept recording with the First National Band, and their second album was released in November.

LOOSE SALUTE (MN)
Released: November 1970
Highest Chart Position: #159

Silver Moon (Michael Nesmith)
I Fall to Pieces (Harlan Howard, Hank Cochran)
Thanx for the Ride (Michael Nesmith)
Dedicated Friend (Michael Nesmith)
Conversations (Michael Nesmith)

Tengo Amore (Michael Nesmith)
Listen to the Band (Michael Nesmith)
Bye Bye Bye (Michael Nesmith)
Lady of the Valley (Michael Nesmith)
Hello Lady (Michael Nesmith)

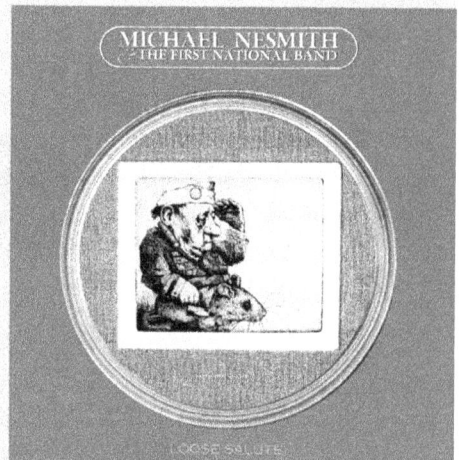

Silver Moon (Michael Nesmith) / Lady of the Valley (Michael Nesmith) (MN) (November 1970) *Highest Chart Position: #42*

The material for the first two First National Band albums consisted of many tracks originally intended for The Monkees. Michael also recorded a solo version of "Listen to the Band." Many of The Monkees' versions, however, did not see the light until The Monkees' Missing Links collections of the 1980s and 90s.

Michael made the following appearances this year with The First National Band: May 19: The Ice House, Pasadena, California; June 3 and 7: The Troubadour, West Hollywood, California; August 25-30: The Troubadour, San Francisco, California; November 27: Alabama State Coliseum, Montgomery, Alabama.

Michael and Phyllis had a daughter named Jessica Buffler on September 10, but he admitted that his personal life was in shambles. "Phyllis was resolute and kept trying to make our marriage cohere," Michael wrote in *Infinite Tuesday*. "Nurit was resolute in making me take responsibility for my child. In both cases, these women were on higher moral ground than I. In addition to all the other lapses of ethics, I fell into yet another sordid and awful affair with a friend's wife, and that affair made me unfit for any relationship on any terms, and I knew it."

Peter was still off the radar after having left The Monkees at the end of 1968, but he performed a series of shows at the famed Troubadour in Los Angeles on April 16 and April 19, and performed May 29-30 at McCabe's Guitar Shop in Santa Monica, California. He also joined Micky and Davy on what would turn out to be the final known Monkees concert during their original tenure at the Valley REC Center in Van Nuys, California on November 21.

"At the time, we were all thinking that we could go on and have our own careers," Micky said in the 1990s. "But basically, when Peter quit that was kind of the end of The Monkees. It just kind of wound down. There wasn't any great last moment."

Davy appeared on an Australian show called *GTK* (Get to Know) late in the year and explained that he was now a solo artist getting a touring group together. He also stated emphatically said that he was an actor first, unlike, say, Ringo Starr of The Beatles, who was a musical performer first but at the time was pursuing an acting career.

Davy also said that he and Micky were still getting together to record new tracks for the Saturday morning version of *The Monkees* TV show, and expressed no regrets of not being part of Mike's First National Band or their hit "Joanne."

He also made his first appearance on the ABC sitcom *Love, American Style* in an episode entitled "Love and the Elopement," which aired on October 23. He would appear again on the show in 1973. He also appeared as himself on the sitcom *Make Room for Granddaddy*, on December 30 on ABC.

Micky visited the Fermi National Accelerator Laboratory in 1970 when it was first being built at the same time he was starring in a play at the Pheasant Run Playhouse. He would visit the Batavia, Illinois lab site again in 2017. Micky, a self-professed physics geek, would continue to show his love for science over the years.

1971

While Micky and Davy seemed to be plugging away as the final nails of the Monkees coffin were being hammered, and Mike was having success with his First National Band albums and singles, Peter seemed to have dropped off the face of the Earth. This was in evidence with the March 1971 issue of *'Teen Magazine*, where a letter from Susan Harrison asked the question: "There has been a rumor going around in school that Peter Tork died of an overdose of sleeping pills recently. Is this true?"

The response was, "Dear Susan: No, thank goodness; there is *no* truth to this rumor at all. Peter is very much alive and well in Los Angeles."

What this response failed to mention was that Peter was having a terrible time signing a record deal, with or without Release. He also ran out of money and was apparently living in David Crosby's basement at the time, and soon found himself behind bars, having been caught with $3 worth of hashish while crossing the border from Texas to Mexico. Luckily for him at a time when Texas state courts were legendary for locking up drug offenders and throwing away the key, Peter was prosecuted by federal authorities and allowed to serve a short sentence under a special leniency program for first offenders. After three months in an Oklahoma prison, Peter said, "They realized I was not a criminal type, and they let me out." The conviction was later removed from his record, according to an Indianapolis radio interview Peter gave in the 1990s.

The Monkees' last gasp as a group was with a one-off single with Micky and Davy (listed as by "Mickey" as was Micky's preference around this time) called "Do It In the Name of Love." This single was recorded in September 1970 and released to virtually no fanfare in April 1971 by Mickey Dolenz and Davy Jones in the US and by The Monkees in Japan, by which time the Davy Jones solo promotion was in full swing.

Micky seemed to be the obvious one to break out with a great and sustainable solo career, but two things stood in his way. One, Micky was still thinking of himself as an actor and not a musician or singer at this point and two, Micky's self-confidence was eroded due to the extreme rise and fall of his career during the past six years. Micky really wanted to get another acting gig, but somehow could only muster the likes of a voiceover role for the character of Skip Gilroy for the Hanna-Barbera cartoon series *The Funky Phantom*, which was basically another *Scooby-Doo, Where Are You?* clone that H-B littered the airwaves with during the 1970s.

42

Despite trying out for significant roles such as Fonzie for *Happy Days* within the next couple of years, Micky really could not seem to get his career jump-started again after the twin past successes of *Circus Boy* and *The Monkees*. Of his Fonzie audition, Micky said in *I'm a Believer*, "I did manage to get considered for the role of Fonzie on *Happy Days*, but they gave the part to this new kid, Henry Winkler. Henry has told me that he remembers seeing me at the interview and thinking, 'Oh shit, Micky Dolenz is here. I'll never get the part!'"

The First National Band's third album in twelve months didn't make the top 200 chart at all, even though the songs were becoming much more layered, well-written, and better produced.

NEVADA FIGHTER (MN)
Released: May 1971
Highest Chart Position: #218

Grand Ennui (Michael Nesmith)
Propinquity (I've Just Begun To Care) (Michael Nesmith)
Here I Am (Michael Nesmith)
Only Bound (Michael Nesmith)
Nevada Fighter (Michael Nesmith)

Texas Morning (Mike Murphy, Boomer Castleman)
Tumbling Tumbleweeds (Bob Nolan)
I Looked Away (Eric Clapton, Bobby Whitlock)
Rainmaker (Harry Nilsson, Bill Martin)
René (Red Rhodes)

Nevada Fighter (Michael Nesmith) / **Here I Am** (Michael Nesmith) (MN) (April 1971) *Highest Chart Position:* #70

Texas Morning (Mike Murphy, Boomer Castleman) / **Tumbling Tumbleweeds** (Bob Nolan) (MN) (June 1971)

I've Just Begun to Care (Propinquity) (Michael Nesmith) / **Only Bound** (Michael Nesmith) (MN) (October 1971)

Interestingly, this song was known as "Propinquity (I've Just Begun to Care)" on the album and reversed for the single.

Michael and The First National Band performed at the Bistro in Atlanta, Alabama in early September for four days. He also appeared on *American Bandstand* on May 8 on ABC and on the US version of *The David Frost Show* on October 14 and December 16.

Despite all the media push, the First National Band failed to catch on, and Michael started worrying.

It's interesting to see that it was Davy that was given the initial post-Monkees push from Bell Records rather than Micky, despite the fact that Micky had more lead vocal hit singles with the group. Bell assigned him Jackie Mills, Bobby Sherman's producer, who saw Davy as a bubblegum singer and picked the songs for the album for him. Davy was not happy with the final result or the terrible album cover, which featured his face looking confused along with a track listing—something that had fallen out of favor for album covers years earlier.

DAVY JONES
Release: Bell 6067, May 1971
Highest Chart Position: #205

Road To Love (Carol Carmichael)
How About Me (John Carrington)
Singin' To The Music (Danny Jannsen)
Rainy Jane (Howard Greenfield, Neil Sedaka)
Look At Me (David Gates)
Say It Again (Ed Welch, Carl Simmons)

I Really Love You (Bob Gundry)
Love Me For A Day (Tony Rossine)
Sitting In the Apple Tree (Douglas Trevor)
Take My Love (Gordon Marron, Reid Reilich, Loren Newkirk)
Pretty Little Girl (Gloria Sklerov, Harry Lloyd)
Welcome To My Love (Steve Goldman)

2012 Friday Music reissue CD bonus tracks:
Girl (Charles Fox, Norman Gimbel)
I'll Believe In You (James Stover)
Take My Love (mono) (Gordon Marron, Reid Reilich, Loren Newkirk)
Road to Love (B side) (Carol Carmichael)
How About Me (mono) (John Carrington)
I Really Love You (mono) (Bob Gundry)

44

Singles released from or at the time of this album:

Rainy Jane (Howard Greenfield, Neil Sedaka) / **Welcome To My Love** (Steve Goldman) (Bell 111, May 1971) *Highest Chart Position: #52*

I Really Love You (Bob Gundry) / **Sitting In the Apple Tree** (Douglas Trevor) (Bell 136, September 1971)

Girl (Charles Fox, Norman Gimbel) / **Take My Love** (Gordon Marron, Reid Reilich, Loren Newkirk) (Bell 159, December 1971)

I'll Believe In You (James Stover) / **Road to Love** (Carol Carmichael) (Bell 178, February 1972)

This is a pretty good album for Davy. Fortunately, Bell picked songs for him and instead of the Broadway-influenced work he was writing in the final days of The Monkees' career, these were good pop songs of the type that were hits for The Partridge Family (another pre-made TV pop group on Bell). "Rainy Jane" made the charts but never the top 40, and should have done better, perhaps with more of a promotional push from the label. "Look at Me" (a cover of a Bread song) and "Take My Love" are also highlights.

What is strange is this album's lack of success despite four singles being released from the album. Equally strange is that there was not a follow-up album, but as Davy said in his autobiography, he was not pleased with the direction that his record career was going post-Monkees.

Davy wanted to continue to be an all-around entertainer, but that occupation was slowly going away. He should have made a choice to do all music like Mike did, or to do (virtually) all acting like Micky did. It might have been all for naught, as being a Monkee by this time was a serious liability.

Perhaps it was due to Davy (and Micky) still being screened each and every Saturday morning through 1973 romping with his former bandmates, but the more likely scenario is that Davy was strongly dissatisfied with Bell Records and their management in comparison to Colgems and how he was being marketed. Eventually, though the calendar years of 1971 and 1972, as Davy's star power eroded on the pages of even supportive magazines as *16* and *Tiger Beat*, he was slowly being eclipsed and replaced by the likes of David Cassidy, Bobby Sherman and Donny Osmond.

Davy appeared as himself and performed "French Song" in a Filipino film called *Lollipops, Roses and Talangka*, released June 5, and on *American Bandstand* on ABC on September 4 where he sang "Rainy Jane".

In the middle of all of this, Davy had another daughter with wife Linda.

Davy performed live on October 23 at the Kleinhans Music Hall in Buffalo, New York, but amazingly, didn't tour more at this time to promote his album. He also appeared on *The Merv Griffin Show* on December 13.

At the tail end of the year, Davy returned to acting with an eponymous cameo appearance on *The Brady Bunch* on the episode entitled "Getting Davy Jones" (original airdate: December 10) on ABC, singing "Girl" which was to have significantly positive repercussions in future decades. At the time, it was yet another appearance designed to reignite Davy's faltering career. His song "Girl" also appeared in the comedy feature film *Star Spangled Girl* starring Sandy Duncan, released December 22.

Sometime in 1971, Micky signed with MGM and recorded 28 songs over the next three years, many of which were not released until 2016, the rest apparently lost to history. The first single from this period came out in October.

Easy on You (Micky Dolenz) / **Oh Someone** (David Price) (MD) (MGM K-14309) (October 1971)

This was produced by Micky Dolenz with an arrangement by David Price, Micky Dolenz and Peter Tork. It's definitely identifiable as a Micky-written song, and has a weird little synthesizer running like a crazy buzzing bee throughout which is clever at first but gets kind of annoying after a listen.

1972

Micky appeared on the penultimate episode of *My Three Sons* called "Barbara Lost," airing on April 6. A review on IMDB says, "'Barbara Lost' stars former Monkee Micky Dolenz as Chip's boyhood pal Brian Lipsker, who has since become the leader of a successful rock group under the name John Simpson. Charlie invites John over for dinner, serving him his favorite chili dogs, and asks how much he makes per year. 'Under two million' has Charlie wondering if he means 'dollars or trading stamps!' Now Chip has notions of giving up chemical engineering for the glamorous life of a rock star, playing his acoustic guitar around the house. After the dinner scene, we see Micky working the mixing board at the recording studio, listening to the group's performance and making corrections. Sadly, he doesn't perform any songs, so this episode can't hold a candle to *The Brady Bunch's* 'Getting Davy Jones'."

Micky also appeared as a character named Oiler on the *Adam-12* episode "Dirt Duel," which aired on September 13. If you ever wanted to know what Micky would look like as The Fonz if he got the role on *Happy Days*, check this episode out with Micky's hair all slicked back. Here, and on *My Three Sons*, he is billed as Mickey Dolenz.

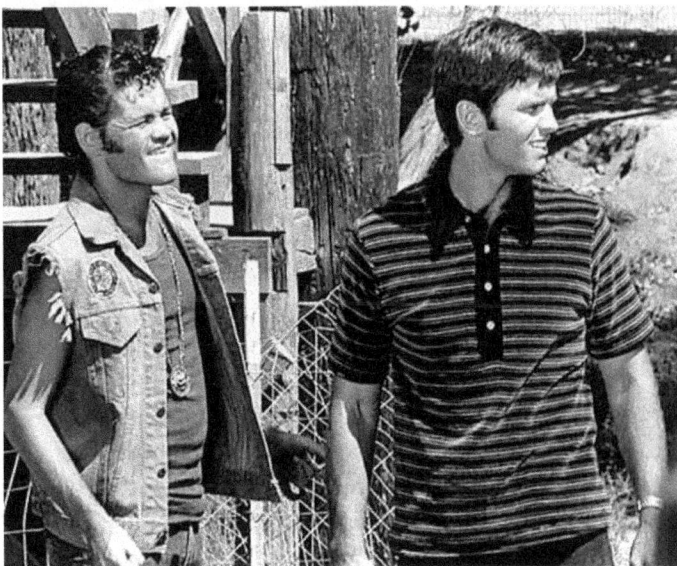

He also appeared on *Cannon* in an episode entitled "Bitter Legion" which aired September 27, and in the feature film *Night of the Strangler* as Vance, released on October 1. In 2018 he was asked about this film on Twitter and he laughingly said "Actually, I have spent the last 45 years blocking it out."

"When I saw that the first three FNB albums were not going to be successful," Michael wrote in *Infinite Tuesday*, "instead of changing the environment of the management or the administrative overhead, where were where the problems lay, I changed the band. The Second National Band came and went in a flash, with only one album. At this point, the powers at RCA gave me notice that I were to continue there, I needed to concentrate on making hit records."

TANTAMOUNT TO TREASON VOL. 1 (MN)
Released: February 1972
Highest Chart Position: #211

Mama Rocker (Michael Nesmith)
Lazy Lady (Michael Nesmith)
You Are My One (Michael Nesmith)
In the Afternoon (Michael Nesmith)

Highway 99 With Melange (Michael
Cohen)
Wax Minute (Richard Stekol)
Bonaparte's Retreat (Pee Wee King, Redd
Stewart)
Talking to the Wall (Bill Chadwick)
She Thinks I Still Care (Dickey Lee, Steve Duffy)

2000 reissue bonus tracks:
Cantata and Fugue in C&W (Michael Nesmith)
Smoke! Smoke! Smoke! (That Cigarette) (Merle Travis, Tex Williams)
Rose City Chimes (Michael Nesmith)

Mama Rocker (Michael Nesmith) / **Lazy Lady** (Michael Nesmith) (MN) (January 1972)

This is the best of the early Michael Nesmith albums—well produced, with interesting songs and lyrics, and more accessible than his earlier country albums. Many of the songs meld into each other so that the album has a completeness missing from previous efforts. Side one is all Nesmith originals, with the highlight being "Mama Rocker," and side two is all covers, with the highlight being "Talking to the Wall."

The album cover itself is interesting, especially because on the back cover, instead of your standard liner notes, Michael includes a recipe for making beer.

And no, there was never a Volume 2.

Micky's next MGM single was a strange little ditty that has "Micky" stamped all over it—quirky and imaginative and not at all the kind of thing you would hear on the radio in 1972. So you didn't.

Unattended in the Dungeon (Bobby Jones) / **A Lover's Prayer** (Randy Newman) (MD) (MGM K-14395, June 1972)

When *Tantamount to Treason* also failed to chart, Michael called in Red Rhodes and the two of them rushed out an album of acoustic songs with an ironic title.

48

AND THE HITS JUST KEEP ON COMIN' (MN)

Released: August 1972
Highest Chart Position: #208

Tomorrow and Me (Michael Nesmith)
The Upside of Goodbye (Michael Nesmith)
Lady Love (Michael Nesmith)
Listening (Michael Nesmith)
Two Different Roads (Michael Nesmith)

The Candidate (Michael Nesmith)
Different Drum (Michael Nesmith)
Harmony Constant (Michael Nesmith)
Keep On (Michael Nesmith)
Roll with the Flow (Michael Nesmith)

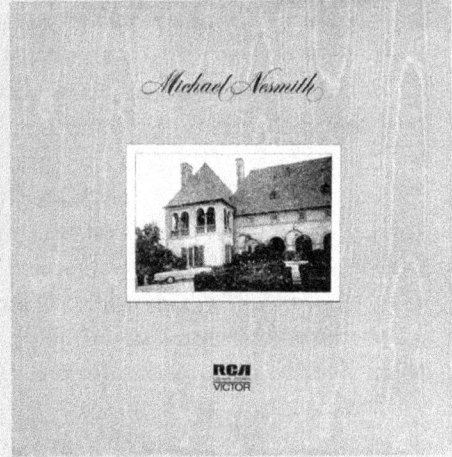

Roll With the Flow (Michael Nesmith) / **Keep On** (Michael Nesmith) (MN)
(August 1972)

This album is the first time Michael recorded "Different Drum," the song he wrote for Linda Ronstadt who had a hit with it a few years earlier. Michael performed a solo concert at McCabe's Guitar Shop, Santa Monica, California, on May 11.

After being part of Colgems, then Bell, Davy finally made his break and landed at MGM Records but had even less success. It is a mystery why no album was attempted while he was at MGM—just two singles which went nowhere.

You're a Lady (Peter Skellern) / **Who Was It?** (Gilbert O'Sullivan) (DJ) (MGM 14458, November 1972)

This A-side is not the 1973 Flo and Eddie single. Theirs was upbeat; Davy's is more of a standard ballad. A Japanese-sung version of this was also recorded. The B-side was done in a kind of a similar in style to "Daddy's Song" but is not very memorable. It was written by Gilbert O'Sullivan, best known for his own hit "Alone Again (Naturally)," also from 1972.

Johnny B. Goode (Chuck Berry) / **It's Amazing To Me** (Mickey Dolenz) (MD as Starship) (Lion 132) (October 1972)

Micky's next single was the old Chuck Berry classic "Johnny B. Goode," which he had played at his audition to be in The Monkees. It was the early 1970s and The Monkees were anything but cool, so perhaps in an effort to hide the fact, the record was credited to "Starship." (This predates Jefferson Starship, of course.) That may have worked but

Johnny B. Goode has been recorded by so many performers over the years that no one was really interested in listening to a version that didn't add something new, and the single went nowhere. To make it even worse, Micky isn't singing lead!

The B-side was a bit more interesting. Micky sings a laid-back song with some excellent harmonies, it might have gotten some attention had it not been on some minor little label that did nothing to promote it. Micky is credited as writer as Mickey Dolenz.

Taking a lead from Micky, Davy, too, started lending his voice to animated cartoon work, starting in 1972. His first assignment was appearing as himself in Hanna-Barbera's *The New Scooby-Doo Movies*, in the episode entitled "The Haunted Horseman in Hagglethorn Hall," which originally aired on December 2 on CBS. Davy even sang a song! "I Can Make You Happy" eventually appeared on CD on the September 5, 1998 collection called *Scooby-Doo's Snack Tracks: The Ultimate Collection*.

Davy also appeared on *The Mike Douglas Show* on August 21, once again on *American Bandstand* on July 15, and on *The Merv Griffin Show* on June 26, where he sang "Consider Yourself." Perhaps he was hoping for an *Oliver!* reunion show.

1973

Rubberene (Alan O'Day) (DJ) (promo only, mono/stereo) (MGM 145242, January 1973)

Davy's next single is an an ode to a rubber sex doll, however, its dixieland style seemed totally out of step with the type of music that was generally being released during 1973. The song has shades of "Cuddly Toy" and perhaps that's what they were going for with this release. However, it didn't even get a proper stock copy release, which is how badly it fared. This was the end of Davy Jones' solo career until after the Dolenz, Jones, Boyce and Hart years and his subsequent team-up with Micky. His next solo release would be his Christmas album in 1977.

Davy then provided the voice Filmation's animated *Treasure Island* in which Davy portrayed Jim Hawkins. It was released theatrically on July 11, and then aired on television the first time on NBC on April 29, 1980.

Davy didn't shy away from live-action episodic television work at this time, returning to *Love, American Style* on November 30, airing on ABC, in the episode called "Love and the Model Apartment."

According to Davy's *They Made a Monkee Out of Me*, he was offered a six month theatre engagement in England in December, appearing in the play *Forget-Me-Not Lane* which got him away from the turmoil he was suffering in California. "My life with Linda seemed ages away," Davy recalled, "and I was glad to be back in England working in the theatre again."

There he made friends with fellow actor Tom Owen, and when the play ended, Tom accompanied Davy back to the states, where Davy got a job at L.A.'s Music Centre in (wait for it) a revival of *Oliver!* with Ron Moody, who reprised his role as Fagin from the film version. After six weeks in L.A., the play moved to the Curran Theatre in San Francisco.

Micky continued his voiceover work, voicing Harvey in Hanna-Barbera's animated *Butch Cassidy and the Sundance Kids*, airing during the 1973-1974 season on Saturday mornings. He appeared on *Owen Marshall, Counselor at Law* in the episode called "The Camerons Are a Special Clan," airing on October 4. On both series, Micky is billed as Mickey Dolenz.

Micky also appeared on *Top of the Pops* on December 27, and he took time out in 1973 to film a well-remembered commercial for *The #1 Hits of the 60s*, a four-record set from Tele House, also available on 8-track tapes!

Daybreak (Harry Nilsson) / **Love War** (Mickey Dolenz) (MD) (Romar RO-710) (May 1973)

"Daybreak" is a song from the movie Harry Nilsson made with Ringo Starr called *Son of Dracula*. It's a terrible home-movie kind of film memorable only for Nilsson's music. Micky had become quite a friend of Nilsson around this time, and you can even see pictures of him on Nilsson's 1975 album *Duit on Mon Dei* although it doesn't appear that Micky performed with Nilsson at all.

In any event, this single is quite well done, but there really was no need for it given Nilsson's own version. The B-side is terribly recorded, with a tinny guitar and hardly any enthusiasm from the musicians, but underneath it all, it's a well written song with country influence. You could almost hear Michael singing it... Again, Micky is credited as Mickey Dolenz on both sides, but there are some pressings where he is Micky Dolenz.

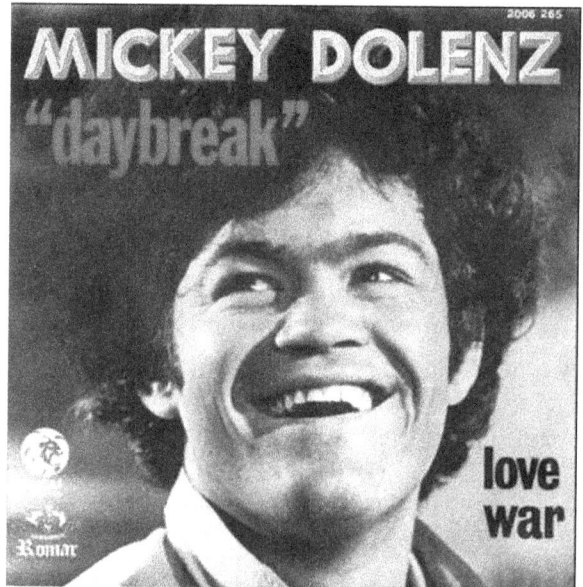

Michael's final album with RCA was *Pretty Much Your Standard Ranch Stash* while at the same time, he was starting his own label Countryside. "Countryside came about when Jac Holzman, who was then president of Elektra Records, and I put together a deal where I would start a label that would in essence be Elektra's country division," he wrote in *Infinite Tuesday*. His new band of Countryside performers did an excellent job, and *Ranch Stash* is a fine album which, sadly, had poor sales.

Strangely, no singles were released from the LP, despite there being some fine song selections that could have been hits. "Some of Shelly's Blues" had been recorded by the Nitty Gritty Dirt Band in 1970 and was a crowd favorite, and "Continuing" is a fine country ballad that should have gotten more attenton.

However, RCA wasn't about to take a risk anymore and was saving their money on their final Nez release.

MICHAEL A. VENTRELLA AND MARK ARNOLD

PRETTY MUCH YOUR STANDARD RANCH STASH (MN)
Released: September 1973

Continuing (Michael Nesmith)
Some of Shelly's Blues (Michael Nesmith)
Release (Michael Nesmith)
Winonah (Michael Nesmith, Linda Hargrove, James Miner)

Born to Love You (Cindy Walker)
The Back Porch and a Fruit Jar Full of Iced Tea
      a. The F.F.V (Trad. Arrangement by Michael Nesmith)
      b. Uncle Pen (Bill Monroe)
Prairie Lullaby (Billy Hill)

Michael also made a concert appearance on August 18, at McCabe's in Santa Monica, California, that became the basis for the 7a Records album *Cosmic Partners* by Michael Nesmith and Red Rhodes. The CD and LP of the show was released in 2019, and contains some great performances of Michael's best songs. (More on that when we get to 2019.)

1974

Countryside as a label did not last long. David Geffen came into power at Elektra and decided there was no need for Countryside. Geffen was nice enough to Michael and didn't just kick him out the door. He allowed him to stay in the studio and use it for a while, but Michael was in a quandary. His sales were weak, money was disappearing, and he couldn't afford to just move on. "I had no opportunities as an actor, a player, a singer, a songwriter, or a producer, given my sales history with RCA and my recent crisis of confidence in any ability I might have to pursue goals along those lines," Michael wrote in *Infinite Tuesday*.

He turned to his mother, who had started the Liquid Paper Corporation. (Yes, it's absolutely true—Michael Nesmith's mother invented Liquid Paper. Not an urban myth.) Her Board of Directors took one look at Michael's career—not to mention his chaotic personal life (he was no longer with his wife or either of his mistresses but had fallen in love with a new woman named Kathryn)—and decided he was not a good risk.

Michael and Kathryn decided the best thing to do was to finish recording a new album while he had access to the Countryside studio and then move north to Carmel, where they could live in his mother's vacation home. Maybe they could start a new business there.

Michael asked for a divorce on February 1. So now he also had alimony and child support payments due on top of all his other commitments.

So what did he do? Did he try to make the most accessible record possible to regain his audience and make lots of money?

No. He wrote a meaningful new-age concept album.

THE PRISON: A BOOK WITH A SOUNDTRACK (MN)
Released: 1974

Opening Theme (Life, the Unsuspecting Captive) (Michael Nesmith)
Dance Between the Raindrops (Michael Nesmith)
Elusive Ragings (Michael Nesmith)
Waking Mystery (Michael Nesmith)

Hear Me Calling? (Michael Nesmith)
Marie's Theme (Michael Nesmith)
Closing Theme (Lampost) (Michael Nesmith)

No singles were released from this album, but "Life, the Unsuspecting Captive" was issued as the B-side to "Rio" in 1977.

The Prison was a book with a soundtrack, recorded it in just over a week, with Red Rhoades. It was a tremendously important record for him personally but a terrible one to present to the public. No major record distributor was interested in it, and it only sold a few hundred copies.

Michael decided the way to promote it was through a concert in San Francisco at the Palace of Fine Arts. "On opening night, it didn't take long into the performance for me to have the feeling that I was a sitting duck," Michael later wrote. "The critics were out in force, and it was a massacre. Fortunately, such critical reception didn't hurt the record sales, since there were no record sales. *The Prison* opened and closed in one night."

Michael later appeared live at The Roundhouse in London, England, on April 28 to celebrate the fifth anniversary of *Zig Zag Magazine*. This performance was finally released on *The Amazing Zig Zag Concert* on October 11, 2010 in a five CD box set. Nesmith with Red Rhoades takes up the entire fifth disc. John Stewart, the composer of "Daydream Believer," performed this and other songs on disc three. The rest of the discs are comprised of other performers.

Michael established Pacific Arts later in 1974. Given his recent track record, he had no idea at the time that it would become successful.

Micky continued his voiceover work, doing various voices for Hanna-Barbera's animated *These Are the Days* and on H-B's *Devlin* and *The Partridge Family 2200 A.D.*, all airing during the 1974-1975 season on Saturday mornings. He also released another single which went nowhere—a medley of "Peggy Sue," "Every Day," "Maybe Baby" and "That'll be the Day." It was well performed and sung, with the songs flowing into each other just fine. This should not be confused with "Tribute to Buddy Holly" by Mike Berry and the Outlaws, which is actually a song composed in tribute to Holly.

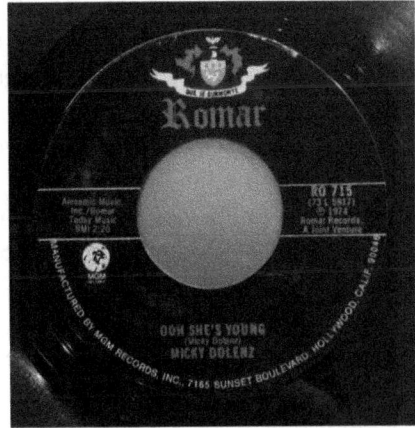

Buddy Holly Tribute (Norman Petty, Jerry Allison, Buddy Holly) / **Ooh She's Young** (Micky Dolenz) (MD) (Romar RO-715) (April 1974)

Davy reprised his role of The Artful Dodger for an animated version of *Oliver Twist*, released theatrically on July 10 and airing on television on NBC on April 14, 1981. It is highly likely that Davy recorded his voiceovers for both features at the same time, since both sport similar voice casts as 1973's *Treasure Island*. He also appeared on a show called *In Session* with Peter Noone.

1975

Peter got married for a third time in January to Barbara A. Iannoli, which conflicts with the fact that his divorce had not completely gone through with Reine E. Stewart, with whom he was married until June. He and Barbara had a child named Ivan Joseph Ianolli, born December 22. They remained married until 1987.

Michael's divorce from Phyllis was finalized on March 21.

Micky, Davy, Michael and Peter gathered together early in the year to consider several offers to reunite The Monkees. "We met up at my house, up in the Hollywood Hills," Micky told Monkees archivist Andrew Sandoval. "I think it was William Morris Agency or something expressed an interest in putting the act back together. Everybody was very enthusiastic about it on the surface. You know, 'Oh great, great idea,' but when it got down to the nitty gritty there were too many conflicting feelings and attitudes ... Actually I remember it being really exciting. We all got together for the first time in quite a few years in the same room and there was a hell of a buzz."

They were offered a lot of money as well for a McDonald's commercial, but Peter refused (being a vegetarian) and Michael also said he wasn't interested (which is interesting given his economic situation at the time).

The reunion never happened, but it led to Micky and Davy teaming up with Tommy Boyce and Bobby Hart, to form Dolenz, Jones, Boyce and Hart. They promoted themselves as the "Guys who sang them and the guys who wrote them" even though Boyce and Hart had only written some of their various hits.

The DJB&H Tour lasted from June 21, 1975 through August 27, 1976, performing 86 dates before Boyce and Hart bowed out.

It's probably easy to see why Micky agreed to do the reunion since his recent film roles were of "You Know" in *Keep Off My Grass*, released in March, and "Lt. Fenwick" in *Linda Lovelace For President*, released in April. Neither film was memorable and Micky would probably prefer that these were forgotten.

Micky also appeared on *The Hoyt Axton Country Western Boogie Woogie Gospel Rock and Roll Show*, airing on March 22. His marriage to Samantha also ended this year.

The DJB&H tour was doing well, so an album was quickly recorded, with a single being released in December.

I Remember the Feeling (Tommy Boyce, Bobby Hart) / **You and I** (Micky Dolenz, Davy Jones) (DJB&H) (December 1975)

Micky commented on the DJB&H experience in *I'm a Believer*: "DJB&H were touring pretty steadily, and we eventually got booked on an extensive Far East tour. Like an idiot, I went hang-gliding two days before the tour and broke my arm! I did the entire tour with my arm in a sling and my brain on painkillers."

Meanwhile, Michael performed solo at the Paris Theatre in London, England on November 27. His song "The World is Golden Too" appeared on the *Blue Angels* soundtrack.

BLUE ANGELS SOUNDTRACK (MN with Fred Myrow, Jim Connor) One track only.
Released: 1975

Dawn: Eagle Call/The World Is Golden Too

Blue Angels as a movie is a pretty straightforward documentary, but for those interested in the subject, it is very good. Michael's song on the soundtrack really enhances the film.

57

1976

DOLENZ, JONES, BOYCE AND HART (DJB&H)
Released: May 1976

Right Now (Tommy Boyce, Bobby Hart)
I Love You (and I'm Glad That I Said it) (Tommy Boyce, Bobby Hart)
You and I (Micky Dolenz, Davy Jones)
Teenager in Love (Doc Pomus, Mort Shuman)
Sail on Sailor (Doug Trevor)
It Always Hurts the Most in the Morning (Tommy Boyce, Micky Dolenz)

Moonfire (William E. Martin)
You Didn't Feel That Way Last Night (Don't You Remember?) (Tommy Boyce, Bobby Hart)
Along Came Jones (Jerry Leiber, Mike Stoller)
Savin' My Love For You (Micky Dolenz, Davy Jones)
I Remember the Feeling (Tommy Boyce, Bobby Hart)
Sweet Heart Attack (Tommy Boyce, Bobby Hart)

I Love You (and I'm Glad That I Said It) (Tommy Boyce, Bobby Hart) / **Saving My Love** for You (Micky Dolenz, Davy Jones) (DJB&H) (May 10, 1976)

Right Now (Tommy Boyce, Bobby Hart) / **You Didn't Feel That Way Last Night** (Tommy Boyce, Bobby Hart) (DJB&H) (1976, Japan only)

DJB&H made an appearance on Dinah Shore's talk show *Dinah!* airing January 21 in syndication. They performed "(Theme From) The Monkees," "Last Train to Clarksville," "I Wanna Be Free," "Pleasant Valley Sunday," "I'm A Believer," "Daydream Believer," "Keep On Singing," and "I Remember The Feeling." DJB&H also appeared (ironically) on *Don Kirshner's Rock Concert* on February 14, *The Mike Douglas Show* on February 27, and on *American Bandstand* on March 13 on ABC.

"It was a much needed change," Davy said about the tour in *They Made a Monkee Out of Me*. "I'd felt as though I was stagnating, 90 miles from LA, surrounded by all Linda's fashion-conscious people in their trendy wine-bars. We were pretty much leading separate lives by now, tolerating each other only for the childrens' sake. So while I was on the road with Micky, Boyce and Hart, I did all the things I never did when I was 15, 16, 21. Women, booze... I went crazy. After a year on the road, I came back and there was nothing there between Linda and me, so I stayed in LA with Micky in his place, up on Lookout Mountain in Laurel Canyon. On the night of the Grammy Awards, Linda came back there and started talking about getting a separation. I said, no, it's divorce or nothing."

The song "You and I" (sung by Micky) was later re-recorded by The Monkees for their *Justus* album with Davy handling the lead vocals.

Michael composed the music for the film *Northville Cemetery Massacre*, a low-budget Roger Corman-esque film, released in March. He didn't get paid for it, which he didn't mind. It was mostly the leftover stuff from Countryside recordings, anyway.

He married Kathyrn Bild on Leap Day in a civil ceremony.

During this same period of time, approximately 1973-1976, Michael got heavily involved with the Christian Scientist religion, due to encouragement from his mother. He was introduced to a leading Christian Science teacher named Paul Seeley.

Peter, meanwhile, became a teacher. Mr. Thorkelson taught English, math, drama, Eastern philosophy and Rock Band Class at Pacific Hills, a private secondary school in Santa Monica. He lived in a small house with Barbara, their 8-week-old son, Ivan Iannoli-Thorkelson, and his daughter Hallie, 6, from his first marriage.

Peter joined Dolenz, Jones, Boyce and Hart for one concert in Disneyland on July 4 for a bicentennial celebration, then later in the year recorded "Christmas Is My Time of Year" with Dolenz and Jones for an ersatz Monkees reunion single for the Davy Jones Fan Club. (This song was later remastered for the Monkees *Christmas Party* album in 2018.)

Micky appeared solo on the TV game show *Break the Bank*, airing on May 19.

1977

After DJB&H ran its course after 1975 and 1976, Micky and Davy continued on touring during 1977. They performed ten dates in Hollywood and New York from March 24 to April 17. As Micky commented in *I'm a Believer*, "The DBJ&H situation lasted for a few more months, and then Davy and I struck out on our own as Dolenz and Jones. Davy and I always worked well together on stage, and we continued to tour around the States dressed up in funny suits and singing the old songs over and over again. Coco even came out with us on the road for a while and added a bit of class to the proceedings."

"We opened in a punk club in LA," Davy recalled, "then headed for Reno, Nevada, where Micky fired the brass section and two of the singers—leaving his sister, Coco, and his girlfriend, Trina, whom he'd met on the DJB&H tour in Chicago. She was shooting pictures for a *Playboy* spread and Micky went all over town buying up every copy he could lay his hands on."

Meanwhile, Davy appeared as "Davey Sanders" in "The Bluegrass Special" episode of *The Wonderful World of Disney*, airing May 22 on NBC. This episode is available on DVD through the Disney Movie Club.

The Micky and Davy team continued on during the year, performing in a musical version of *Tom Sawyer* in Sacramento, California. Despite being way older than the characters they portrayed, Micky was Huck Finn and Davy was Tom. "You haven't lived until you've heard Tom Sawyer with a thick, North Country English accent," Micky said.

Micky and Davy appeared together on Tom Snyder's *Tomorrow Show* on September 1. They did not perform, but answered many questions about The Monkees and their solo careers that had not been discussed much to that point. They insisted that the four did get along. They also appeared together on *Our Show*, to promote *The Point!* in the UK, airing on December 17.

The Point!, of course, was Harry Nilsson's musical that had been turned into an animated special a few years earlier. "Harry Nilsson decided he couldn't live without me playing Oblio in the London production of *The Point*," Davy said, "and Micky decided we should keep the partnership intact. 'Hey, we could be like

Crosby and Hope, Martin and Lewis, Morecambe and Wise.' So Micky was written into the show that debuted in November 1977."

"I honestly thought that the run of *The Point* was going to be one of the highlights of my career. I thought that I would finally be able to break out of the mold that The Monkees had fashioned around me," Micky said. However, it was during this run of *The Point* that Davy and Micky had such a major falling out that they wouldn't even speak to each other for nine years.

Micky felt that Davy was "determined to sabotage his own success" and had become an unhappy, bitter misanthrope. This was a complaint that followed Davy even through the various reunions, and was borne out by Davy's actions which would later destroy their MTV-led resurgence in the late 80s.

THE POINT! (MD & DJ)
Released: 1977, UK; July 1, 2016, US

Overture – Orchestra (Harry Nilsson)
Everything's Got 'Em – Company (Harry Nilsson)
Me and My Arrow – Davy Jones (Harry Nilsson)
Poli High – Company (Harry Nilsson)
Remember – Veronica Clifford (Harry Nilsson)
To Be a King – Noel Howlett and Company (Harry Nilsson)
He's Leaving Here This Morning (Bath) – Micky Dolenz, Colin Bennett, Clovissa Newcombe (Harry Nilsson)
Think About Your Troubles – Davy Jones and Company (Harry Nilsson)

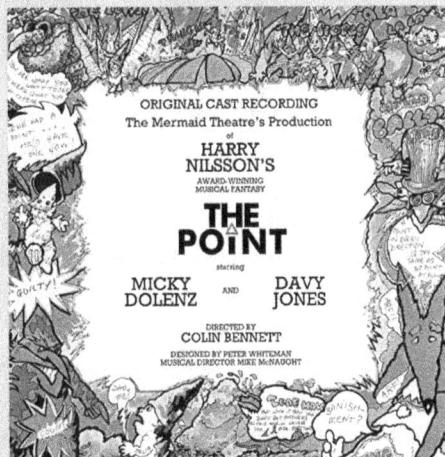

ORIGINAL CAST RECORDING
The Mermaid Theatre's Production
of
HARRY NILSSON'S
AWARD-WINNING
MUSICAL FANTASY
THE POINT
starring
MICKY DOLENZ AND DAVY JONES
DIRECTED BY
COLIN BENNETT
DESIGNED BY PETER WHITEMAN
MUSICAL DIRECTOR MIKE McNAUGHT

Blanket For a Sail – Davy Jones (Harry Nilsson)
Life Line – Davy Jones (Harry Nilsson)
Thursday (Here's Why I Did Not Go to Work Today) – Felix Rice (Harry Nilsson, Danny Kortchmar)
It's a Jungle Out There – Micky Dolenz (Harry Nilsson)
P.O.V. Waltz – Davy Jones and Company (Harry Nilsson)
Are You Sleeping? (Song Title) – Davy Jones and Company (Harry Nilsson)
Gotta Get Up – Davy Jones, Micky Dolenz (Harry Nilsson)
Reprise Overture – Orchestra (Harry Nilsson)

Life Line (Harry Nilsson) (DJ) // **It's a Jungle Out There** (Harry Nilsson) (MD) / **Gotta Get Up** (Harry Nilsson) (MD & DJ) (January 27, 1978, UK only)

This is quite a good album and perfect for Micky and Davy (since Davy had sung Nilsson's "Cuddly Toy" and "Daddy's Song" for the Monkees). The play adds extra Nilsson songs that were not heard in "The Point" movie, such as "Bath," "It's a Jungle Out There" and "Gotta Get Up" (not to mention "Remember" which Micky would later cover on two separate albums years later).

In happier news, Micky married Trina on June 18 (like his first wife, also British), and decided to stay in England for a while. He resumed his voiceover work, voicing Willy Sheeler on the animated *Wonder Wheels* segment of Hanna-Barbera's live-action *The Skatebirds*, airing during the 1977-1978 season on Saturday mornings, where he is billed as Mickey Dolenz. He also performed various voices on H-B's *Captain Caveman and the Teen Angels* animated series airing during the 1977-1978 season.

On July 31, Peter played at CBGB's, the legendary Manhattan music club that featured rising stars of punk and new wave. Legendary critic Lester Bangs, from *Rolling Stone*, *Creem* and *The Village Voice*, wrote an extremely negative review of the show, as well as negative reviews on the previous year's DJB&H shows.

Peter continued teaching English and math and began writing his autobiography which, since his death, may never see the light of day. It had the working title of *Monkee Business (or Why I Pawned My Gold Records)*.

Michael appeared on the UK *Top of the Pops* on March 31, and played a solo show on November 10, at The Palais, in Melbourne, Australia. This concert was the source for Michael's 1978 album *Live at The Palais*.

But most importantly, in 1977, he had an idea.

He was working on his next album, *From a Radio Engine to a Photon Wing*, which would be released from his new company Pacific Arts. He gathered some great musicians, including many who had worked with him in The Monkees days: David Briggs, the keyboardist on "Listen to the Band," Jerry Carrigan and Larrie London on drums, Weldon Myrick on steel; and David MacKay on bass.

He presented the finished product to Chris Blackwell from Island Records who would be distributing the album. Blackwell thought "Rio" was a winner, and asked Michael to trim it down a bit to make it more palatable to radio stations. "Oh, and can you make a promotional clip for it?"

In Europe, artists would often make promo clips for their singles—cheap little lip-sync performances where the band pretended to play the song like they used to do on *American Bandstand*. Blackwell expected Michael to stand in front of a microphone, look into the camera, and move his mouth to the words.

Michael had other ideas.

"In my mind, the assignment triggered a remembrance of scenes of every Hollywood musical I had ever seen all the way up to and including *A Hard Day's Night* and *The Monkees* TV shows," Michael said in *Infinite Tuesday*. "Island Records had no allowances for this."

Michael took royalties received from radio play of his songs while in The Monkees and was able to gather up $25,000, which is about 100 times more than record companies paid at the time to record these little clips. Gathering some talented friends, he recorded a wonderful, entertaining mini-movie of the song. And no one in America knew what to do with it.

Meanwhile, the album was released.

FROM A RADIO ENGINE TO THE PHOTON WING (MN)
Released: March 1977
Highest Chart Position: #209

Rio (Michael Nesmith)
Casablanca Moonlight (Michael Nesmith)
More Than We Imagine (Michael Nesmith)
Navajo Trail (Majorie Elliot)
We are Awake (Michael Nesmith)
Wisdom has its Way (Michael Nesmith)
Love's First Kiss (Fred Myrow, Michael Nesmith)
The Other Room (Michael Nesmith)

Rio (Michael Nesmith) / Life, the Unsuspecting Captive (Michael Nesmith) (MN) (April 1977)

We Are Awake (Michael Nesmith) / Love's First Kiss (Fred Myrow, Michael Nesmith) (MN) (1977. New Zealand only)

Navajo Trail (Majorie Elliot) / Love's First Kiss (Fred Myrow, Michael Nesmith) (MN) (July 1, 1977, UK only)

This is an excellent album, one of Michael's best. The transition from strict country to a more pop sound at this point in Michael's career really served him well (and will be even more pronounced on his next album). Michael properly credits the great musicians who performed on this record for making it sound so good, and specifically David MacKay, whose bass really pushed "Rio" forward, and Lonnie Mack on guitar.

The "Rio" clip was well received in Europe, but there really wasn't an outlet for such a thing in America. Michael decided there had to be a way. "After all," he though, "audio records are played on the radio, so a video record should be played on video—on television."

Meanwhile, "Rio" became a hit in Australia, and became Michael's first gold record. He gathered a band and went there to perform. Upon arriving, he was told by the locals that they loved his popclip, referring to the video in a term Michael had never heard before.

"I thought *Popclips* would make a wonderful daily afternoon show right after school," Michael said. He was able to find a few other promo clips he could use and prepared a pilot for a proposed syndicated show he could take to the distributors.

1977 also saw a "Greatest Hits" collection.

COMPILATION (MN) (compilation)
Released: 1977

Some of Shelly's Blues (Michael Nesmith)
I Fall to Pieces (Harlan Howard, Hank Cochran)
Born to Love You (Cindy Walker)
Different Drum (Michael Nesmith)
Harmony Constant (Michael Nesmith)
Prairie Lullaby (Billy Hill)

Joanne (Michael Nesmith)
Propinquity (I've Just Begun to Care) (Michael Nesmith)
Silver Moon (Michael Nesmith)
I Looked Away (Bobby Whitlock, Eric Clapton)
Continuing (Michael Nesmith)
Roll With the Flow (Michael Nesmith)

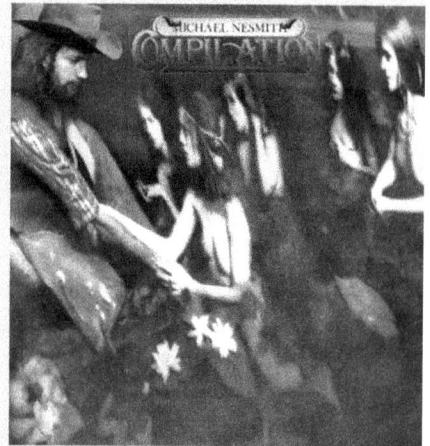

Davy meanwhile reunited with Chip Douglas, who had produced two of The Monkees' best albums as well as "Daydream Believer" and "Pleasant Valley Sunday." This resulted in a little-known Christmas album for his fans. "Mele Kalikmaka" and "Christmas is My Time of Year" were later remastered for The Monkees' *Christmas Party* album, released after Davy's death. Most of the songs recorded here were redone or re-recorded in the 1990s. The cover on the next page is the one used by Davy when he reissued this in 2005.

CHRISTMAS JONES (Davy Jones) Recorded 1976 in Hawaii with Chip Douglas. *Released:* December 1, 1977

When I Look Back On Christmas (Martin Jackson)
Winter Wonderland (Richard B. Smith, Felix Bernard)
Rudolph, the Red-Nosed Reindeer (Johnny Marks)
Silver Bells (Jay Livingstone, Ray Evans)
God Rest Ye Merry Gentlemen (traditional)
Hark, the Herald Angels Sing (Felix Mendelssohn)
White Christmas (Irving Berlin)
Mele Kalikimaka (Robert Alexander Anderson)
This Day in Bethlehem (Davy Jones)
Silent Night (Franz Xaber Gruber)
Rockin' Around the Christmas Tree (Johnny Marks)

It's Christmas (Davy Jones) (Reissue Bonus Track)

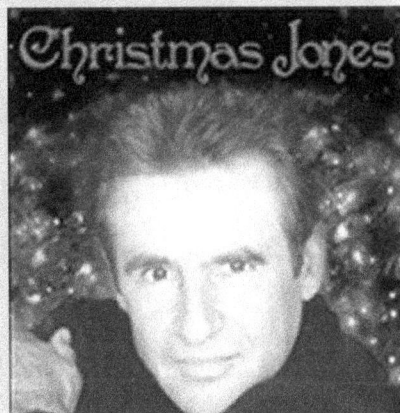

Singles released from or at the time of this album:

Christmas is My Time of Year (Howard Kaylan, Chip Douglas) / **White Christmas** (Irving Berlin) (DJ; MD; PT) (A-side technically The Monkees / B-side DJ)

The rendition of "White Christmas" on this single's B-side is a different version and is a minute shorter than the one on *Christmas Jones*.

1978

Before friction split them up again until 1986, Micky and Davy appeared together on the UK show *Tiswas*, airing on January 28.

Micky voiced The Diabolical Disc Demon on the November 17 episode of Hanna-Barbara's animated *The Scooby-Doo / Dynomutt Hour*. He also signed a contract with Chrysalis Records and took publicity photos, but only managed to get the "Love Light" single released in 1979.

Michael, with his *Popclips* pilot in hand, went to a convention in Anaheim for TV program distributors and station owners, which were mostly old white men who couldn't understand how pop music would sell on TV. None were interested—something they all would later regret.

He released a live album and kept pitching his *Popclips* idea. Though this album was always well-received by fans, it was not highly regarded by Michael, as he wasn't fond of his performance. As a result, it eluded release on CD until 2004.

LIVE AT THE PALAIS (MN)
Released: August 1978

Grand Ennui (Michael Nesmith)
Calico Girlfriend (Michael Nesmith)
Propinquity (Michael Nesmith)
Joanne (Michael Nesmith)
Roll With the Flow (Michael Nesmith)
Some of Shelly's Blues (Michael Nesmith)
Silver Moon (Michael Nesmith)
Nadine (Is It You?) (Chuck Berry)

2004 reissue bonus tracks:
Grand Ennui (Michael Nesmith)
Capsule (Michael Nesmith)
Crippled Lion (Michael Nesmith)
Listen to the Band (Michael Nesmith)

Roll With the Flow (Michael Nesmith) / **I've Just Begun to Care (Propinquity)** (Michael Nesmith) (MN) (1978)

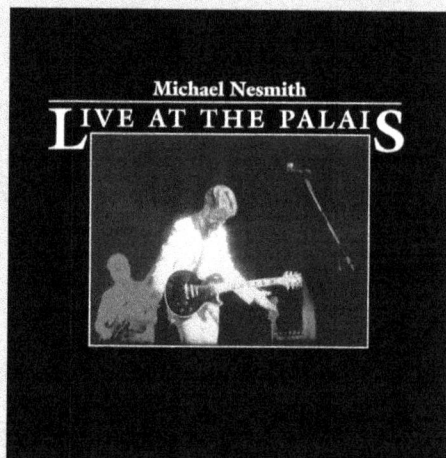

Davy, meanwhile, was hired by Disney to sing happy birthday to Mickey. No, not Micky—*Mickey.* It's a simple song that is quite instantly forgettable. The only significance is of Davy's lead vocals; otherwise it sounds like any other generic Disney children's song in release at that time.

(Hey Ra Ra Ra) Happy Birthday Mickey Mouse (Al Kasha, Joel Hirschorn) (DJ and a Million Kids) / **You Don't Have to Be a Country Boy to Sing a Country Song** (Tommy Boyce, Davy Jones) (Warner 17161, May 26, 1978)

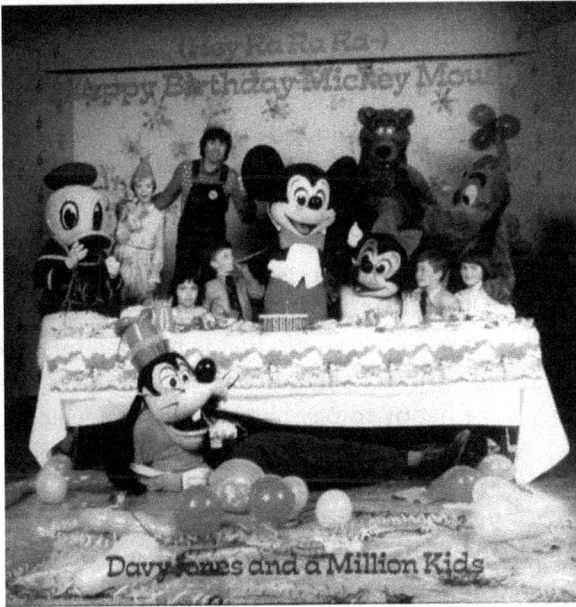

1979

Nickelodeon finally decided to take a bite at Michael's idea for the *Popclips* show, and work began for a series of half-hour clips that would begin to air later that year. Michael approached the record companies to seek videos but found that only a few bands were producing these, and mostly "new wave" bands without much of a following. However, perhaps inspired by "Rio," these clips were getting more professional and interesting than the standard "band plays and one camera records them" clips that had come before.

He was able to put together eight episodes, which included not only "Rio" but music from Squeeze, Graham Parker, Split Enz, The Tourists, The Police, Pretenders, Huey Lewis and the News, and others.

To the amazement of everyone, the ratings were sky-high. Even though there were only enough videos for eight shows, the videos were rotated so each episode seemed new.

Michael was thrilled, and began discussing with the studio heads his idea for a 24-hour channel showing videos. He had no interest in actually running the cable channel, despite them offering it to him, and they were happy to pay him for the idea which, of course, later became MTV.

Meanwhile, his next album *Infinite Rider on the Big Dogma* was released.

According to the book *Total Control*, "To promote the *Infinite Rider* album, Pacific Arts launched a promotional campaign with posters, T-shirts, postcards and even life-size and miniature stand-ups of Nesmith. Pacific Arts also sent records to radio stations of *The Michael Nesmith Radio Special*, which featured Michael being interviewed by KSAN DJ Steven Seaweed. The radio special featured all the tracks from the album, as well as dry anecdotes in-between each song told by Michael."

INFINITE RIDER ON THE BIG DOGMA (MN)
Released: May 1979
Highest Chart Position: #151

Dance (Dance & Have a Good Time) (Michael Nesmith)
Magic (This Night Is Magic) (Michael Nesmith)
Tonite (The Television Song) (Michael Nesmith)
Flying (Silks & Satins) (Michael Nesmith)
Carioca (Blue Carioca) (Michael Nesmith)

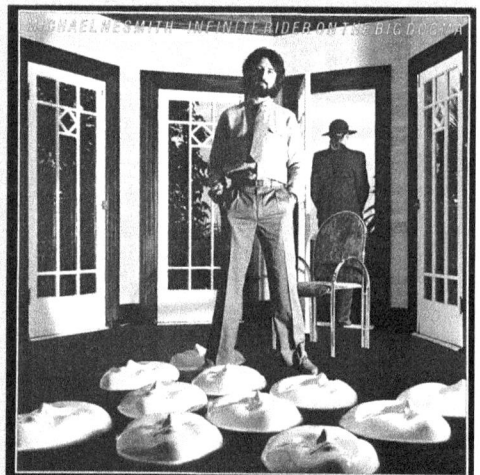

Cruisin' (Lucy and Ramona and Sunset Sam) (Michael Nesmith)
Factions (The Daughter of Rock n' Roll) (Michael Nesmith)
Light (The Eclectic Light) (Michael Nesmith)
Horserace (Beauty and Magnum Force) (Michael Nesmith)
Capsule (Hello People a Hundred Years from Now) (Michael Nesmith, Al Perkins, David MacKay, Paul Leim, John Hobbs, Lenny Castro)

Bonus tracks from Videoranch:
Walkin' in the Sand (Shadow Morton)
Rollin' (Michael Nesmith)

Magic (This Night is Magic) (Michael Nesmith) / Dance (Dance and Have a Good Time) (Michael Nesmith) (MN) (June 1979)

Cruisin' (Lucy and Ramona and Sunset Sam) (Michael Nesmith) / Horserace (Beauty and Magnum Force) (Michael Nesmith) (MN) (August 1979)

This was Michael's most accessible album to date, with hardly any country songs, although the influence is still there. These are wonderful pop songs that should have grabbed much more attention than they did. Some are convinced that the lick from "Cruisin'" was sped up and became the, um, *inspiration* for Rick James' "Super Freak" a few years later.

Michael did a tour to promote the album, but was dogged by fans demanding Monkees songs. He refused, which did not endear him to his audience, and only once gave in grudgingly, performing "Listen to the Band" which, of course, had also been recorded by the First National Band.

Michael appeared live on October 4 for a concert at The Old Waldorf in San Francisco, California. It would be his last solo concert until 1992. He also appeared on *Don Kirshner's New Rock Concert* which was recorded earlier but broadcast on August 11.

Micky, meanwhile, was enjoying life in England and doing well for himself. He resumed his directing career in the UK by directing seven episodes of the TV series *Pop Gospel* as well as directing the December 13 episode of *Premiere* entitled "Story Without a Hero."

In front of the camera, he appeared on *Top of the Pops* on February 8 and has a cameo in the Paul McCartney and Wings documentary *Wings Over the World*, which aired on March 16 and is about the 1976 tour. He also appeared on the UK music series *Get it Together*, airing on May 15, and two episodes of the UK game show *Star Games*, airing on December 4 and 25.

In the middle of all this, his single "Love Light" was released in Britain. Micky directed himself in the promotional video (which also featured his wife Trina). The video is interesting only for the last chorus, where it turns into a "bouncing ball" sing-along to the lyrics, except the ball is Micky's head. It's a fairly simple song (for Micky) but fits in the sound of the day. However, it failed to attract any attention. It never played on Michael's *Popclips*. It was later released in Japan in 1981.

Love Light (John Brown, Gerald Brown) / **Alicia** (Micky Dolenz) (MD) (June 1979, UK only)

Meanwhile, Peter appeared on California Public Access TV in Santa Monica for a 30-minute interview called *Reasonably Spontaneous Conversation* with Dennis Tardan. In it, Peter revealed that he felt not worthy of the success that he had and that was the reason he didn't pursue it so strongly after the breakup of The Monkees. He admitted having therapy and analysis over the years. He also expressed strong socialistic views towards the direction he felt society should take in order to survive.

On October 27, the TV short *Southside Johnny and The Asbury Dukes at The Asbury Park Convention Center* was released. Peter was assistant director.

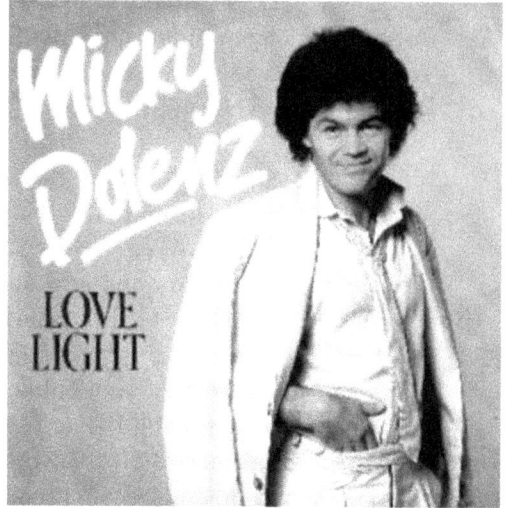

Davy appeared at three live dates at Six Flags Magic Mountain in Valencia, California on September 30, and Kips South in Toledo, Ohio on October 23 and 31. His backing band on this tour was named Toast, and this tour came to be known by the band as the "Davy Jones Alimony Tour."

He also appeared on two episodes of the UK children's *Horse in the House* called "Stable Girl" as Frank Tyson, which aired March 12 and 19.

1980

With his new band, The New Monks, Peter recorded several demos in 1980 and 1981 for Sire Records. "Since You Went Away" was later re-recorded and released on the 1987 Monkees album *Pool It!* He performed with his group at Max's Kansas City on May 13 and The Lone Star Cafe on May 15, both in New York, doing mostly covers of old songs but intermixed with the Monkees songs he knew people came to hear. He later made his first appearances on TV's *Uncle Floyd Show* in New Jersey on July 25 and again on September 25.

THE MONKEES SHOW

Featuring **PETER TORK**

Author Comment from Michael: I saw Peter at a small club in Boston with the New Monks around this time, and got to pat him on the back as he walked to the stage.

Michael's mother, Bette Clair Graham, died on May 12 at the age of 56. Michael inherited her fortune of over $50 million, which he said was like receiving "a cross between a tsunami and a Category 5 hurricane."

He remembered his mother in *Infinite Tuesday* and wrote of how much he admired her. "She was held back in the ordinary job market because she was a woman, and she was always looking for an opportunity to rise out of this economic prison. She made her living by keeping two active jobs; one as a secretary and the other and the other as a commercial artist. These two skill sets would combine in her invention of Liquid Paper."

Between this inheritance and the royalties from *Popclips* (soon to be MTV), Michael would never have to worry about money again.

But the artist in him wanted to create. And now he had the funds to do whatever he wanted.

He gathered some friends and comedians come along to help write material, and hired directors and producers with the goal of making a show that would go directly to video.

"What?" people said. "No one does that."

Michael did. He recorded videos for songs from *Infinite Rider*, including "Magic," "Cruisin'," "Light," and "Tonight" and then interspersed those with humorous skits (along with the video of "Rio") to make a fun, hour-long show that would be released early the next year.

Davy acquired his jockey's license on September 19. He rode his first race aboard Speed of Light at Newberry Race Track. Davy recalls in *They Made a Monkee Out of Me*, "All the time I was at Basil's stables, I learned a lot about riding, but I actually never took part in a race. So what if it's a bit late to start. It's something I always wanted to do."

At this same time, Davy was starring in many British "pantos" or pantomime plays, including *Cinderella*, *Dick Whittington* and *Puss in Boots*—a bit of a step down from having an Emmy-winning television show and #1 records.

Micky produced the 1980-1983 UK TV comedy sci-fi series *Metal Mickey* under the name of Michael Dolenz. He also directed 21 of the series' 39 episodes. "It was a sitcom starring Irene Handl about a kid who builds a robot in his basement and it suddenly comes alive (the robot, not the basement)," Micky wrote in *I'm a Believer*. "The series was very successful and ran for a number of years. It also firmly established me as a bona fide programmaker."

He also started using "Michael" for his directorial duties, saying that he felt like a new person. "The British don't have nearly the same problem with typecasting as they do here in the States. Providing that I could prove that I knew what I was doing, the industry was quite happy to accept me as a director, and I was soon working full-time."

Micky also appeared in the audience on the UK comedy TV special *An Evening with Dame Edna Everage*, airing on December 26.

1981

Two of Michael's videos from his hour-long video, now called *Elephant Parts* (from the old adage about blind men touching different parts of the elephant and finding it means something unique to each) appeared on the January 10 and 24 editions of *Saturday Night Live*. Elephant Parts was released in July and, to the surprise of many, was an immediate hit, once more proving that Michael was a video visionary. It even won the Grammy the following year for the new category "Video of the Year."

And on August 1, the 24-hour music video station that Michael pioneered as *Popclips* debuted as MTV and was also an immediate success.

He even did some acting, portraying "Foyer the Butler" in *An Evening with Sir William Martin*, a comedy short released this year. He was also listed as the executive producer.

Davy divorced Linda and married Anita Pollinger in England on January 24. They had a daughter, Jessica Lillian, born on September 4.

The Monkees around this time were becoming a hit in Japan. Davy was the first to take advantage of this, appearing live at Shiba Yubinchokin Hall in Tokyo on May 1. This concert was the basis for his *Davy Jones Live* album. This was a highly sought after album at time of release, as it was only released in Japan, plus it was the only Monkees-related live album released to date, as Michael's *Live at the Palais* avoided Monkees songs. It was later re-released in 2019 in the US for the first time. The cover shown below is from the 1981 release.

DAVY JONES LIVE (DJ)
Released: 1981, Japan only

Last Train to Clarksville (Tommy Boyce, Bobby Hart)
I'm a Believer (Neil Diamond)
Cuddly Toy (Harry Nilsson)
How Do You Know? (Davy Jones)
(I'm Not Your) Steppin' Stone (Tommy Boyce, Bobby Hart)
Star Collector (Gerry Goffin, Carole King)
I Wanna Be Free (Tommy Boyce, Bobby Hart)
A Little Bit Me, A Little Bit You (Neil Diamond)
Valleri (Tommy Boyce, Bobby Hart)
It's Now (Davy Jones)

73

Daydream Believer (John Stewart)
(Theme from) The Monkees (Tommy Boyce, Bobby Hart)
1988 bonus tracks:
I'll Love You Forever (Davy Jones)
Sixteen Baby, You'll Soon Be Sixteen (Alan Green)
You're a Lady (Peter Skellern)
Dance Gypsy Dance (Davy Jones)
Rainy Jane (Howard Greenfield, Neil Sedaka)
Baby Hold Out (Andy Sears, Davy Jones)

It's Now (live) (Davy Jones) / **How Do You Know? (live)** (Davy Jones) (DJ) (1981, Japan only)

Dance Gypsy Dance (live) (Davy Jones) / **Can She Do it Like She Dances** (Gerry Robinson, Steven Duboff) (DJ) (1981, Japan only)

Unbelievably, Davy's version of the B-side song is even more disco than Ringo Starr's version on *Ringo the 4th*.

In February 1981, Peter finally released his first record since leaving The Monkees—a cover version of "(I'm Not Your) Steppin' Stone." Though it had absolutely no chart action, it was nice to see that—as the picture sleeve said—"Peter's Back!"

(I'm Not Your) Steppin' Stone (Tommy Boyce, Bobby Hart) / **(Your Love Keeps Lifting Me) Higher and Higher** (Carl Smith, Raynard Miner) (PT and The New Monks) (February 1981)

Peter then took off for Japan as well, and with the New Monks performed four shows at Shinjuku Koseinenkin Kaikan in Tokyo from August 16-19. He also made another appearance on *The Uncle Floyd Show* on December 18.

Micky had a daughter with Trina named Charlotte Janelle on August 8, and continued to expand his British career behind the camera. He wrote and directed a weird comedy short called *The Box* which consisted entirely of two large boxes being moved from a warehouse to the beach while the voices of Monty Python's Terry Jones and Michael Palin portrayed the Pope and a British Minister trapped in the boxes.

He also directed the comedy short *Gateway to the South*, released in November.

74

Micky was in front of the camera briefly as an audience member on the UK comedy TV special *An Evening with Dudley Moore*, which aired on December 26.

Meanwhile, to capitalize on the Japanese Monkees revival, a recording of a live concert of Dolenz, Jones, Boyce and Hart was released. Like Davy's recent live album, this was originally a Japanese-only release, and a highly sought after import, as they were the first live release of Monkees songs.

CONCERT IN JAPAN (DJB&H) Recorded live on July 20, 1976. Not released in US until 1996.
Released: August 1981 in Japan

Last Train To Clarksville (Tommy Boyce, Bobby Hart)
Medley: Valleri (Tommy Boyce, Bobby Hart) / **Daydream Believer** (John Stewart) / **A Little Bit Me, A Little Bit You** (Neil Diamond)
I Wonder What She's Doing Tonight (Tommy Boyce, Bobby Hart)
(I'm Not Your) Steppin' Stone (Tommy Boyce, Bobby Hart)
I Wanna Be Free (Tommy Boyce, Bobby Hart)
Savin' My Love For You (Micky Dolenz, Davy Jones)
Pleasant Valley Sunday (Gerry Goffin, Carole King)
I Remember The Feeling (Tommy Boyce, Bobby Hart)
Teenager In Love (Doc Pomus, Mort Shuman)
Cuddly Toy (Harry Nilsson)
Medley: Come A Little Bit Closer (Tommy Boyce, Bobby Hart, Wes Farrell) / **Pretty Little Angel Eyes** (Curtis Lee, Tommy Boyce) / **Hurt So Bad** (Teddy Randazzo, Bobby Hart, Bobby Weinstein) / **Peaches 'N' Cream** (Steve Venet, Tommy Boyce) / **Something's Wrong With Me** (Danny Janssen, Bobby Hart) / **Keep On Singing** (Danny Janssen, Bobby Hart)
I Love You (And I'm Glad That I Said It) (Davy Jones, Micky Dolenz, Luke Harshman, Tommy Boyce)
Action (Steve Venet, Tommy Boyce)

75

1982

Micky was convinced to join in the Japan craze and performed a single solo show in Japan on January 20. It would be his final solo show until 1991.

He also directed episodes of the UK children's series *Murphy's Mob*, first airing on March 1 but running through 1985. He was also accidentally shot by a kid with a BB gun while hunting with his daughter, Ami. He sustained no major damage.

He then recorded another single.

To Be Or Not To Be (Britten, Robertson) / **Beverly Hills** (Micky Dolenz) (MD) (January 1982, Japan only)

"To Be Or Not To Be" is a very Phil Spectorish wall-of-sound-meets-the-80s sound. Quite catchy, with catchy lyrics about Shakespeare. "Beverly Hills," penned by Micky himself, is better and probably should have been the A-side.

Davy spent the better part of the year recovering from a broken hand. And then there was a very bizarre release with a lengthy genesis. In short, the duo Jan and Dean were working sporadically on a new album from 1966 to 1968 called Carnival of Sound. It was to be very different from their typical releases which had a Beach Boys-like surf sound. Jan's car crash on April 12, 1966 slowed down production on the album, and it was eventually shelved, but a few songs escaped as single tracks in 1968, including "Laurel and Hardy" without Davy vocals. Davy Jones contributed a lead vocal in 1968, but his version was not officially widely released until 2010 on *The Birds, The Bees and The Monkees Deluxe Edition*. This Australian edition from 1982 had a limited edition of 250 copies.

Carnival of Sound (Jan Berry, Roger Christian, David Weiss) / **Mulholland** (Jan Berry, Roger Christian) / **Stay** (Maurice Williams) // **Girl, You're Blowing My Mind** (Jan Berry, Steve Gaines, Paul Freese) / **Louisiana Man** (Doug Kershaw) / **Laurel and Hardy** (Jan Berry, Roger Christian) (all Jan Berry of Jan and Dean except last track DJ) (1982, Australia only)

Sixteen Baby, You'll Soon Be Sixteen (live) (Alan Green) / **Baby, Holdout (live)** (Andy Sears, Davy Jones) (DJ) (1982, Japan only)

"Baby, Holdout" is an uptempo rocker with a heavier guitar break that is kind of atypical for Davy to sing, but the Japanese fans seemed to dig it in the live version released from a 1981 concert there. It probably could have been a hit, unlike the sappy ballad A-side that is a more typical Davy Jones release. These two tracks were among those added when *Davy Jones Live* was reissued in 1988.

This is a different live concert recorded in Japan than Davy's *Live in Japan*, which was the basis for *Hello Davy*, a Japanese-only laserdisc that was finally released in the US in 2019 as a CD and DVD.

HELLO DAVY (DJ)
Recorded live in August 1981. Not released in US until 2019.
Released: March 27, 1982 as a video laserdisc in Japan only.

Dance Gypsy Dance (Davy Jones)
Last Train to Clarksville (Tommy Boyce, Bobby Hart)
I'm a Believer (Neil Diamond)
Star Collector (Gerry Goffin, Carole King)
I Wanna Be Free (Tommy Boyce, Bobby Hart)
Rainy Jane (Howard Greenfield, Neil Sedaka)
You're a Lady (Peter Skellern)
Can She Do it Like She Dances (Gerry Robinson, Steven Duboff)
Cuddly Toy (Harry Nilsson)
I'll Love You Forever (Davy Jones)
Daydream Believer (John Stewart)
Sixteen Baby, You'll Soon Be Sixteen (Alan Green)
It's Now (Davy Jones)
Baby Hold Out (Andy Sears, Davy Jones)

Peter continued making semi-regular appearances sans New Monks on *The Uncle Floyd Show* on February 5, and October 9 and 30. This was the year that *The Uncle Floyd Show* went into limited syndication in 17 markets allowing many to finally see Peter perform nationally for the first time since The Monkees.

Peter also appeared on *Late Night with David Letterman* on July 8. He good-naturedly participated in a "Win a Dream Date With Peter Tork" segment, as the winner, Esther Pollack, was significantly older than Peter was at the time. Peter was a good verbal sparring partner with Letterman, and later in an interview segment, spoke more about Jimi Hendrix than The Monkees. He also gave a shout out to Mike, gloating about being on national television, saying, "If you're watching this, Mike, eat your heart out!"

Michael, freed from worries about money, indulged in his creative endeavors. He wrote and produced a feature length film called *Timerider: The Adventure of Lyle Swann*—and he also appeared in a short cameo.

Finding a distributor for the finished project proved to be more difficult. He found a small company in Utah that took the risk on the distribution and went out of business within a month after the film opened. The film remained unseen until released on video from Michael's own company Pacific Arts, although it has shown up at various film festivals and science fiction conventions. A soundtrack to the film was finally released in 2000.

1983

Michael appeared on *Late Night with David Letterman* on January 13, but didn't mention Peter at all. He wrote some material for the *Playboy Video Magazine, Volume 1*, and presented an award for Paul McCartney (who doesn't appear) on *The First Annual American Video Awards* which aired on April 6. He also executive produced a music video for Lionel Richie's "All Night Long," which was directed by former Monkees producer Bob Rafelson. It was released in September and became a hit.

Micky remained busy behind the scenes in England, doing quite well. He produced and directed episodes of the 1983-1985 comedy series *No Problem!*, a situation comedy created by Micky and a black theater group in London. It began airing on January 7. He also directed the comedy talk show series *For 4 Tonight*, which ran for six episodes beginning October 1.

He was most proud of his science fiction comedy *Luna*, which debuted in January and ran for two years. It was something he had imagined years earlier and was thrilled when it was finally made. He produced and directed a number of the episodes. "*Luna* was a very special show for me," he said in a later interview. "It was about a little girl living in the future—kind of a cross between *The Jetsons*, *Alice in Wonderland* and *Brazil*."

Micky took to the theater to direct a stage version of the 1976 film *Bugsy Malone*, which ran for over 300 performances. His version featured a 14-year old Catherine Zeta-Jones as Tallulah, the part played by Jodie Foster in the film. He also recorded a song from the show which was released as a single. Not a bad song, and of course, Micky sure can sing.

Tomorrow (Paul Williams) (MD) / **Fat Sam's Grand Slam** (Paul Williams) (The Bugsy Malone Gang) (MD) (1983, UK only)

In front of the camera, Micky appeared on the UK game show *Pop Quiz*, which aired on June 11.

And on July 25, he was thrilled to have another addition to his family: a daughter named Emily Clare.

Peter performed solo at Ripley's Music Hall in Philadelphia, Pennsylvania on July 6, and Bogart's in Cincinnati, Ohio on October 23. These were Peter's final solo concerts until 1992.

1984

Micky continued to direct *No Problem!* and *Luna* throughout the year, and welcomed another daughter named Georgia Rose on September 3.

Davy appeared on the UK shows *The Little and Large Show*, airing January 14; *Pop Quiz*, airing on October 2; and *Saturday Superstore*, airing on October 13.

Michael's next film venture was much more successful. *Repo Man*, released on March 2, didn't become a blockbuster, but has a huge cult following which keeps it constantly shown on TV and in film festivals.

"When I delivered the movie to Universal," Michael said in *Infinite Tuesday*, "they immediately deemed it unreleasable ... Fortunately, one small theater in Cambridge, Massachusetts, got a print and started playing it. It ran in that theater for a year. The deal I made with the studio turned out to be wonderful. I got all the production money back, the picture started performing and the royalty checks got bigger and bigger. The picture went into profit and still makes money for all as I write this."

> Author comment from Michael: I was living in Boston at the time and recall seeing *Repo Man* in Cambridge where it was part of a science fiction marathon. The audience appreciated it!

Michael also portrayed an Academy Award Presenter in the thriller *An All Consuming Passion*, released on November 14.

1985

Due to the success of *Elephant Parts*, Michael was approached by Brandon Tartikoff, head of the entertainment division of NBC, who wanted Michael to turn it into a weekly TV show, with the idea being that besides the sketches and musical numbers, Michael would get big name comedians to do short stand-up bits. "Of course, I could not just 'call up' Steve Martin and Robin Williams, except to hear them say no," Michael recalled. "They were big, expensive stars and had no intention of wasting their fame on my little TV show. I would have to search comedy clubs to find the talent."

Among the talented comedians he brought to greater attention were Garry Shandling, Martin Mull, and Bill Martin (who is mostly known today for his voice-over work for animated films and video games).

Michael also hired a well-known director from England calling himself "Michael Dolenz" who gathered some British comedians to do a few skits.

Michael Nesmith in Television Parts debuted on March 7. Michael also appeared in some of the sketches and songs, and promoted it on *Entertainment Tonight* on March 6 and on *The Today Show* on NBC on March 7. Despite fairly good reviews, the ratings were awful, and the show only lasted the original eight episodes. Still, it was the first (and only) time an ex-Monkee appeared regularly on a prime-time American TV show other than the original *Monkees* show.

Television Parts has never been released to home video in its entirety. Michael explained why in an interview in 1992 with Ken Sharp from Monkee Business Fanzine: "The unions changed the laws on me. There was some basic change-up in the law, so that it makes the shows uneconomic to ever release again. It is too bad, isn't it? They shot their foot off."

At the end of 1985, Michael moved his entire Pacific Arts operations from Carmel, California, to Beverly Hills.

Micky's stepfather, Dr. Robert Leroy Scott, died in February. Micky kept busy producing and directing episodes of the UK TV comedy series *From the Top*, which aired beginning September 23. Micky also composed the show's theme song.

Davy began touring the UK in a new production of *Godspell*. The show ran from July to November 23, took a break, and then resumed for a four-week run at the Fortune Theatre from December 16 through January 11 with a final charity performance given on January 15, 1986. This final performance was enlivened by an audience member's dive from the balcony, causing Davy to temporarily halt the show. No one was seriously injured.

According to the *Monkee Business Fanzine* #35 in December of 1985, "*Godspell* has been great for Davy. The theatres are packed and the cast receives standing ovations at every performance. The overwhelming majority of reviews have been fantastic, and they have improved as the tour progressed. In addition, Davy has been very visible, doing TV interviews in every city on the tour to publicize the show.

"The eight show per week schedule has been a grueling one, and David's chronic sinusitis began to plague him. He missed a few shows in October to have a very minor operation on his sinuses."

Ten days before his 40th birthday, Davy granted an interview for *Monkee Business Fanzine* #36 which was published in March 1986. "The only thing in England is the theatre," he said. "You can get in the charts and cut a record, but you can't expect to have a couple of hits a year and keep it going and going and going. My career's been going for 29 years now, and that's because I change countries regularly. I'm 40 years old this month, so maybe in the next five to ten years, I can establish myself as a grown-up.

"I went to America and made my fortune and my career, although it was basically in The Monkees. My only problem is, and I shouldn't say it, people don't know how good I am. They don't know until they see me. I just can't go out and do garbage, because I've worked too long to do that."

Peter played two shows at Musikfest in Bethlehem, Pennsylvania on August 20. He also did a telephone interview for a radio station on WNEW-FM's *Saturday Morning 60s* show on November 16, and appeared on WFMZ, channel 69, in Allentown. He also performed at Club Bené in Sayreville, New Jersey on November 2, Northampton, Massachusetts on November 7 at the Iron Horse, and November 16 at the Speakeasy in Greenwich Village in New York.

Peter was scheduled to appear as a villain in a film called *Dream Demons*, but it ended up not being released (at least with that title). Davy, Micky and Michael were also approached to appear, with Michael flatly declining.

Also that year, Peter attended a concert in New York City featuring the 'Happy Together' tour that showcased several regrouped sixties rock and roll bands, led by Howard Kaylan of the Turtles. Tour promoter David Fishof went to Peter with the idea of a Monkees reunion. Peter agreed to consider it, and Fishof quickly began an effort to reunite the band, little aware that Michael Nesmith's creation MTV would play a large role in making that happen.

1986

Davy appeared on the UK children's show *Blue Peter* on January 6 and on *Good Morning Britain* the next day. On *Blue Peter*, Davy performed "All For the Best." He was scheduled to be on *Saturday Superstore*, but canceled. He also appeared on *The New Love, American Style* on January 10 on ABC.

Davy was also asked to participate in a "Spirit of the 60s" concert during Labor Day weekend at the Magic Mountain theme park, but Davy declined when the promoter did not provide transportation to California. Ads appeared in the LA area claiming that Davy, Peter and Micky would be performing. Then, a few days before the show, the promoter vanished with the money, and needless to say, the concert did not occur.

A second video of segments from the 1985 series *Michael Nesmith in Television Parts* was released this year as *Doctor Duck's Super Secret All-Purpose Sauce*. Michael served as executive producer. He also appeared in some of the sketches and songs.

Then, on February 26, MTV did a Monkees marathon, showing all their shows for what they called "Pleasant Valley Sunday." The response was tremendous, and a new generation found Monkeemania.

Peter and Davy were on the other side of the planet when this happened, performing 17 shows in Australia from February 25 through March 19. The tour was called "Hey, Hey, It's the Sound of The Monkees featuring Davy Jones and Peter Tork."

Peter later appeared at the Rock 'n' Roll Flea Market Convention in Albany, New York on April 20 along with Bobby Hart. He performed his last solo show before rejoining Davy and eventually Micky on April 22 at The Bitter End in Greenwich Village, New York.

While this was going on, Nickelodeon (sister network to MTV) began to show Monkees episodes daily, and by May, an old Greatest Hits album was back on the Billboard charts. Promoter David Fishof was able to book Micky, Davy and Peter into a "20th Anniversary Tour" across North America, which started in late May and grew in size as it progressed, with performances almost every day through December. It started playing small theaters and grew to fill huge arenas, and was one of the more successful and profitable tours of the year.

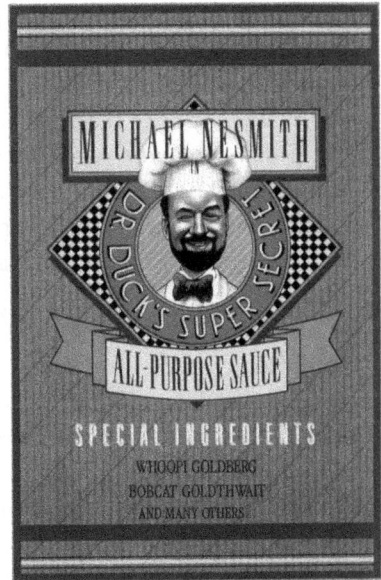

To promote the tour, Micky and Peter went into the studio, recording three songs very quickly, which were added onto a new greatest hits album called *Then and Now*. The single "That Was Then, This is Now" was released in June, eventually reaching #20 on the Billboard charts. The single was credited to Micky Dolenz and Peter Tork of The Monkees. Davy was still angry at Arisia records (which used to be Bell records which used to be Colgems records) for failing to promote his solo career, so he refused to sign the contract. In concert, Davy would even leave the stage when the song was performed. A follow-up single of "Anytime, Anyplace, Anywhere" from the Micky and Peter recordings was planned but apparently when Davy protested, a remixed "Daydream Believer" was re-released instead, but it barely charted. Many top 40 stations considered it something that belonged on the oldies station.

Rhino Records, which had in the meantime purchased the rights to the Monkees catalog and had lovingly reissued the albums, was thrilled to find all of the original albums back on the charts (with the exception of *Head, Instant Replay*, and *Present*, for some reason).

This led to more publicity appearances. Micky and Peter were interviewed together on *CBS News Nightwatch*, which aired on July 16, and then Micky was interviewed solo on the TV Generation spot between shows on Nickelodeon's Nick at Nite, on September 28. Two Monkees conventions were quickly arranged, one in Philadelphia in August, and one in Los Angeles in September, scheduled to coincide with the tour dates to allow Peter, Micky and Davy to make appearances.

A live double-album was prepared but never made publicly available to stores. However, it was sold during future tour appearances and Rhino later made it available as a mail order CD.

Michael did not tour with the others. He was originally interested, but when it blossomed from 20 dates to 200, he bowed out. He did make a surprise appearance for their performance at the Greek Theatre in Los Angeles on September 7 and joined in on a few songs, much to the delight of the audience. He also appeared on *Good Morning America* on ABC on September 9, and was on the cover of the September 1986 issue of *Music Connection*.

Meanwhile, Michael test marketed *Overview*, a video magazine that was sold in videocassette form. There was supposed to be a second issue released in June 1987, but

20th Anniversary Tour 1986

sales of the first issue were so bad, the concept was dropped, despite financial backing from Coca-Cola and NBC.

"*Overview* was a magazine on videocassette that just brought previews and reviews and things of coming attractions, "Michael told *Monkee Business Fanzine* about his latest venture. "It was designed as kind of a video guide. I think that hews closer to the form. At the end of the day, I've got to tell you I think home video is an entertainment medium and it's going to occupy the same place in the minds of future people as records kind of do now. That's where it's going to extend from, not from motion pictures." Was he predicting the rise of Netflix and online movie watching 20 years later?

After The Monkees tour, Davy had start wearing knee braces and was looking at possible surgery on his knees due to the abuse given them during all his travels. He started wearing the knee braces onstage and started a regimen of special exercises to strengthen his knees, so surgery would no longer be necessary.

In December, Micky, Davy and Peter appeared on an MTV Christmas special, singing a medley of Christmas favorites as Santa and others danced around and sang with them. The medley ended, and Santa took off his beard, revealing himself to be Michael all along.

1987

Michael started work on his next film *Tapeheads* and was planning *Zippyvision*, a live action movie based upon Zippy the Pinhead as well as *Motorama*, an absurd metaphoric drama about the human condition set in the future. There was talk with Brandon Tartikoff to do a movie based upon the *Weekly World News* tabloid with its characters such as Bat Boy, but nothing came of it.

He discussed these films in *Infinite Tuesday*. "Brandon and I started talking casually about setting up a movie partnership between Pacific Arts and NBC. He wanted to make movies like *Repo Man*. NBC Films and I made two movies together: *Square Dance* and *Tapeheads*. *Tapeheads* was my favorite of the two because it was silly and adolescent fun. The kind of kid-anxiety comedy that was perfect for its time."

Square Dance premiered at the Sundance Film Festival on January 16, and appeared in theaters soon thereafter. Michael's name does not appear in the credits. This introduced Winona Ryder and also starred Jason Robards, Jane Alexander, and Rob Lowe. It garnished fair reviews but was not a success at the box office.

Michael made a personal appearance on February 14 at Sound Warehouse in Dallas, Texas, to promote and sign copies of his *Dr. Duck's* video tape compilation. On March 20, he could be seen as a cabbie in the Whoopi Goldberg film *Burglar*. He also appeared on *Show Biz Today* on June 22 to discuss *Television Parts*, and he appeared on *Getting Fit with Denise Austin* during June.

Davy had released the first Monkees-related autobiography on February 2, though his own publishing company, Dome Press, along with co-author Alan Green. Davy was to make multiple book stops, but Monkee business got in the way, so Green had to make many of those appearances instead.

Davy filmed a TV commercial for the book that originally aired on *Night Tracks* in November. He also announced a second book called *Evolution* and made Multiple Sclerosis his official charity, as a member of his family was diagnosed with the disease earlier this year.

David Fishof, who had arranged the tours, told MTV that The Monkees would perform on an MTV Super Bowl Sunday special. Unfortunately, he didn't tell The Monkees that, and Davy refused to make the trip. MTV took it as a snub and stopped running Monkees TV episodes, and later refused to play any videos from their reunion album. The Monkees tour later in the year may have been even bigger had this not happened.

-DAVY JONES-

They Made a *MONKEE* Out Of Me

THE ONLY AUTHORIZED STORY

Davy and Peter headed for Australia and New Zealand for another duo tour that ran from February 9 through April 5. Davy appeared solo on *Cartoon Company* and *The Early Bird Show* on March 28, on *Sounds* on April 4, and on *Hey Kids*.

Davy and Peter appeared together on *The Midday Show* in early March, where they performed "Daydream Believer" and on *Young Talent Time*. Back in the States, they appeared together on *Noonday*, a local talk show on channel 11 in Atlanta, Georgia.

Micky had a busy few months at the start of the year. He started work on a Monkees feature film and a Broadway show that both ended up unproduced. He did, however, go on a series of personal appearances on the car show circuit from January 2 through March 8, along with the Monkeemobile. He also appeared on *Good Day!*, a local Boston TV talk show on January 9.

He was interviewed on *The Larry King Show* on February 24. On February 25, he acted on the "Deadly Collection" episode of *The New Mike Hammer* and appeared on *Entertainment Tonight* as well as *Show Biz Today* and on MTV's music news (as was Michael, discussing *Square Dance*).

On his March 8th birthday, he appeared on the Easter Seals Telethon and called in to Rodney Bingenheimer's KROQ radio show that day. On March 18, he was seen on *Nightlife*. On April 11, he appeared on Nickelodeon's movie review show *Rated K for Kids by Kids*, and was interviewed by sister Coco on radio station KATD on April 19.

Micky, Peter, and Davy went into the studio individually during May through July to record songs for what would become an album called *Pool It!* There's not one song on the album that features more than one Monkee. Producer Roger Bechirian had been behind some of the biggest albums of the "new wave" (Elvis Costello, Squeeze, Nick Lowe) that tried to recapture the fun of the 60s music so he seemed like a perfect fit. However, pressure from the Monkees (and especially Davy, who had screaming arguments with Bechirian) forced him to make an 80s sounding album, which did not appeal to many listeners.

Since Davy refused to sign with Arista, the album was issued by Rhino, which did not have the budget to promote it. The album was released in August and reached #72 on the charts before disappearing after a few weeks.

The three of them went on a massive tour which lasted from July 1 through October 24. The first part of the tour concentrated on the older material, but after *Pool It!* was released, the second part of the tour included some of those songs. Opening act was Monkees fan "Weird Al" Yankovic, who years later sang "Hey Hey We're the Monks" in the satirical TV show "Galavant."

As the tour ended, the Monkees found themselves being sued by David Fishof who claimed that he was owed a lot of money. The suit was eventually thrown out by the judge.

In the meantime, Rhino put out the first of the *Missing Links* albums, which featured Monkees tracks that had been recorded and never released.

Micky and Peter were the mystery guests on *The Howard Stern Morning Radio Show* in New York on August 20, talking about the album and the reunion tour.

Davy appeared at the Make-a-Wish Foundation's All-Star Charity Banquet and Celebrity Auction on November 19, at the Museum of Broadcast and Communications in Chicago, Illinois. He attended and auctioned off clothing from the 1986 Monkees tour, and autographed copies of his book.

Davy appeared solo on December 12 at the Hickory Hallow Mall in Antioch, Tennessee. He also purchased another racehorse he named Daydream Believer, and bought a farm in central Pennsylvania, where he relocated. He also appeared briefly on Chicago's channel 5 news on December 2 to talk about The Monkees and his theatrical work over the years.

Peter performed a solo show on June 6 at a benefit function for Impact Hospital in Pasadena, California. He announced at a Monkees convention that he was going to go out solo with his band in November. However, In August, he scraped his right arm pretty badly when he went down a water slide at a resort area in Michigan, and had to wear bandages. The promised tour never happened. (Also Davy bruised some ribs around the same time in a water-skiing accident.)

Peter appeared on WCBS-FM radio on December 31 in a surprise visit where he played guest DJ.

Michael appeared as the keynote speaker to the First American Video Conference sponsored by *Billboard* magazine and the American Film Institute on November 19-21, at the Hollywood Roosevelt Hotel in Los Angeles, California. On December 15, he was interviewed on the ESPN exercise program *Getting Fit.*

1988

INCREDIBLE (DJ)
Recorded between February 1986 and July 1987.
Released: January 8.

Look Inside Yourself (Davy Jones, Mark Clarke, Wreckless Eric)
Make the Woman Love Me (Davy Jones, Mark Clarke, Wreckless Eric)
You're Only Dreaming (Davy Jones, Mark Clarke, Wreckless Eric)
Black and White (Davy Jones, Mark Clarke, Wreckless Eric)
After Your Heart (Chuck Bianchi, Pat Taylor)

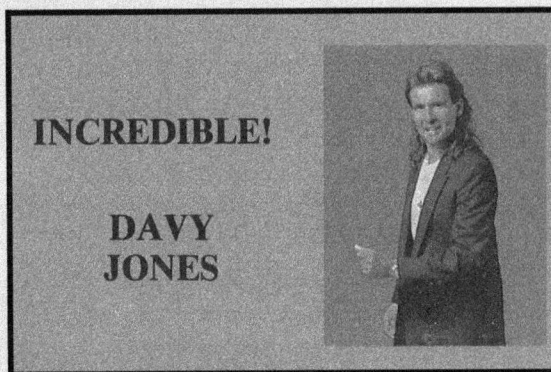

INCREDIBLE!

DAVY JONES

Incredible (Davy Jones, Mark Clarke, Wreckless Eric)
Hippy Hippy Shake (Chan Romero)
She Believes (Davy Jones, Mark Clarke, Wreckless Eric)
How Do You Know? (Davy Jones)
It's Now (Davy Jones)

I'll Love You Forever (Davy Jones) (DJ) (cassingle)
Valleri (Tommy Boyce, Bobby Hart) (DJ) (cassingle)
After Your Heart (Chuck Bianchi, Pat Taylor) / **Hippy Hippy Shake** (Chan Romero) (DJ) (cassingle)
Don't Go (Davy Jones) (DJ) (cassingle)

Davy's cassette-only album *Incredible* is thoroughly immersed in the 80s, with that synthesizer and echo drum sound popular at the time. You'd think he would have learned from the failure of *Pool It!* (which was largely his fault). Nothing from this album is very memorable (and especially not the cover), although Davy does a fine job singing.

In mid-January, Davy met in London, England, with the producers of *Me and My Girl* about the possibility of taking the lead role, but he eventually decided against it. The producers wanted Davy's commitment for a year, and Davy couldn't spare that much time due to touring commitments in the US and Australia.

He spent much of the year promoting his book. He appeared at Faneuil Hall in Boston on January 23, and on March 5 at Samuel French in Hollywood after a couple of weeks of vacation in Malaga, Spain. He came back to Samuel French on October 26 to introduce the audio version of his book.

Davy did additional book signing appearances throughout the year and could be seen on many local TV station entertainment shows.

He had a few acting jobs as well. He appeared on the comedy show *Sledge Hammer!* in an episode called "Sledge, Rattle and Roll" which aired January 15 on ABC. He also appeared on the sitcom *My Two Dads* on the episode "The Wedge" which aired February 7 on NBC (and reprised the character the following season.) He also tried out for a similar character to head up his own NBC TV series, but lost out to another actor.

Davy and family flew back to England on May 17, where he became a father for the fourth time on June 26, with Annabel Charlotte Jones.

Davy did commit to performing in (wait for it) *Oliver!* from August 8-14 in Kansas City, Missouri. This time Davy portrayed Fagin, with a ton of make-up to make him appear much older. Peter saw Davy's performance on August 9, and they spent time together the next day before Peter flew back to California.

Davy's mare Chrissy gave birth to a colt named Hackenbush, named after Groucho Marx's character in *A Day at the Races*. Anita also gave Davy a horse for Valentine's Day, a year-old thoroughbred filly named Atlantic Valentine.

He acquired the rights to the book *Mister God, This is Anna*. He planned to produce it as a stage show and eventually a movie, and to write songs for it, but nothing came of the project.

Davy, Micky and Peter did another tour of Australia from September 21 through October 15, which even featured an encore of "Ditty Diego" from *Head*.

Other than the tour, Peter spent most of the year relaxing at his home in Northern California, recovering from the pandemonium of the past two years. He performed solo at the Vic Theatre in Chicago on August 20 and at The Speakeasy in New York from November 25 to 27, performing six shows. He also added the Post and Beam in Kingston, Rhode Island on December 2; The Town Crier in Pawling, New York on December 3, 1988; and the Iron Horse in Northampton, Massachusetts on December 4.

Peter auditioned for the same TV series and same role that Davy did. Peter ultimately turned the role down as it was for a dumb sidekick role and he didn't want to play "another dumb character."

Peter made a surprise appearance at a PBS's *Rockathon* fundraiser for channel 13 in New York on March 19. He also appeared at Caesar's Hotel & Casino on October 27 to speak about drug and alcohol abuse. At the conference, Peter said, "If I could tailor the story so that each of you would receive exactly the right thing, we would be there for a couple of centuries. It's no good to sit around and think about my problems when my problem is my thinking."

Michael appeared on *Lifestyles of the Rich and Famous* on April 17 and filmed a TV commercial for Liquid Paper. His film *Tapeheads* was released on October 21, and he appears as "the water man." He appeared on VH-1's *Watch Bobby Rivers*, on November 2, discussing music videos and *Tapeheads*. He also appeared on NPR's *Fresh Air* on December 1.

During this time, Michael's marriage to Kathryn dissolved, as he became involved with Victoria Kennedy, 24 years his junior and, as Michael reported, "One of the few people in the world who saw *Television Parts*."

Micky appeared as himself in the video documentary called *Your Alcohol I.Q.* He continued work on *Repossessed* and visited his mother on Mother's Day, then left for England with his family on May 9, staying for three weeks suffering from a case of mononucleosis. He also appeared with daughter Ami at the Los Angeles Stars Polo Benefit on September 6, and he appeared on *This Morning* in the UK while directing a pop video on November 3.

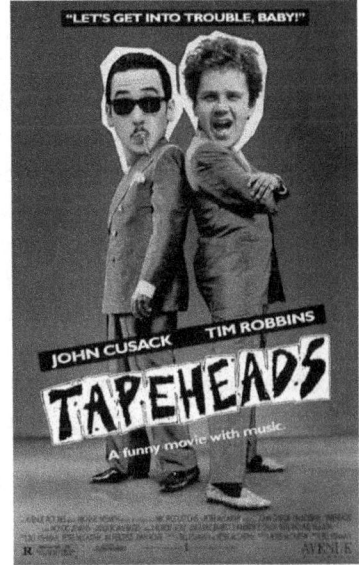

1989

Davy, Micky and Peter continued their reunion tour in England from March 17 through April 24. To promote it, Davy and Micky appeared on BBC's *Daytime Live* on February 1, and on *The Steve Wright Show* on Radio 1, on February 6.

Davy appeared on *The Gloria Huniford Show* on Radio 2 on February 6 and reprised his role as Malcolm O'Dell on the sitcom *My Two Dads* on the episode "Fallen Idol" which aired February 15 on NBC. He also appeared on *Crook and Chase* again on March 3, *Good Morning Britain* on March 8, Nickelodeon's *Don't Just Sit There* on March 29, and *My Generation* on July 4.

Davy taped an interview for *Entertainment Tonight* in England in early February that aired in two parts on February 11-12, in conjunction with the 25th anniversary of his and The Beatles appearance on *The Ed Sullivan Show*.

Davy also did a short promotional tour for his audio book of *They Made a Monkee Out of Me*. He traveled to the US where he did book signings around the country, often appearing on local radio and TV shows to promote the appearance.

Health-wise, Davy a very unlucky year. He had surgery to repair his broken cheekbone from a soccer accident, and he wasn't sure if he would rejoin Micky and Peter for the 1989 Monkees tour, but doctors did give clearance and the tour proceeded without incident. Then he broke his ring finger on his left hand and doctors had to cut off his wedding ring before setting the finger. During the tour, he fell backwards off a revolving stage but was able to break his fall and wasn't seriously hurt.

After the tour, he appeared in a revival of (wait for it) *Oliver!* from November 17 through January 14 at the Hirschfeld Theatre in Miami Beach, Florida, again playing Fagin. He appeared in local media often promoting the show.

Davy was offered a gig hosting a new music video TV series. He taped the pilot on December 11, but the series was not picked up.

Peter was interviewed by British talk show host Michael Aspel on Channel 3 of British Airways' inflight radio show Skysound in July, talking about The Monkees recent British tour.

He was in his Northern California home on October 17 when the major earthquake that hit the San Francisco Bay Area. He and his sister Anne, plus Micky's mom and sisters who all live in the general area (Los Gatos), were fine—however, there was a lot of broken glassware to sweep up.

Michael appeared again on *Showbiz Today* and on *Headline News* and *Crook and Chase*, all on March 21. He also attended the Grammys on February 22 and attended the Cammtron video seminar in Des Moines, Iowa, on May 23, where he spoke for about 20 minutes. Pacific Arts and Nesmith Video Publishing were present at the annual VSDA video dealers trade show in Las Vegas, Nevada, August 6-9, where Michael held a press conference.

In March, he released a greatest hits collection called *The Newer Stuff* for Rhino Records since he had the rights to these. (The older stuff was still under contract with RCA.) He told Rhino that he didn't think anyone would play this record, and their response was "We specialize in marketing records that don't get played."

"When I put together *The Newer Stuff*," Michael recalled, "I realized that I had music videos on seven or eight of them and I had also been getting a lot of requests to combine all those music videos on one videocassette, so I put it together and called it *Nezmusic*." *Nezmusic* was released in April.

THE NEWER STUFF (MN) (compilation)
Released: March 28, 1989. Original title was to be *New Stuff.*

Total Control (Michael Nesmith)
Tanya (Michael Nesmith)
I'll Remember You (Michael Nesmith)
Formosa Diner (Michael Nesmith)
Dreamer (Michael Nesmith)
Eldorado to the Moon (Bill Martin)
Tahiti Condo (Michael Nesmith)

Chow Mein and Bowling (Bill Martin)
Magic (Michael Nesmith)
Cruisin' (Michael Nesmith)
Light (Michael Nesmith)
Carioca (Michael Nesmith)
Rio (Michael Nesmith)
Casablanca Moonlight (Michael Nesmith)

Rio (Michael Nesmith) / **I'll Remember You** (Michael Nesmith) (MN) (June 1989, UK only)

Micky appeared by himself on the *1989 MTV Video Music Awards*, airing on September 6, and on *Nashville Now*, airing on October 16, where he talked about the 1st Annual Celebrity Music Golf Invitational he played in Dallas. He even joked about his bald spot!

He and his family finally relocated back to California, where he had hoped to continue his producing and directing career and embark on a solo tour. He took advantage of the LA culture, attending the September 4 Ringo Starr and his All-Starr Band concert in Los Angeles as well as a Paul McCartney concert on November 29, and then a Donny Osmond concert on December 16. He also became involved with celebrity polo tournaments and played at various events over the year.

1990

Davy appeared on *What's Up, Dr. Ruth?* on January 26, *The Oprah Winfrey Show* on February 26 in a program about teen idols, the UK *This is Your Life* salute to Sir Harry Secombe (whom Davy co-starred with onstage in *Oliver!*) on March 7 and on *Almost Live!* on December 1. Davy appeared on *The Story Behind the Story* on May 13, speaking about being on *The Ed Sullivan Show* on the same night as The Beatles in 1964.

On May 22, Davy appeared in an infomercial about a 1960s hit song collection assembled by Don Kirshner called *The Don Kirshner Rock Awards* to celebrate Don's 35 years in the music business. Davy did an interview on KYW-TV's noon *Eyewitness News* on May 22, about the infomercial, and Davy and Don appeared together on WPVI-TV's *AM Philadelphia* on that same day to also talk about the project. They were also on hand at Bobbysox, a Philadelphia nightspot, on May 21, given by radio station WMGK.

He continued racing his horses, but August 11, his horse suffered a fatal heart attack and Davy's shoulder was broken in the fall.

Davy spent much of the year continuing to try to get his *They Made a Monkee Out of Me* book into a TV-movie.

Davy performed a number of solo shows this year as well: The annual Summerfest in Merrifield Park, Indiana on June 23; the Bismarck Hotel in Chicago on August 18; the Oak Lawn Pavilion in Chicago on August 24; Lulu's Roadhouse in Kitchener, Ontario, on October 12-13; and the Hartford Civic Center in Hartford, Connecticut on November 16. He was interviewed on Muchmusic, Canada's music channel, on October 11.

He finished the year appearing in (wait for it) *Oliver!* from December 1-16, in the Fifth Avenue Musical Theatre productions, in Seattle. Then, when he flew back from Seattle to England, stopped in Port Chester, New York, to film a scene for an upcoming *ABC Afterschool Special* called "It's Only Rock and Roll", which was shown in March of 1991.

Peter appeared on *What's Up, Dr. Ruth?* on February 9, as part of an episode about drugs and alcohol.

He did a short concert tour of Japan from July 18 through 21, performing at Expo '90 in Osaka ABC Kaikan Hall in Tokyo.

Back home, he put together a group called Sleep of Reason, and later called The Dashboard Saints, which performed in his local area. They appeared regularly at clubs in Fairfax and San Rafael, California, but he made a surprise solo appearance at a club in Mt. Vernon, New York, on June 22.

Peter appeared on VH-1 to countdown the top 20 videos in the US on September 27.

Determined to get back on the road on his own merits, Peter signed up to be managed by Onstage Management Group run by Jack Yoger. In discussions about 1991 venues, Peter disclosed that he was working on an album with his old friend James Lee Stanley. He wanted to tour without playing Monkees tunes, but his agent said, "Where's your hit?"

He also spent a few days in New York in mid-April 1990, appearing as a celebrity co-host at New York University's *Beyond Vaudeville* stage show on April 19, and was interviewed on April 20, on the Flo and Eddie radio show on WXRK 92.3 FM.

Michael announced on February 7 that his company, Pacific Arts, has signed a home video distribution deal with PBS, and addressed the annual conference of the Public Broadcasting Service on June 17-21 in Dallas, Texas, Michael's home town. He also appeared August 6-12, in Las Vegas for the annual VSDA video trade show.

Michael appeared on *Crook and Chase* again on March 8. He was also profiled in *Business of Film* magazine and appeared as a keynote speaker at the NARAS conference on music video at the Loews Vanderbilt Hotel in Nashville, Tennessee, on February 26.

In May, Michael was at Lion Share recording studio to clean up the tracks of his old RCA albums for inclusion on the upcoming *The Older Stuff* CD. He also remixed and reissued *The Prison* onto CD on November 19. Michael also appeared on *Entertainment Tonight* on November 30, during a segment where Don Kirshner discussed The Monkees' refusal to record "Sugar, Sugar."

Micky had a very busy year.

He spent much of late January and February directing a live-action TV movie for The Disney Channel called *Aladdin*, which aired in October. This musical, starring Barry Bostwick, predated the 1992 animated version from Disney starring Robin Williams. There's no way you'd get them confused; it has a very different plot (Aladdin goes to China!).

Micky decided to install a telephone hotline so fans could know what he is currently doing. It only lasted a few months until fans overloaded the voicemail. Micky never bothered to get another number.

Micky appeared on the March 9 edition of *A.M. Los Angeles*; the May 1 edition of *Inside Edition*; *Lifestyles of the Rich and Famous* on May 6; and the August 11 edition of *Dennis Norden's Pick of the Pilots* on ITV. He called in to Flo and Eddie's radio show on K-Rock 92.3 on his birthday, March 8. On March 26, Micky was a guest at Milton Berle's post-Oscar charity gala, from which he appeared on *Entertainment Tonight* on March 27.

SILVER SERIES

From the mystical fables of 1001 Arabian Nights...

Aladdin

A timeless family classic returns in a magical new musical

He also sang on an all-star charity single called "Forgotten Eyes," released on Motown (He's listed on the cover as "and many more"), and in August, released an audio cassette in the UK where he read *Memoirs of a Sword Swallower*, an autobiography of Dan Mannix. Extracts were played on BBC Radio 4.

Micky told *Monkee Business Fanzine* in June that he was recording an album for CBS Records, but the deal must have gone through as it never appeared. "The album will be quite different from what you'd expect from Micky Dolenz," he said. "It will be more rock 'n' roll, more mature. I'm 45 years old. I can't sing about little girls and puberty. I'd probably get arrested."

Micky planned to direct *Runaway Bay* in the Caribbean, but by summer, those plans were shelved. He also bought the remake rights to make a UK version of Norman Lear's *Fernwood 2-Night*, a parody talk show. He also bought the remake rights to *The Comedian*, and was working on two pilots for Chris Beard Television.

He was on hand at the star-studded invitation-only opening of singer Donna Summer's art show at Circle Gallery in Beverly Hills and attended a BMI dinner honoring Michael Jackson in May. He appeared on Paul Rodriguez's syndicated television show and on the BMI Pop Music Awards on May 22.

Micky attended a New Kids on the Block concert in Costa Mesa, California, on September 13, where he appeared onstage during the encore.

On November 25, Micky appeared for the third time in the Hollywood Christmas Parade. The first time was in 1955 during *Circus Boy*, when he rode an elephant. The second time was in the 1960s as a Monkee.

Micky hosted the *Hawaiian Tropic Beauty Pageant* in the fall of 1990, but it wasn't shown until June 9, 1991. He was featured on the *Cruisin' America* syndicated radio show on August 19 and attended the MTV Music Video Awards on September 6.

Micky made a special guest appearance on Flo and Eddie's radio show on October 23. They asked Micky about *The New Monkees* television series. Micky responded, "They wanted us to be in it, to kind of hand the torch over to the young guys, hand it over to the new generation, and we said, 'Get outta here! You crazy? Let these guys have all the fun.' They asked me to direct it, and I read the scripts, and it was pretty abysmal. I said it's a good idea to do something like this, but they wanted to try to do *The Young Ones*. They were trying, I think, to capture that kind of originally, but they just didn't have a prayer."

When asked about The Monkees breakup, Micky said, "It ended mainly because musically, there wasn't a vision. When we got control after battling to get control of our music, we just started going off on our own musical directions. It was four separate, entirely separate, musical visions. It wasn't a group anymore. It was four solo acts, doing three tracks each and sticking them all on the album. It lost its cohesiveness because Tommy Boyce and Bobby Hart and Carole King and Bert and Bob, the producers, they

were the group, too. That's why it fell apart. I regret it to a degree. We could have had a couple more years on television. Who knows? Since there was no musical vision after the show went off the air, there wasn't anything keeping it together, except the old hit records, which I usually sang. Every time we'd get back together, Davy would get pissed off singing backgrounds for Micky. I don't blame him. I hadn't chosen to be the lead singer. They made me the lead singer. Mike had a country-western feel, Peter was folk-rock, and Davy was Broadway. The only thing holding us together was the old songs, which we had to do. We'd get out on the road and the first couple of weeks it would be, 'It's good to see you again,' and two weeks later, it was, 'Grrr! Asshole!'"

Micky appeared as quite the celebrity athlete for various charities over the year, which was something that just was not done much in jolly old England. On April 7-8, he played tennis in the 9th annual Michael Landon Celebrity Tennis Classic in Tucson, Arizona. He played a charity softball game in Palm Spring, California on May 4. On June 3, he played in the Love Match tennis tournament in Westlake Village, California. He played at the Peninsula Humane Society's Celebrity Sports Classic from June 29-July 1. The Roy Clark Celebrity Weekend in Tulsa, Oklahoma was held on September 15-16. The Children's Discovery Museum fundraiser in San Jose was on September 23. A tennis tournament for the Children's Wish Foundation found Micky on September 28-30. The Cliff Robertson Tennis Tournament in Scottsdale, Arizona, was held on November 16-18. And celebrity polo matches were held on December 9 and 16, in Indio, California. Whew!

1991

Micky performed at the 1991 New Year's Eve Bash at Bally's Casino in Reno, Nevada, in a show called *30 Years of Rock 'n' Roll*. He then went on tour with his new backup group, performing at least 36 dates between April 18 and September 27. This group appeared briefly on the Arthritis Foundation Telethon on April 21, broadcast live from Bally's. A home video of the tour was available from Midnight Gold Productions.

At this point, with no Monkees 25th anniversary tour, Micky insisted emphatically that The Monkees were behind him with no more reunions. He insisted that this tour was his first serious solo tour.

Micky was interviewed on the syndicated show *Personalities* on January 8 and on *The World Through Celebrity's Eyes* on the Travel Channel on January 21.

Micky continued to attend and participate in many celebrity sports fundraisers over the year, showed up on many local TV stations promoting the events, and performed a solo show at the New York State Fair on August 24, and a concert at the San Diego Zoo for the zoo's 75th anniversary in October.

On September 30 and October 1, Micky was in Vancouver, British Columbia, to tape episodes of the Canadian game show *Acting Crazy*.

Micky claimed to still be working on a rock 'n' roll album with producer David Foster, but in the meantime, recorded the vocals for his first children's album called *Micky Dolenz Puts You to Sleep*. It's a wonderful album, excellently produced, with Micky's soothing voice. There are two Monkees songs hidden within, re-recorded for the sleepy set. The song "Sugar Mountain" was released as a promotional video.

MICKY DOLENZ PUTS YOU TO SLEEP (MD)
Released: October 22, 1991

Pillow Time (Janelle Scott, Matt Willis)
Dream a Little Dream of Me (Fabian Andre, Gus Kahn, Wilbur Schwandt)
Beautiful Boy (John Lennon)
Blackbird (John Lennon, Paul McCartney)
Lullaby to Tim (Graham Nash, Alan Clarke, Tony Hicks)
Fool on the Hill (John Lennon, Paul McCartney)
Good Night (John Lennon, Paul McCartney)
St. Judy's Comet (Paul Simon)
The Moonbeam Song (Harry Nilsson)
Remember (Harry Nilsson)
Sugar Mountain (Neil Young)
The Porpoise Song (Gerry Goffin, Carole King)

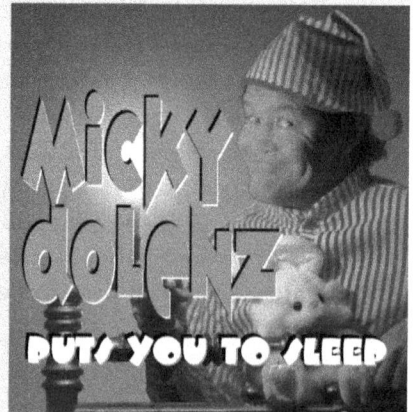

Later in October, he performed a series of concerts in Florida, including the Rainbow Festival in Stewart; at a club called "Midnight Gold," also in Stewart; and at the Coconuts Festival in Miami Beach.

On October 31, he showed up to the *Spinal Tap* press conference in Los Angeles. A week later he could be found in Austin where he did an interview with KLBJ radio and signed copies of *Micky Dolenz Puts You to Sleep*.

He performed a concert in Norfolk, Virginia at the Scope Coliseum on November 17, signed autographs at the Home and Design Showcase in Sayreville, New Jersey on the same day, and headed to New York on the 18th, where he attended Paul McCartney's *Liverpool Oratorio* at Carnegie Hall. The next day, he taped interviews for *Entertainment Weekly* syndicated radio; *Streetbeat*, a cable TV show; a segment for VH-1; a segment for *The Real Story* for CNBC; and appeared with Howard Stern on KXRK-FM radio in New York. Micky talked about the album in Marillyn Beck's syndicated column on November 19.

The next few weeks were filled with many radio station interviews and local appearances to promote the album, with another solo date in Florida on December 8 at the Sarasota Winter Music Festival.

He also appeared on New Year's Eve on *Super Gold*, an oldies radio show.

In sadder news, Micky divorced his second wife, Trina Dow.

Davy performed live for four dates from February 21 to July 26, and for a 1991 US tour called The Davy Jones Flash Tour that lasted 15 dates from July 3 through August 17. Davy continued with a three week tour of Australia starting September 12 for twelve dates, lasting till October 6, 1991. He arrived in the US on June 27 to rehearse his touring band in Beavertown, Pennsylvania, where he was living on his horse farm. He also signed autographs at the Philadelphia Fan Fair and Collectibles Extravaganza at the Valley Forge Convention Center in King of Prussia, Pennsylvania, on August 4. Davy also performed a short six date tour in the US from November 2 through December 7. Along the way, he did many radio interviews.

As an actor, Davy appeared on *Country Kitchen* on March 30 and in the UK drama series *Trainer* in an episode called "No Way to Treat a Lady" that aired November 24 on BBC. Davy was scheduled to take on the role of The Sly Fox in American Family Theatre's musical production of *Pinocchio* beginning in April, but it never happened. Davy even taped a TV commercial on August 5 to air in every city where *Pinocchio* was to be performed.

Add a broken hand and a broken toe to the list of Davy's injuries, thanks to his horses. He rode his own horse in an amateur race in Warwick, England, on May 25 and someone else's horse for Red Nose Day in March.

Davy appeared on the May 7 edition of *Personalities*, and in the background on a segment interviewing Jeremy Irons on the March 25 *Barbara Walters Special*. He also made a surprise appearance at the Pulsations nightclub in Glen Mills, Pennsylvania, on November 8, performing a 45-minute set.

Other concert appearances included The Hop in Totowa, New Jersey in November; Pleasure Island in Walt Disney World on November 14; and a fundraiser shows on December 1 for the Shikellamy High School cheerleaders in Sunbury, Pennsylvania! On December 14, he performed at the Big Five Club in Miami, Florida, and a week later was interviewed by an Apeldoorn, Netherlands radio station.

Around this time, Davy's 1977 Christmas album was re-released by Dome Press, which also released *Davy Live at Lulu's* on videocassette on October 5. The recordings were either re-recorded or remixed with some new recordings. Material from this session ended up on the 2018 Monkees *Christmas Party* release.

Davy patted himself on the back about this album. "I've always been a great believer in endorsing my own ideas. I made a Christmas album. I spent my own money doing that. It'll take a long time to recoup that. That's only because I want to communicate."

Davy's self-released albums may sound fine, but he clearly wasn't spending anything on hiring a good design department to take care of the artwork.

IT'S CHRISTMAS TIME AGAIN (DJ)
1991 reissue of 1977 *Christmas Jones* album with slightly different track order. Released on cassette only at this time, then CD in 1997, and again on CD in 2005.
Released: December 1991 (although it didn't make it out until January 1992)

Winter Wonderland (Richard B. Smith, Felix Bernard)
Rudolph, the Red-Nosed Reindeer (Johnny Marks)
Silver Bells (Jay Livingstone, Ray Evans)
God Rest Ye Merry Gentlemen (traditional)
Hark, the Herald Angels Sing (Felix Mendelssohn)

White Christmas (Irving Berlin)
Mele Kalikimaka (Robert Alexander Anderson)
This Day in Bethlehem (Davy Jones)
Silent Night (Franz Xaber Gruber)
Rockin' Around the Christmas Tree (Johnny Marks)
When I Look Back On Christmas (Martin Jackson)

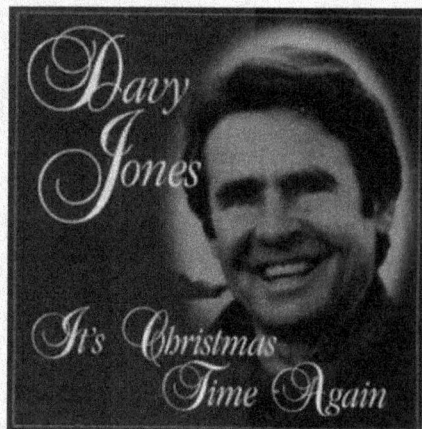

Peter performed live with his band The Dashboard Saints at 19 Broadway in Fairfax on New Year's Eve/Day, and then again on January 26, February 23 and 28, March 29, and April 6 and 11. Their gig at the 4th Street Tavern in San Rafael on April 26 turned out to be the farewell performance of the band.

Peter continued to perform with some of the ex-members of The Dashboard Saints at 19 Broadway with occasional shows starting May 30 and July 25, as well as on August

3 at Buck's in Guerneville, California, as well as shows at Sweetwater in Mill Valley, California.

Peter served as one of the judges in the Harmony Sweepstakes, a national a cappella competition held at the Marin Civic Center in San Rafael on May 18.

After getting the rights back to his earlier albums, Michael refurbished his First National Band material for *The Older Stuff* compilation.

THE OLDER STUFF (MN) (compilation)
Released: November 1991

Joanne (Michael Nesmith)
The Crippled Lion (Michael Nesmith)
I Fall to Pieces (Harlan Howard, Hank Cochran)
Listen to the Band (Michael Nesmith)
Silver Moon (Michael Nesmith)
Propinquity (I've Just Begun to Care) (Michael Nesmith)
I Looked Away (Eric Clapton, Bobby Whitlock)
Nevada Fighter (Michael Nesmith)
Tumbling Tumbleweeds (Bob Nolan)
Here I Am (Michael Nesmith)
Some of Shelly's Blues (Michael Nesmith)
Born to Love You (Cindy Walker)
Different Drum (Michael Nesmith)
Harmony Constant (Michael Nesmith)
Continuing (Michael Nesmith)
Prairie Lullaby Hill (Billy Hill)
Release (Michael Nesmith)
Roll With the Flow (Michael Nesmith)

Awareness Records in England then re-released *Magnetic South, Loose Salute* and *Nevada Fighter* for the first time on CD on March 18. *Tantamount to Treason, And the Hits Just Keep on Comin',* and *Pretty Much Your Standard Ranch Stash* were reissued in September.

Michael also appeared on the cover of the March 1991 issue of *Vidpix,* in honor of the 10th anniversary of *Elephant Parts.* He was also featured on the April 3 edition of *Personalities,* making Peter the only holdout for a story about him on the show. He was interviewed on radio station KFI in Los Angeles on July 23.

Michael's Pacific Arts company moved to 11858 La Grange Avenue, Los Angeles in July. Pacific Arts was awarded a Homer Award in July for Favorite Video Documentary: *The Civil War*, released on the PBS Home Video label.

The TV series Michael was developing for FOX called *Reel Life* was not picked up for FOX's fall schedule.

1992

Michael performed nine solo shows from January 25 to February 29. The June 19 concert in Jacksonville, Oregon was the basis for the *Live at the Britt Festival* album, released in 1999. This was Michael's first solo tour since 1979. It was called The Multi-Purpose Tour. Micky and Peter attended Michael's February 7 concert at The Strand, in Redondo Beach, California.

Michael took a break to record *Tropical Campfires*, and then went on a *Tropical Campfires* Tour from September 16-27, for 16 dates, later reduced to five dates. He was also a guest speaker in March 1992 at Hamilton High School in Los Angeles, California.

Michael attended the annual PBS meeting in San Francisco in June 1992. He also performed on Austin City Limits on September 16 that aired on PBS the following January 16.

Michael discussed *Tropical Campfires* with Mike Hockinson in *Monkee Business Fanzine* #62, September 1992. "*Tropical Campfires* came out of the tour that I finished in February. It was a result of the band I was working with, and the way we started singing. I started writing these songs. I liked them so much and the reaction from the crowd was encouraging enough for me to go back into the studio and make this LP." It's a very pleasant album continuing on the tradition and style of all of Michael's albums since 1977 with "Laugh Kills Lonesome" being a strong standout track.

TROPICAL CAMPFIRES (MN)
Released: September 1992

Yellow Butterfly (Michael Nesmith)
Laugh Kills Lonesome (Michael Nesmith)
Moon Over the Rio Grande (Michael Nesmith)
One... (Michael Nesmith)
Juliana (Michael Nesmith)
Brazil (Bob Russell, Ary Barroso, Russell Sidney)
In the Still of the Night (Cole Porter)
Rising in Love (Michael Nesmith)
Begin the Beguine (Cole Porter)
I Am Not That (Michael Nesmith)
...for the Island (Michael Nesmith)
Twilight on the Trail (Michael Nesmith)

"...Michael Nesmith..."

"...tropical campfires..."

Peter performed live at The Bammies a.k.a. The Bay Area Music Awards at the San Francisco Civic Auditorium, California, on March 7. He also appeared in an episode of *California Dreams* called "Romancing the Tube," which aired on November 14 on NBC.

Sometime during 1992, Peter relocated back to Los Angeles after living a number of years in San Anselmo in Marin County in Northern California. He claimed to be working on more demos and shopping them around to different record labels, and also taking acting classes again.

He did perform with Micky in attendance at the Coconut Teaszer in Los Angeles, on July 30. Other performances in the LA area were on July 1, September 5, October 20, October 31, November 20 and December 19.

Micky appeared with his "30 Years of Rock 'n' Roll Show" at the Country Club in Reseda, California, on February 14, and then embarked on a solo tour that was scheduled for twenty performances between March 6 through September 5, but many performances after May 23 were canceled. He would not perform another solo show until 2001.

He also played solo backed with Cannibal and the Head Hunters at Club La Bamba at Harrah's in Laughlin, Nevada, on September 12, and played selections from *Micky Dolenz Puts You to Sleep* in Dallas, Texas, on October 4. He was scheduled to play on October 17, but that was also canceled.

Micky claimed to have penned at least ten new songs at this point, and started shopping around his demos to record labels. Meanwhile, he began working on his autobiography.

He did a few acting appearances on various TV shows during the year. He voiced the characters "Min" and "Max" on the "Two-Face, Part II" episode of *Batman: The Animated Series*, airing on September 28. He actually had to audition for the role.

Micky's appearance on *The Ben Stiller Show* on November 15 is a wonder to behold. The skit involves a group called "The Grungees" which is an obvious satire of the Monkees with a grunge band of Seattle rockers. (Micky shows up as a turtle-necked agent from Pretentious Records offering The Grungees a lot of money if they sign with the label).

Micky also provided the voice of a dog in a live-action Kibbles 'n' Bits commercial. Micky was considered for a voice role in Disney's fully animated *Aladdin*, but the part went to another actor. As himself, he appeared on *Bear Country* on January 31, and the April 3 edition of *Breakfast Television*. He was interviewed from Hollywood on WZLX in Boston, on July 8.

Micky continued to attend celebrity sport fundraising events, including playing softball at the Santa Monica Girls' Club on May 9; the Jimmy Stewart/Robert Wagner Marathon at Griffith Park in Los Angeles on May 17; the celebrity charity tennis tournament at Placerita Junior High in Santa Clarita on May 31; the celebrity softball game at Pepperdine University in Malibu on June 13; the T.J. Martell Rock 'n' Roll Celebrity Softball game at Dedeaux Field at USC on June 14; the celebrity tennis tournament at the The Woodlands Resort in Houston, on July 11-12; a golf tournament in Tulsa, Oklahoma on July 13; the Celebrity Surfing Contest in Malibu on July 26; and the Mazda Tennis Classic at Lacosta Resort in Carlsbad on August 29. Micky also appeared at Kid Around, a fundraiser for battered women and children, which was held in Dallas on October 4. Whew!

Micky also dabbled in painting, and his work, along with other celebrity works of art, were exhibited May 16-21, at the Director's Guild in Los Angeles.

He also spent time recording, producing and mixing music of his own at The Recording Studio in Sunnyvale, California, in September. He recorded a version of "O Little Town of Bethlehem" for Nordstrom's Christmas anthology album called *A Gift of Life*.

Davy performed live in concert on January 31 at the Cambria County War Memorial in Johnstown, Pennsylvania, for two shows. He then embarked on a tour with the backing band Breakway, which ran (with certain breaks away) from February 15 through August 22.

He appeared on *New York at Night* at the end of March, and performed at the Village Gate in New York in *The Real Live Brady Bunch* show from April 2 – 8 and was interviewed on WCBS radio on April 8. He also performed at shows at the Westwood Playhouse in Los Angeles from May 21 - 24, and was asked back there for the week of July 16 - 22. Peter attended Davy's May 24 performance after reading about it in *Monkee Business Fanzine*! After the performance, Peter and Davy posed for pictures together.

Davy's second autobiography with Alan Green was finally released in September, and his book tour started soon thereafter. Its title was *Mutant Monkees Meet the Masters of the Multimedia Manipulation Machine!*

Davy continued to try to interest major labels into releasing a new solo album, but he did find time to record the song "Free," which was given away free with copies of his new book.

He appeared on the June 4 episode of *Live! With Regis and Kathie Lee* and found himself on "Howard Stern's Tribute to Breasts" on *The Howard Stern Show* on April 25. "It was not my idea," Davy said about the Howard Stern appearance. "I didn't know what the topic was until I was there. He was alright. I understand that a lot of people seem to have a hard time with him, but it all depends on how you go into these things. I had no intention of going into it with my tail between my legs. Improvisation, I think, is what I do best. It afforded me the opportunity and the cues. He didn't bother me at all. Everyone says I did pretty good on it."

Other appearances that year included *The Jerry Lewis Telethon* on September 7; a performance of "Daydream Believer" and "Hippy Hippy Shake" on *Nightcap* on November 11; a fundraiser on November 20, in Port St. Lucie, Florida; the Broward County Fair in Gulf Stream Park in Hallandale, Florida, on November 26; and a televised all-star benefit in Helsinki, Sweden, in December 29.

As an actor, he appeared on the sitcom *Herman's Head* in an episode entitled "The One Where They Go On The Love Boat" on November 22.

Davy purchased two more horses to add to his stable at his Beaverton, Pennsylvania farm, an appaloosa and a two-year-old Arabian.

The Dolenz, Jones, Boyce and Hart studio album as well as the live album which was only released in Japan were scheduled for release onto compact disc in 1992. The DJB&H album was scheduled to be released by Capitol Records in the US, but was shelved indefinitely, because they could not find the master tapes! The *Live* album eventually came out on Varese Sarabande in 1996, and the studio album came out on Cherry Red Records in the UK only in 2005.

1993

Davy's live performances in 1993 included appearances in Boston on February 6; Toronto's "Rockin' Back to the 60s" concert at the Skydome on April 16; eleven other concerts from May 2 through August 9; and the Belgrave Hotel in Torquay, England on October 14. He continued touring through the rest of the year into early 1994.

He was scheduled to perform on August 22 at Holiday Park in Fox Lake, Illinois, but he cancelled due to a payment dispute. The promoter had tried to get Davy to perform a shorter set for less money at the last minute, but Davy chose not to perform at all given the breach in contract. Fans were disappointed. Another show was scheduled for November 12 in Waukegan, Illinois, where the promoters started selling tickets in advance without a contract from Davy confirming that he'd attend. Since they would not meet his price, he did not perform and the tickets had to be refunded.

When asked about the possibility of a Monkees reunion tour in 1996 for the 30th anniversary, Davy said, "I don't see why that would be a problem. It would be a lovely payday."

He was a guest on the August 4, edition of *Sally Jessy Raphael* and appeared as himself on *Bradymania: A Very Brady Special* which aired on May 19 on ABC.

He rode in Comic Relief Race Day at Cheltenham Racecourse in Cheltenham, England, on March 19.

As an actor, he once again portrayed Fagin in *Oliver!* from July 4 through August 8, but the shows after July 11 were canceled, so he spent a week on vacation in England instead.

Peter performed five US concerts from March 13 through June 5 and then performed two shows in Santa Monica on October 30.

He spent most of the rest of 1993 recording and completing the tracks for his first solo album, which was released in 1994. In *Monkee Business Fanzine* #65, June 1993, Peter attributes the delays "to his long-time friend James Lee Stanley, who is also a working musician who frequently must go out on the road on tours of his own. While he's away, of course, nothing gets done in the recording studio! In addition, there are other unexpected problems that bring further delays; intense technical difficulties—lots of gremlins—in the recording studio with the computers that do the sequencing."

Since Davy and Micky had written their autobiographies, MBF asked if Peter would write one next? "If I'd really wanted to write a book," Peter responded. "I would have done so a long time ago!" Of course, Peter never did get around to writing that book.

Michael responded to the same question by saying that biographies are for the end of one's life and are inappropriate any sooner. (His book was finally published in 2018.)

He appeared on *Austin City Limits* on January 16; on *Showbiz Today* on January 27; and on *The AFI Life Achievement Award: A Tribute to Elizabeth Taylor* on May 6.

Michael spent most of 1993 recording his next album *The Garden* while releasing a new collection. Despite being billed as the "complete" recordings of the First National Band, the two-disc set does not include "First National Rag" from *Magnetic South*, "First National Dance" (a bonus track on *Loose Salute*) or "Rose City Chimes," the B-side to "Little Red Rider."

Michael later said in an interview from *The Nashville Banner* published on February 27, 1995, "The First National Band albums were to be considered as a unit. I just didn't have the medium that I could get all of that music on at the same time. It was too long. I didn't write it all at the same time, but I conceived it all at the same time. I thought maybe what I could do was fashion it so that all the first sides of those albums had a continuity to them. I was not successful at that. Once I finally got them all done, I realized that the continuity had really emerged by just playing them in a straight line. If you just play one right after the other, it works. It almost creates the overall work that I wanted."

THE COMPLETE FIRST NATIONAL BAND RECORDINGS (MN) (compilation)
Released: September 28, 1993 (See individual volumes for track listing.)

Micky finished up his tour with *A Funny Thing Happened On the Way to the Forum* on January 24 at the Stage West dinner theatre in Calgary, Alberta and resumed the tour to Stage West in Edmonton, Alberta from January 27 through March 21.

He performed at the Classic Rock Super Jam on April 22 held at the Queen Mary in Long Beach, California. He didn't do much touring the rest of the year due to his other commitments, including recording a second children's album. He was scheduled to perform the week of August 16 - 23 at the Cristy Lane Theater in Branson, Missouri, with The 30 Years of Rock 'n' Roll tour, but had to cancel at the last minute. He did

appear in concert at the Trump Taj Mahal Casino/ Hotel in Atlantic City, New Jersey on September 5.

Micky appeared with his daughter Ami on *Vicki!* which aired on June 18; and alone on the September 3 edition of *The Today Show.*

Acting-wise, he had a small part in the film *Deadfall* with Nicolas Cage, which was released on October 8. Director Tim Burton said that he wanted Micky to portray The Riddler in the upcoming *Batman 3*, but then Burton dropped out of the project. Eventually, the third Batman movie came to be known as *Batman Forever*, with Jim Carrey in the role of The Riddler, and was released in 1995.

Micky was approached by a group of London theatre producers to write and direct a stage adaptation of the US TV series *Happy Days*, but nothing came of it.

Micky's autobiography, *I'm a Believer: My Life of Monkees, Music and Madness*, was released in August. He then went on a 14-date book signing tour from September 8 through October 2. (The picture above is from the revised 2004 edition.)

Author Note from Mark: I saw Micky and got his autograph at the September 16, 1993 date at The Booksmith in San Francisco, California.

Micky was guest of honor at the book premier party held at the Hard Rock Café in New York on September 7, 1993. Based on photographs, Micky apparently wore the exact same outfit to every book signing on the tour.

He made *many* TV and radio appearances to promote the book, a listing of which would take an entire page to recount. Basically, from late August through December, Micky was on the air somewhere in the country almost every day, culminating in an appearance on the December 16 edition of *Late Night with Conan O'Brien.*

He finished up recording vocals to *Broadway Micky* on November 2. It was titled *Micky Does the Musicals* at this point.

Micky's artwork traveled the country during the year at places like The Image Makers Rock 'n' Roll art exhibit; the University Mall in South Burlington, Vermont; and the Maryland State Fairgrounds.

On December 7 and 8, Micky and Davy got together to record a radio advertising campaign for Monsanto floor covering products.

1994

Plans were this close for another Monkees reunion tour in 1994, but were scrapped at the last minute. Micky and Davy, however, performed a "Together Again" tour that ran from July 19 through October 7.

Acting-wise, Micky was seen on the "My Dad Could Beat Up Your Dad" episode of *Monty* and on the "Band On the Run" episode of *Boy Meets World*, which aired on November 11. He filmed a hilarious TV commercial for *Jeopardy!* where he is sitting in his living room watching the show and shouting, "I know this one! Davy Jones' locker! Davy Jones' locker!" The chest he's sitting on then starts to wobble and Micky says, "Calm down, Davy."

In April, his second album aimed at children was released. It is every bit as charming as Micky's first album. And yes, Charlie Smalls, the composer of "Ease On Down the Road," appeared at the end of The Monkees episode "Some Like it Lukewarm" with Davy.

BROADWAY MICKY (MD)
Released: April 5, 1994

Supercalifragilisticexpialidocious (Richard Sherman, Robert Sherman)
Talk to the Animals (Leslie Bricusse)
Somewhere Out There (James Horner, Cynthia Well, Barry Mann)
Put On a Happy Face (Lee Adams, Charles Strouse)
You're Never Fully Dressed Without a Smile (Charles Strouse, Martin Charmin)
Never Ending Story (Giorgio Moroder, Keith Forsey)
My Favorite Things (Richard Rodgers, Oscar Hammerstein II)
Ease On Down the Road (Charlie Smalls)
I Whistle a Happy Tune (Richard Rodgers, Oscar Hammerstein II)
Chim Chim Cher-ee (Richard Sherman, Robert Sherman)
Me and My Arrow (Harry Nilsson)
When You Wish Upon a Star (Leigh Harline, Ned Washington)

As himself, he appeared on the talk show *Marilu*, airing on February 14; *Entertainment Tonight* on June 17 and then on December 15; and on *The Tonight Show with Jay Leno* on August 10.

Micky's artwork continued to be shown at showings at different venues, with the December show lasting the entire month at Imagemakers Gallery in Strafford, Pennsylvania.

He directed the "Turnaround" episode of *Boy Meets World*, which aired on December 16.

He continued his celebrity sports run by participating in the annual Connie Stevens Celebrity Ski Extravaganza in Jackson Hole, Wyoming, on March 11-12; the LA Open Golf Tournament in Los Angeles on February 6; the Empire Polo in Palm Springs, on February 12-13; the celebrity polo match at the Equestrian Center in Burbank on May 8; and the Richard Karn Celebrity Golf Classic at Echo Falls Country Club in Snohomish, Washington on June 11-12. A brief appearance of Micky on the golf course appeared on ESPN's special about Richard Karn's Golf Tournament on December 18.

Michael performed a solo show at the West End Marketplace in Dallas on July 16 with The Hellecasters, and planned to play with The Hellecasters again at Humphreys in San Diego on August 7, but that date was canceled. He did play two more shows in Oregon on August 18 and 20.

He also appeared on an episode of *Later* on December 1.

Having had enough of California, he moved to Santa Fe, New Mexico this year.

His album *The Garden* was released in August. "*The Prison* had mixed two media—text and music—years earlier, in 1974, and had given me enough insight into a mixed-media format that I was comfortable juggling ideas across multiple platforms," he wrote in *Infinite Tuesday*. "In 1994, I wrote *The Garden* around the same approach, listening to music and reading text, and had two parts of a trilogy. But the virtual world moved me into another dimension and opened new possibilities."

THE GARDEN (MN)
Released: August 30, 1994

Garden's Glow (Michael Nesmith)
Ficus Carica (Michael Nesmith)
City (Michael Nesmith)
Hills of Time (Michael Nesmith)
Flowers Dancing (Michael Nesmith)
Wisteria (Michael Nesmith)
Life Becoming (Michael Nesmith)

THE GARDEN MICHAEL NESMITH

This release was for Michael's new label, Rio Records. It was issued as a standard CD and as a CD-ROM version which will allow you to read the book on your computer screen as you listened to the music.

Michael later said in an interview in *The Nashville Banner* published on February 27, 1995, "When I recorded it, I certainly didn't think of it as being new age … I suppose it's closer to new age than it is any other kind of music, in that it is instrumental. It's got elements of new age in it, but I sure didn't design it for that."

The album didn't sell well at all, but at this point in his life, Michael had no money worries and instead just continued to create what he wanted to.

Peter appeared on the July 4 episode of *The Geraldo Rivera Show* and the July 11 episode of *The Steven Banks Show* on PBS. He was also on *The Fog City Theater* radio show on KQED-FM in San Francisco, on April 30.

Peter performed at the June 4 Salute to Parks and Recreation Festival in Northridge, California, and at a pre-release party for his first solo album at 19 Broadway in Fairfax, California, on August 27.

The album features Michael and Micky singing backing vocals on the track "Milkshake," and Michael singing backing vocals for "MGB-GT." Monkees fans will note that the songs "MGB-GT" and "Gettin' In" had been recorded with The Monkees around the time of the *Pool It* album. They may also notice the absence of Davy Jones. A re-recording of The Monkees' "Take a Giant Step" is also featured.

STRANGER THINGS HAVE HAPPENED (PT)
Released: June 15, 1994

Stranger Things Have Happened (Rudetsky, Levin)
Get What You Pay For (Peter Tork)
Sea Change (Peter Tork)
Take a Giant Step (Gerry Goffin, Carole King)
Milkshake (Martin Briley)
MGB-GT (Peter Tork)
Miracle (Peter Tork)
Pirates (Nick Thorkelson)
Gettin' In (Peter Tork)
Tender is (Peter Tork)
Higher and Higher (Carl Smith, Gary Jackson, Raynard Miner)

Davy started 1994 with multiple shows from January 10 through February 5 at the Starcase Theater, Resorts International in Atlantic City, New Jersey, and other US shows on March 5 and 26 and May 21, plus ten more from May 29 through September 10. Some of these dates previously announced as Davy solo shows became Davy-Micky shows and a few dates were canceled.

Davy also made over two dozen various appearances portraying himself in *The Real Live Brady Bunch* show from February 7 through May 1. He appeared as Vince Fontaine, the DJ, in a touring revival of *Grease* for lengthy stretches from September 23 through the end of 1994, plus some dates in January and February 1995.

Davy appeared on the April 2, 1994 edition of *Entertainment Tonight*, the September 16, 1994 edition of *Good Morning America* on ABC, and on the October 12, 1994 edition of *Show Biz Today* talking about his role in a stage version of *Grease* and his lifelong hobby of being a jockey racing horses.

He also did an autograph signing at Wherehouse Records in San Francisco, California, during his run with *Grease*. He later made a personal appearance at the Arlington Height Bowling Lanes (Seriously. A bowling alley) in Illinois on December 16, 1994, and he hung around the Kentucky Derby race track when *Grease* was in town in Louisville, Kentucky, during November 1994,

Davy filmed his scenes for *The Brady Bunch Movie* on July 15, 1994, after rehearsals on July 13-14, 1994. He also recorded a new version of "Girl" for the film soundtrack that was issued as a cassingle as the B-side of a new version of "Daydream Believer."

"You're In My Heart" is described on Davy Jones' Bandcamp page as having a light Latin feel.

"It's Not Too Late" is a Davy solo song that was rerecorded by The Monkees for their 1996 reunion album *Justus*.

Daydream Believer (John Stewart) / **Girl** (Charles Fox, Norman Gimbel) (DJ) (cassingle)
You're In My Heart (Davy Jones, Johnny J. Blair) (DJ) (cassingle)
It's Not Too Late (Davy Jones) (DJ) (cassingle)

In sadder news, longtime Monkees collaborator Tommy Boyce and member of Dolenz, Jones, Boyce and Hart committed suicide on November 23 at age 55.

Once again, before The Monkees started their second official reunion from 1996 to 1997 (and almost 1998), Micky and Davy tested the waters with a "Micky and Davy Together Again" tour which lasted for 29 dates and 33 shows from July 19 to September 18 and then from June 10 to October 7, 1995.

1995

January started on a good note when Michael's *The Garden* was nominated for a Grammy for Best New Age Album, but sadly it didn't seem to help sales much—nor did it win the award. He performed at the NAMM music industry trade show on January 22, and on March 18 at the Wadsworth Theater in Los Angeles, which would be his last concert (apart from The Monkees) until 2012.

Michael then reissued all of his solo albums again on Rio Records except for the elusive *Live at the Palais*.

Peter appeared on *Boy Meets World* episode called "Career Day" on May 12, having taped his appearance in February. He reprised the role in an episode airing on November 17, along with Micky and Davy in an episode called "Rave On" but none of whom played themselves. He also appeared on the November 13 episode of *The Stephanie Miller Show*, and as himself on the TV sitcom *Wings* in an episode called "She's Gotta Have it", which aired on November 14. In this episode, he gets into a bidding war at an auction where the Monkeemobile is for sale!

Peter also filmed scenes for the Pamela Anderson film *Barb Wire* on July 21, but his scenes were cut before the 1996 release, which may have been a blessing in disguise.

Peter was quite busy during this year, performing live concerts across the states, appearing on various radio shows, signing copies of his CD at record stores, and even singing the National Anthem for the Portland Sea Dogs baseball game in Portland, Maine, on April 6.

Davy appeared on *The Tonight Show with Jay Leno* on January 5; *TV's All Time Favorites* on May 19 (where he co-hosted with Dawn Wells and Jerry Mathers); and *The Oprah Winfrey Show* on September 21.

Meanwhile, he continued his role as Vince Fontaine, the DJ in *Grease - The 50s Musical* through February 5, and then some actor named Micky Dolenz took over the role!

Davy was also interviewed for *Brady: An American Chronicle*, a Nickelodeon special which premiered on February 12, 1995.

The Brady Bunch Movie featuring Davy was released on February 7. Peter and Micky make cameo appearances.

THE BRADY BUNCH MOVIE SOUNDTRACK (one track by DJ)
Released: February 28, 1995

Girl (Charles Fox, Norman Gimbel)

Davy was scheduled to do more *Oliver!* in summer 1995, but nothing materialized. Instead, he performed three more solo live dates on June 18, July 28-29, August 2, 10, and October 28, 1995, and also shows in Japan from March 27 through April 8.

Davy's *Just for the Record, Volume 2* was the first of his self-released multi-box set, released sometime in June 1995. The full box set was released in 1999. Now, don't ask us why Volume 2 came out before Volume 1, and please don't point out the obvious photoshopped "straw" in Davy's mouth on the cover.

JUST FOR THE RECORD, VOLUME 2 (DJ) (compilation)
Released: June 1995

Man We Was Lonely (Paul McCartney)
Rainy Jane (Howard Greenfield, Neil Sedaka)
King Lonely The Blue (Bobby Andriani)
Bye Bye Brown Eyes (Anthony Newley)
Dragonfly (Davy Jones)
Kansas (Davy Jones)
Leavin' Here This Morning (Davy Jones)
Was It A Dream? (Davy Jones)
Fire And Rain (James Taylor)
Staying Here With You (Davy Jones)
Blossom (Davy Jones)
Rainmaker (Harry Nilsson, Bill Martin)
Opening Nite (Davy Jones)
The Girl I Left Behind Me
(Instrumental) (Davy Jones)
No Regrets (Davy Jones)
So In Love With You (Davy Jones)
Fallen Hero (Special Edit Version)
(Davy Jones)
Leaving It Up To You (Davy Jones, Johnny J. Blair)
Baby Hold Out (Special Edit Version) (Davy Jones)
I'll Love You Forever (Davy Jones)
Proud Proud Man (Davy Jones)
Can't Believe You've Given Up On Me (Davy Jones)
I'll Survive (Davy Jones)
Thank Heaven For Little Girls (Take Two) (Alan Jay Lerner, Frederick Loewe)
Yeah Be Yeah (Davy Jones)

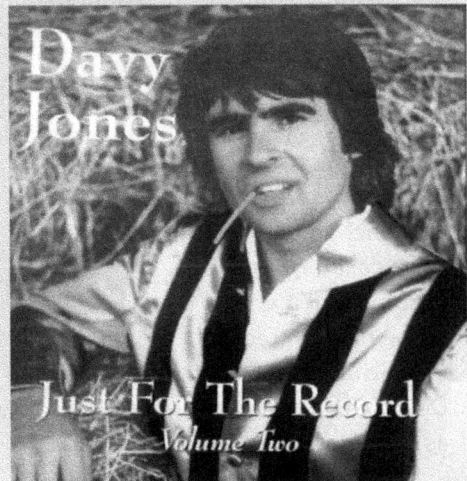

Micky also remained busy this year. He voiced Jed and Kilowog on the "Simon Strikes Back" / "The Ickis Box" episodes of the animated series *Aaahh!!! Real Monsters*, airing January 21. He also appeared as himself in the made-for-video documentary *You Can't Do That!: The Making of A Hard Day's Night* and on Marilu Henner's syndicated talk show on February 14, talking about the traveling show *Grease*, where he performed in Davy's old role from February 7 through August 2. He made personal appearances to promote the show on many local TV stations, including a joint appearance with Peter on WABC-TV's *Eyewitness News* on February 14.

Micky's artwork continued to tour with *The Image Makers Rock 'n' Roll Show* from March 15 through May 31 at six week-long engagements. Micky made a personal appearance on May 6 at the Renaissance Gallery in Strafford, Pennsylvania since the art schedule coincided with his *Grease* schedule. On his way to the gallery, Micky stopped by WMMR-FM radio for a brief interview and KYW-TV on *News 3 Weekend* for a surprise visit.

Micky was scheduled to record the voice of Arthur for a second season of 13 episodes of *The Tick*, but touring commitments prevented him from resuming the role in summer 1995, and he was replaced with voice actor Rob Paulsen.

Micky was approached to direct a film called *Boys Will Be Boys*, but it ended up being directed by comedian Dom DeLuise and released as a TV movie in 1999.

Micky and Davy toured together again from June 10 through October 7 for 16 dates. One of these was a free lunchtime concert performed at the base of the World Trade Center in New York on August 3.

Author comment from Mike: I was there at the World Trade Center show! To make it even better, August 3rd is my birthday. There's video of the show on the web, but you can't see me in the audience.

Micky also made a brief archival appearance in the *American Masters* episode of *Rod Serling: Submitted For Your Approval*, airing on PBS on November 29.

In sadder news, Micky's mother, Janelle Johnson passed away on December 2, at the age of 72.

1996

Michael was using his new webpage to promote and cyber-publish his novel *The Long Sandy Hair of Neftoon Zamora*, which he planned to put into book form later. He also planned to record an album to accompany the book, although that never happened.

As an actor, Micky appeared as "Mayor Micky Dolenz" on the "Pilot" episode and the "No Man's Land" episode of the crime drama TV series *Pacific Blue* which aired on March 2 and March 16 respectively. He also directed the "Moving Target" episode of the show, which aired on April 27.

He directed a music video for PJ and Duncan's recording of "Steppin' Stone" in March.

On April 4, he appeared on *Muppets Tonight*, where he interrupted a Muppet performance of "I'm a Believer" and then joined in.

He was interviewed on *George and Alana*, which aired on February 20; appeared on the February 14 and October 23 editions of Bill Maher's *Politically Incorrect*; the February 29 edition of *Showbiz Today*; the March 1 edition of *Good Day L.A.*; and the October 11 edition of *Midday*.

Meanwhile, Micky's artwork with *The Image Makers Rock 'n' Roll Art Exhibit* continued its exhibition tour around the country.

The *Dolenz, Jones, Boyce and Hart: Live in Japan* album that was previously only released on LP in Japan in 1981 was finally released on CD in the US on June 18 on Varese Sarabande.

Davy and Peter performed a one-off concert at the Flint Center in Cupertino, California, on April 12, two months before a full-blown Monkees reunion tour began, and Davy and Micky performed on April 27, at the Sports Palais, in Antwerp, Belgium.

Davy also performed solo during the year at a number of places, including The Mint in Sun Valley, Idaho, on January 26-27; February 17 at The Palace of Auburn Hills in Detroit, Michigan; April 13 at Seattle Center in Washington; May 18 at the Georgia Dome in Atlanta; and Le Bar Bat in New York on April 4.

On February 20, he appeared on *Prime Time Country*, where he sang "It's Not Too Late," "I'll Love You Forever" and "Daydream Believer." A British TV documentary called *Hollywood Kid$* featured him which aired on June 15 on TV4. He also recorded some TV and radio spots for Ames, an East Coast chain of discount department stores.

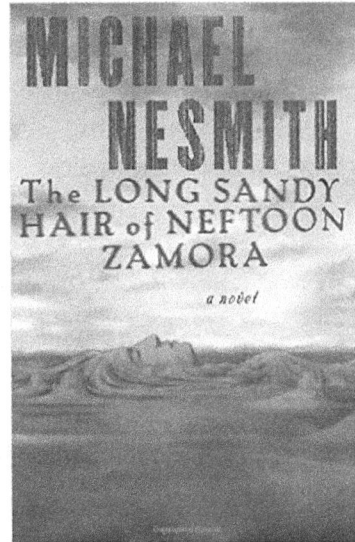

As an actor, he performed on *Crook and Chase* on February 21; the sitcom *Lush Life* on October 14; and as himself on the sitcom *The Single Guy*, which aired on November 21. He was offered the lead in yet another production of *Godspell*, but he had to turn it down due to new Monkees commitments. Japan still loved Davy, so on May 19, he headed there to judge a TV music competition. While there, he recorded a TV special called *Group Sounds Carnival* which aired in May, and then he was back in Japan on November 6 for a concert.

Davy rode his winner Digpast in the Ontario Amateur Riders' Handicap at Lingfield Park racecourse in England on February 1. He raced Digpast again on February 6 and again on May 10 and June 14.

Davy also finished up work on *Just For the Record, Volume 4*, at the end of June. It covered material he had recorded during 1996. Some of these tracks were re-recorded for *Justus*, the Monkees' 1996 reunion CD, while the rest remain in unfinished form. *Volumes 1* and *3* finally saw release in 1998.

JUST FOR THE RECORD, VOLUME 4 (DJ) (compilation)
Released: June 1996

What A Night (Davy Jones)
You And I (Davy Jones, Micky Dolenz)
I Miss You (Davy Jones)
You're In My Heart (Davy Jones, Johnny J. Blair)
I Wanna Fall In Love With Someone (Who's Been In Love Before) (Davy Jones)
Couldn't Have Been Love (Davy Jones)
Variation On Pachebel's Cannon in D (Davy Jones)
It's Not Too Late (Davy Jones)
Rough To the Touch (Robert Mitchum mix) (Davy Jones)
I'll Love You Forever (live) (Davy Jones)
It's Just A Matter Of Time (Davy Jones)
It's Now (live) (Davy Jones)
If I Knew (Bill Chadwick, Davy Jones)
The Only Thing Left (Davy Jones)

Peter performed six shows with James Lee Stanley from January 5 through February 28 and two solo shows at Genesee Theatre in Waukegan, Illinois on January 19, one at New George's on February 1, and at Tin Angel in Philadelphia, Pennsylvania on February 17. His schedule changed constantly with canceled and rebooked shows along the way.

In preparation for their 30th anniversary, all four of the Monkees finally got together and recorded and produced an album called *Justus*, with all songs written by and all instruments played by the band.

Micky, Davy and Peter then went off on a huge and very successful "30th Anniversary Tour" which ran from June 8 through January 19, 1997, with a few breaks in the schedule.

Michael did not participate in The Monkees reunion tour as he was committed to his position as host of The Council of Ideas in Nambe, New Mexico, on July 15-16, plus he was busy with his lawsuits against PBS, but while the other three were on tour, he completed work on *Justus*, which he finished on August 5. He performed live with The Monkees on a short tour in Britain, much to the frustration of his American fans.

The film "A Very Brady Sequel" was released at the end of the summer, and the soundtrack album contains Davy's version of "Girl" as well as the original recording of the Monkees' "Last Train to Clarksville."

A VERY BRADY SEQUEL SOUNDTRACK (one track by DJ; one track by The Monkees)
Released: August 20, 1996

Girl (remake) (Charles Fox, Norman Gimbel)
Last Train to Clarksville (Tommy Boyce, Bobby Hart)

In October, one day away from the 30th anniversary of the release of the album *The Monkees*, *Justus* was released. It failed to make the charts.

Finally, at the end of the year, Peter's album *Two Man Band* was released with Peter's longtime collaborator James Lee Stanley. It contains new versions of Monkees tracks, "MGB-GT" and "Pleasant Valley Sunday", plus a redo of "Milkshake" from Peter's first solo album, from which "MGB-GT" was also featured in yet another version.

TWO MAN BAND (PT with James Lee Stanley)
Released: December 17, 1996

Touch Like Magic (James Lee Stanley)
Pirates (Nick Thorkelson)
Everyday (Rick Ruskin, James Lee Stanley)
MGB-GT (Peter Tork)
Everybody Knows (James Lee Stanley)
Milkshake (Martin Briley)
Two Wrongs (Chris Fradkin, James Lee Stanley)
Miracle (Peter Tork)
All I Ever Wanted (James House, James Lee Stanley)
Pleasant Valley Sunday (Gerry Goffin, Carole King)

1997

Between January 21-28, the four got together and created an hour-long special with the clever concept that they still lived in the same place 30 years later and were still trying to make it as a band. Sadly, it's not a joke you can drag out for an hour-long show even with the songs. Michael was the executive producer and he wrote the script, directed it, and performed with the other three. *Hey, Hey, It's The Monkees* aired on February 17 on ABC. It received low ratings and didn't help the sales of *Justus* much. (At least Michael didn't make Peter play the dummy.)

The final time all four Monkees appeared together publicly was on March 20, live at Wembly Arena in London.

After the failure of *Justus* to gather attention or make the charts, The Monkees continued with their own solo projects.

In an interview with *Hello! Magazine* on March 29, Davy said, "This is the last time we do The Monkees. It's great fun but there's a piece of me that can't wait for it to all be over, so I can get on with the rest of my life."

Davy appeared as himself on the episode of the sitcom *Hitz* called "It Ain't Over Till...", airing on September 2; on a *Sabrina, the Teenage Witch* episode called "Dante's Inferno" which aired October 10; and on *The 1997 Billboard Music Awards*, airing December 8.

He also strolled out on June 23, 1997, during a U2 concert when they were performing a version of "Daydream Believer" in Santa Monica, California, and also performed on October 17-18, at the Lady Luck Casino in Bettendorf, Iowa.

Davy appeared in the music video for Freddy Monday and Sorethumb's "I Want To Be Your Davy Jones", with footage filmed on August 21 and 23.

Peter performed with James Lee Stanley from April 22 through July 12 for 28 dates to promote their *Two Man Band* album. He was also a guest speaker at the annual awards breakfast of the Santa Clara County Committee for the Employment of People with Disabilities at the Sunnyvale Hilton in Sunnyvale, California.

Peter performed three solo shows at Iron Horse Music Hall in Northampton, Massachusetts, on May 19, Tin Angel in Philadelphia on May 20, and Godfrey Daniels in

Bethlehem, Pennsylvania on May 20. He also appeared on *Prime Time Country* on April 29.

He also had a daughter, Erica Marie, born June 15, from a relationship with Tammy Sustek.

Micky appeared solo as Donny Shotz in the TV-movie remake / sequel of *The Love Bug* airing on the November 30 edition of *The Wonderful World of Disney*; the October 20 edition of *Arthel and Fred*; twice on *The Tonight Show with Jay Leno* on April 23 and October 8; the December 1 edition of the game show *Debt*; and the December 19 edition of *Politically Incorrect*.

Micky's "Talk to the Animals" from *Broadway Micky* was also included on the charity compilation *Ben & Jerry's One World, One Heart for Kids*.

LISTEN TO THE BAND (MN) (compilation)
This is a European compilation of RCA recordings.
Released: December 15, 1997

Silver Moon (Michael Nesmith)
Listen To The Band (Michael Nesmith)
Different Drum (Michael Nesmith)
Some Of Shelly's Blues (Michael Nesmith)
Mama Nantucket (Michael Nesmith)
Harmony Constant (Michael Nesmith)
Grand Ennui (Michael Nesmith)
Bonaparte's Retreat (Pee Wee King, Redd Stewart)
I've Just Begun To Care (Propinquity) (Michael Nesmith)
Land Of The Valley (Michael Nesmith)
First National Rag (Red Rhodes)
Keys To The Car (Michael Nesmith)
Two Different Roads (Michael Nesmith)
Nevada Fighter (Michael Nesmith)
I Fall To Pieces (Harlan Howard, Hank Cochran)
Rainmaker (Harry Nilsson, Bill Martin)
Calico Girlfriend (Michael Nesmith)
Nine Times Blue (Michael Nesmith)
Little Red Rider (Michael Nesmith)
Conversations (Michael Nesmith)
Joanne (Michael Nesmith)
Beyond The Blue Horizon (Richard A. Whiting, W. Franke Harling, Leo Robin)

Michael Nesmith
Listen To The Band

1998

Peter performed nine solo shows January 16 to August 7, 1998, performing at times with his brother Nick Thorkelson. Peter performed with Shoe Suede Blues over a dozen times from July 5 through December 17 and two more shoes with James Lee Stanley on August 29-30.

He acted on the TV show *7th Heaven* in the episode called "No Sex, Some Drugs and a Little Rock 'n' Roll", which aired on November 16 on WB. He performed a version of "Sunshine Of Your Love," His would later repeat the role in an episode called "100", which aired on January 29, 2001.

Elephant Parts was released to DVD for the first time on August 18. This first version has a "hilarious" narrative by Michael that has nothing to do with what's going on on-screen. He would do a proper commentary on a later reissue.

Michael also finally published his novel *The Long Sandy Hair of Neftoon Zamora* on November 16. He did an online chat for Barnes and Noble on November 19.

THE MASTERS (MN) (compilation)
Released: March 4, 1998

She Thinks I Still Care (Dickey Lee, Steve Duffy)
Born To Love You (Cindy Walker)
Texas Morning (Mike Murphy, Boomer Castleman)
Tumbling Tumbleweeds (Bob Nolan)
I Looked Away (Eric Clapton, Bobby Whitlock)
One Rose (D. Lyon, L. McIntyre)
Prairie Lullaby (Billy Hill)
Hollywood (Michael Nesmith)
Hello Lady (Michael Nesmith)
Here I Am (Michael Nesmith)
Only Bound (Michael Nesmith)
Thanx For The Ride (Michael Nesmith)
Dedicated Friend (Michael Nesmith)
Bye Bye Bye (Michael Nesmith)
Talking To The Wall (Bill Chadwick)
Lazy Lady (Michael Nesmith)
In The Afternoon (Michael Nesmith)
Release (Michael Nesmith)
Winonah (Michael Nesmith, Linda Hargrove, James Miner)
Mama Rocker (Michael Nesmith)

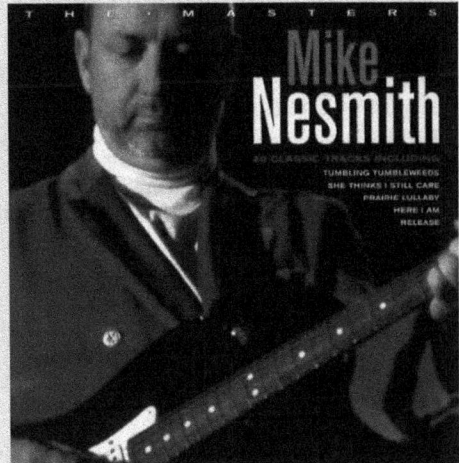

Davy's divorce from Anita was finalized in April, and he celebrated by participating in horse races throughout the month, finishing first in one.

Davy appeared on *The Tonight Show with Jay Leno* on June 9. He was to have appeared with Peter Noone on *Live With Regis and Kathie Lee* on June 23 and *The View* on June 24, but canceled because his voice was hoarse. They did appear together via satellite on *Philly After Midnight* on May 22 and at various local radio stations and newspapers.

His book *They Made a Monkee Out of Me....Again* was scheduled to appear in August, but did not appear. The title was changed to *Davy Jones: Daydream Believing*, and was finally released in 2000.

"The Monkees are behind me now," Davy said in an interview on July 17. "I've done that. I probably should have done that a little less over the last 20 years, and bit more me. I've played parts in the theatre that have nothing to do with The Monkees. I played Jesus in Godspell. When I first started doing it in 1985, when I was singing at the end, 'Oh God, I'm dying...', I was hoping somebody wouldn't shout out from the audience, 'Give us "Daydream Believer" before you go!' I'm not Davy Jones from The Monkees. I'm Davy Jones who entertains and performs and travels around."

Davy appeared in the Marshall Field's Jingle Elf Holiday Parade in Chicago, Illinois, on November 28, as the honorary Jingle Elf ("Just 'cause I'm short, I know...") as well as doing his usual share of radio and TV interviews at local stations over the year.

Then in November, he had knee surgery to compound all the other injuries he had suffered over the years.

Davy undertook his first major US solo tour from April 17 to December 5 for 46 dates. He would continue to perform a few solo shows every year until his passing in 2012. Part of that time from June 17 through September 11 (with four more scheduled dates extending into 1999), was taken up with *The Teen Idols Tour starring Davy Jones, Peter Noone and Bobby Sherman*. Sherman had not toured for 22 years prior to this. An album of songs performed on the tour was sold at concert venues. Talks occurred for the tour to continue through Australia, Japan and England, but they did not.

TEEN IDOLS 1998 TOUR (DJ with Peter Noone and Bobby Sherman)
Released: June 1998

Today's the Day - Davy Jones and Peter Noone (Phil Thornally)
Little Woman - Bobby Sherman (Danny Janssen)
Valleri - Davy Jones (Tommy Boyce, Bobby Hart)
I'm Into Something Good - Peter Noone (Gerry Goffin, Carole King)

Davy Jones   Peter Noone   Bobby Sherman

Mrs. Brown You've Got a Lovely Daughter - Peter Noone (Trevor Peacock)
Julie Do Ya Love Me - Bobby Sherman (Tom Bahler)
Girl - Davy Jones (Charles Fox, Norman Gimbel)
I'll Love You Forever - Davy Jones (Davy Jones)
Can't You Hear My Heartbeat - Peter Noone (John Carter, Ken Lewis)
Seattle - Bobby Sherman (Ernie Sheldon, Hugo Montenegro, Jack Keller)
Cried Like a Baby - Bobby Sherman (Craig Doerge, Paul H. Williams)
I'm Henry VIII - Peter Noone (Fred Murray, R.P. Weston)
It's Not Too Late - Davy Jones (Davy Jones)
Daydream Believer - Davy Jones (John Stewart)
Easy Come Easy Go - Bobby Sherman (Diane Hildebrand, Jack Keller)
There's a Kind of Hush - Peter Noone (Geoff Stephens, Les Reed)

Around this same time, Davy released more of his own collections for his fans, with lots of repeats.

DON'T GO (A COLLECTION OF MUSIC BY DAVY JONES 1979-1996) (DJ) (compilation)
Released: June 1998

Daydream Believer (John Stewart) (soundtrack released only on music video)
Don't Go (unreleased studio take 1986) (Davy Jones)
It's Just A Matter Of Time (Davy Jones)
After Your Heart (Chuck Bianchi, Pat Taylor)
You're Only Dreaming (Davy Jones, Mark Clarke, Wreckless Eric)
What A Night (Davy Jones)
Sixteen Baby, You'll Soon Be Sixteen (Alan Green) (live in Japan 1983)
Variation Of Pachebel's Canon In D / It's Not Too Late (Davy Jones)
Valleri (Tommy Boyce, Bobby Hart)
Black and White (Davy Jones, Mark Clarke, Wreckless Eric)
Manchester Boy (Davy Jones)
I'll Love You Forever (original UK 2-track demo 1979) (Davy Jones)
Girl (live in USA, same source as track 1) (Charles Fox, Norman Gimbel)

He also finally started releasing the earlier numbered volumes of his "Just For the Record" collections. The first one appears to be primarily old Broadway numbers, but we were unable to confirm all of the songwriters, who are not listed on the album.

JUST FOR THE RECORD, VOLUME 1 (DJ) (compilation)
Released: November 1998

Introduction by Mr. Harry Jones (Harry Jones)
"Oliver" Medley (Lionel Bart)
I've Got A Lot Of Living To Do (Lee Adams, Charles Strouse)
More (Riz Ortolani, Nino Oliviero, Marcello Ciorciolini, Norman Newell)
Bandit Of My Dreams (A. Schroeder, A. Orlowski)
Misty (Johnny Burke, Erroll Garner)
Kiss And Hug (?)
Be My Friend (?)
Let It Happen (?)
Donna (Ritchie Valens)
Never Will I Ever (?)
Boy Can't Win (?)
I Want To Love You (?)
Since I Fell In Love With You (?)
Take Me To Paradise (Wine, Venet)
Summertime Is Fun Time (?)
I Love You Anyway (?)
Steppin' Stone Stop (?)
Face Up To It (Atkins, Robinson)
Dream Girl (Van McCoy)
Boom Times Seven (?)
Baby It's Me (Marc Anthony)
This Bouquet (Hank Levine, Barbara Roberds)
What Are We Going To Do? (Henry Levine, Murray MacLeod, Smokey Roberds)
Closing By Mr. Harry Jones (Harry Jones)

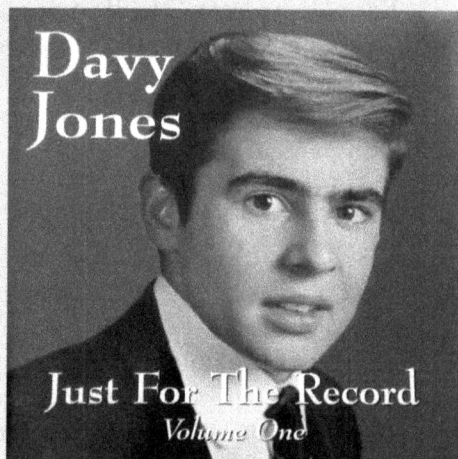

JUST FOR THE RECORD, VOLUME 3 (DJ) (compilation)
Released: November 1998

Manchester Boy (Davy Jones)
Don't Go (Davy Jones)
(Hey Ra Ra Ra) Happy Birthday Mickey Mouse (Al Kasha/Joel Hirschorn)
Hanging By A Thread (Davy Jones)
When I Look Back At Christmas (Davy Jones)
She Believes (Davy Jones, Mark Clarke, Wreckless Eric)
If I Knew (Bill Chadwick, Davy Jones)
How Can I Tell You? (Davy Jones)

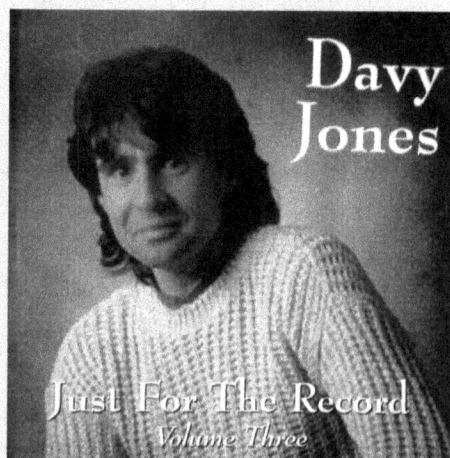

126

Dance Gypsy Dance (Davy Jones)
Star Collector (Gerry Goffin, Carole King)
I Wanna Be Free (Tommy Boyce, Bobby Hart)
Rainy Jane (Howard Greenfield, Neil Sedaka)
You're A Lady (Peter Skellern)
Cuddly Toy (Harry Nilsson)
I'll Love You Forever (Davy Jones)
Daydream Believer (John Stewart)
Sixteen Baby, You'll Soon Be Sixteen (Alan Green)
It's Now (Davy Jones)
Baby Hold Out (Davy Jones)
Bluebird (In My Garden) (Davy Jones)
Butterfly (Davy Jones)
I'm Coming Home (Davy Jones)
Cried My Heart Out (Davy Jones)
Makes Me Feel Fine (Davy Jones)
Goodbye Old Friends (Davy Jones)
Photograph (Of Someone That I Knew) (Davy Jones)
Please Believe Me (Davy Jones)
Don't Go (Davy Jones)

Then there was that song that plays in the background during a typical Scooby-Doo romp and was performed by George A. Robertson, Jr., for a chase scene in the *Scooby-Doo, Where Are You!* episode "Mystery Mask Mix-Up" in 1970. In 1972, the song was re-recorded by Davy and used in *The New Scooby-Doo Movies* episode "The Haunted Horseman of Hagglethorn Hall." This CD was released in 1998 and the episode itself wasn't released onto DVD until 2019.

SCOOBY-DOO'S SNACK TRACKS: THE ULTIMATE COLLECTION (one track by DJ) (compilation)
I Can Make You Happy (Danny Janssen, Austin Roberts)
Released: September 15, 1998

Micky spent most of January in England, visiting his daughters and pursuing directing possibilities there. "My celebrity has always helped me to get through the door, but then I had to prove myself as a technician, and I think I did," he said in an interview from *The Montreal Gazette*, discussing his directing career. "My name is simply in the hopper along with a lot of other TV directors. There's an A list and a B list. I don't know where I am at the moment, but it's great just being in the game."

Micky voiced Ralph and Scribble on *The Secret Files of the Spy Dogs*, an animated series airing on Saturday mornings during the 1998-1999 season. He recorded his lines at various times from January to June. He also appeared on the January 7-9 episodes of the game show *Pictionary*, and appeared on the December 15 edition of *Politically Incorrect*.

Micky sang a promo for *Seinfeld* over the closing credits of *Friends* to the tune of "Last Train to Clarksville" on May 14. He was a celebrity guest on Joy Philbin's *Haven*, airing on November 14-15 in syndication.

Micky served on the nominating committee for the Directors Guild Awards in the category of children's programming and attended the Just for Laughs comedy festival in Montreal, Canada from July 15-26. He also performed on some cruises for The Royal Caribbean Cruise Line during the summer.

Micky was interviewed for a book called *How to Be a Working Comic: An Insider's Guide to a Career in Stand-up Comedy* by Dave Schwensen. He also issued a book called Micky's Secret Snaps in December 1998.

Perhaps inspired by Davy, Micky released *a* self-pressed disc of demos that he had recorded for the aborted rock 'n' roll album he wanted a major label to finance. Some of these songs had ended up recorded by The Monkees on the *Justus* album.

DEMOISELLE (MD)
Released: October 1998

It's the Season (Micky Dolenz)
Never Enough (Micky Dolenz)
Dying of a Broken Heart (Micky Dolenz)
Regional Girl (Micky Dolenz)
Not That Bad (Micky Dolenz)
Lonely Weekends (Micky Dolenz)
Piston Power (Micky Dolenz)
Beverly Hills (Micky Dolenz)
Since I Fell For You (Live) (Micky Dolenz)

1999

Peter performed more than two dozen shows through 1999, as a solo act, with Shoe Suede Blues, and with James Lee Stanley. He also did an autograph signing on July 17 at the Newark Airport Sheraton Hotel in New Jersey for the International Collectable Toy Megashow.

Peter appeared as the Band Leader on *The King of Queens* episode entitled "Best Man" which aired on January 11 on CBS, but was replaced for some reason by actor Michael McKean in the role of Jedediah Lawrence on *Boy Meets World*, a role Peter portrayed twice before on the show.

Michael did a short promo tour for his *Neftoon Zamora* novel, appearing on the January 25 editions of the *KTLA Morning News* and *The Today Show* on NBC as well as other local media outlets over the year. He appeared live at the New York City Barnes & Nobles January 29 to sign books for an appreciative crowd.

During a radio interview, he was asked about why he doesn't participate in all of The Monkees reunions. "The other three guys have been going out on these nostalgia tours for a long time," he said. "They'd been asking me to go, and I had never really been interested in doing one of the nostalgia trips.

"You know, The Monkees is not a real band. It's a television show about a band, and so the band is no more real than the crew of the Starship Enterprise is, so when we work together as a band, it's kind of an odd thing watching a television show come to life, and that had always intrigued me, creatively. I asked them if they would be interested in taking a swing at that, and they all said, yeah, they would. We tried and *Justus* came out and it was sort of too hard. Then we went on tour, and that was harder than any of us thought. To sustain that level of creative energy, there has to be an organic base somewhere.

"For the four of us, when we had the television show, we were thrown together in a way that was like a crucible or a high-pressure environment. It made things happen that wouldn't ordinarily. Once the show was gone, for us to come together naturally didn't really fit, so it was just an effort at that time that in my estimation I didn't think it worked."

In February, after a five week trial, Michael's lawsuit against PBS ended. Michael had purchased the rights to distribute videos of PBS shows in 1990, at a time when no one thought anyone would be interested in buying a video of a show that had already aired. Michael had once again correctly predicted what the public wanted, and the videos had

been tremendously successful to the point where PBS executives realized they had made a mistake. They wanted the rights back and started acting in bad faith, hoping Pacific Arts would go bankrupt so they could obtain the rights again. Pacific Arts crashed and PBS sued to get the rights back. Michael countersued, blaming PBS for its financial problems, and a jury agreed. PBS was ordered to pay Michael $47 million for damages and income he should have received.

"One thing that became clear in the early days of the trial," Michael said in *Infinite Tuesday*. "They were out for blood. They wanted to personally ruin me and told me so. They said they were going to take away everything they could from me: the copyrights of my songs, every royalty I had, every piece of property I owned and be divided among their member stations and producers. They were going to see to it that I was left with nothing."

Despite this, Michael was forced to close Pacific Arts as a video distribution business, which greatly saddened him.

The lawsuit also forced Michael to give up plans to make a movie version of Douglas Adams' *The Hitchhiker's Guide to the Galaxy*. (A feature film version was eventually made by other hands in 2005.)

Another greatest hits compilation was then released.

SIXTEEN ORIGINAL CLASSICS (MN) (compilation)
Released: May 3, 1999

Calico Girlfriend (Michael Nesmith)
Nine Times Blue (Michael Nesmith)
Little Red Rider (Michael Nesmith)
The Crippled Lion (Michael Nesmith)
Joanne (Michael Nesmith)
First National Rag (Red Rhodes)
Mama Nantucket (Michael Nesmith)
The Keys to the Car (Michael Nesmith)
Hollywood (Michael Nesmith)
One Rose (D. Lyon, L. McIntyre)
Beyond the Blue Horizon (Richard A. Whiting, W. Franke Harling, Leo Robin)
Silver Moon (Michael Nesmith)
Lady of the Valley (Michael Nesmith)
Here I Am (Michael Nesmith)
Nevada Fighter (Michael Nesmith)
Tumbling Tumbleweeds (Bob Nolan)

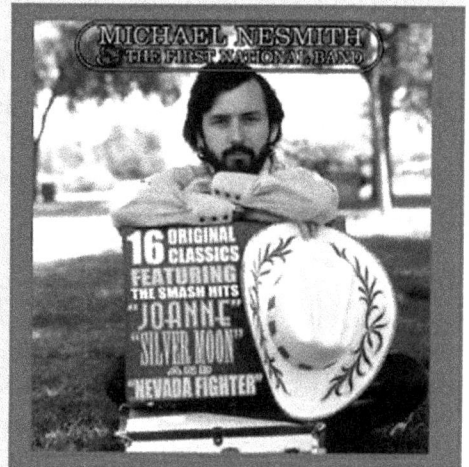

The Britt Music & Arts Festival is a non-profit performing arts festival located in Jacksonville, Oregon each year. Michael performed there in 1992, and it was finally released in July.

LIVE AT THE BRITT FESTIVAL (MN) Concert recorded on June 12, 1992.
Released: July 1999

Two Different Roads (Michael Nesmith)
Papa Gene's Blues (Michael Nesmith)
Propinquity (I've Just Begun to Care)
(Michael Nesmith)
Some of Shelly's Blues (Michael Nesmith)
Joanne (Michael Nesmith)
Tomorrow and Me (Michael Nesmith)
The Upside of Goodbye (Michael Nesmith)
Harmony Constant (Michael Nesmith)
Silver Moon (Michael Nesmith)
5 Second Concerts (Hobbs, Michael Nesmith)
Yellow Butterfly (Michael Nesmith)
Moon over the Rio Grande (Michael Nesmith)
Juliana (Michael Nesmith)
Laugh Kills Lonesome (Michael Nesmith)
I Am Not That (Michael Nesmith)
Rising in Love (Michael Nesmith)
Rio (Michael Nesmith)
Different Drum (Michael Nesmith)
I Am Not That (Reprise) (Michael Nesmith)

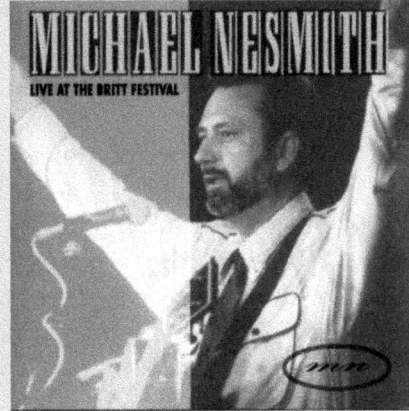

Micky appeared in the direct-to-video movie *Invisible Mom II*, released on August 31, and directed the "Bee True" episode of *Boy Meets World* airing on April 9. He then self-released a live CD that he would sell at his performances, making this a very rare collector's item.

MICKY DOLENZ LIVE (MD)
Released: 1999

Intro/Last Train to Clarksville (Tommy
Boyce, Bobby Hart)
(I'm Not Your) Steppin' Stone (Tommy
Boyce, Bobby Hart)
That Was Then, This is Now (Vance
Brescia)
Randy Scouse Git (Micky Dolenz)
The Girl I Knew Somewhere (Michael
Nesmith)
Bye Bye Blackbird (Ray Henderson, Mort
Dixon)

Different Drum (Michael Nesmith)
A Little Bit Me, A Little Bit You (Neil Diamond)
Too Much Monkey Business (Chuck Berry)
Runaway (Del Shannon, Max Crook)
For Pete's Sake (Joseph Richardson, Peter Tork)
Route 66 (Bobby Troupe)
Purple Haze (Jimi Hendrix)
Dialogue
Since I Fell For You (Buddy Johnson)
Goin' Down (Micky Dolenz, Davy Jones, Peter Tork, Michael Nesmith, Diane Hildebrand)
Circle Sky (Michael Nesmith)
Daydream Believer (John Stewart)
Pleasant Valley Sunday (Gerry Goffin, Carole King)
I'm a Believer (Neil Diamond)

The Teen Idols Tour starring Davy Jones, Peter Noone and Bobby Sherman wrapped up with six shows in 1999 from March 28 through September 4, 1999. The tour eventually broke up due to Sherman's commitments to the LA Police Academy, and then Davy was replaced by Micky and his sister, Coco, in May to finish up the tour.

Davy did another tour performing January 14 through April 10 for six dates touring Japan and the US and on Royal Caribbean Cruise Line. Each Japan show was recorded and, in 2000, the best takes were edited for a CD that was abandoned for unknown reasons. It was finally released in 2011.

Davy also did at least 15 solo dates around the country, as well a number of radio interviews. He served as narrator for the syndicated radio special, *Rock 'n' Roll at the Movies*, airing in May, and appeared on the June 9 edition of *E! True Hollywood Story* about *The Brady Bunch*, and the *Donny and Marie* talk show from December 17.

JUST FOR THE RECORD (DJ) (compilation) (self-pressed four-disc set)
Released: 1999 See individual volumes for track listing.

2000

Michael had been with Victoria Kennedy since 1988 and they finally married in 2000. He devoted most of his time in 2000 developing *Fried Pies*, including writing the screenplay and the music, and working on a second novel called *The America Gene*. Both eventually got placed on hold.

He did finally release the soundtrack to the *Timerider* movie. Don't expect an album of quiet little country-styled instrumentals with a few instruments. This is a full-fledged soundrack album with orchestra, and it's quite exciting (as fits the theme of the film).

TIMERIDER: THE ADVENTURE OF LYLE SWANN (MN) (soundtrack to 1982 movie)
Released: August 7, 2000

The Baha 1000 (Michael Nesmith)
Lost in the Weeds (Michael Nesmith)
Somewhere Around 1875 (Michael Nesmith)
Scared to Death (Michael Nesmith)
Silks and Sixguns (Michael Nesmith)
Dead Man's Duds (Michael Nesmith)
Two Swanns at the Pond (Michael Nesmith)
I Want That Machine (Michael Nesmith)
Escape to San Marcos (Michael Nesmith)
Claire's Cabin (Michael Nesmith)
No Jurisdiction (Michael Nesmith)
Murder at Swallow's Camp (Michael Nesmith)
Claire's Rescue (Michael Nesmith)
Up the Hill to Nowhere (Michael Nesmith)
Out of Ammo (Michael Nesmith)
Reprise (Michael Nesmith)

Peter performed over 35 shows during the year with Shoe Suede Blues, appearing in various local news stations across the country to promote his appearances.

He also had an uncredited cameo in *Daydream Believers: The Monkees' Story* which aired on June 28 on VH-1.

SHOE SUEDE BLUES LIVE! (PT with Shoe Suede Blues) Recorded at Harvelle's in Santa Monica, California
Released: February 2000

Hitch Hike (Clarence O. Paul, Marvin Gaye, William Stevenson)
She Belongs to Me (Bob Dylan)

Crosscut Saw (Tommy McClennan)
Stagolee (Lloyd Price, Harold Logan)
Tough Enough (?)
Shake, Rattle and Roll (Jesse Stone) /
Flip, Flop and Fly (Charles E. Calhoun, Lou
Willie Turner)
Black Drawers (?)
Young Blood (Alexandra Leah Tamposi,
Andrew Wotman, Ashton Fletcher Irwin,
Calum Hood, Louis Russell Bell, Luke
Hemmings)
Madison Blues (Elmore James) / Blue
Suede Shoes (Carl Perkins)
Mojo (?)

Shoe Suede Blues

LIVE

Davy performed thirteen solo shows from January 16 to November 30.

He appeared on various talk shows over the year, including *The Roseanne Show,* *FOX and Friends, Entertainment Tonight, Extra!, Access Hollywood* and the *VH-1 Behind the Music Anniversary Special.* Much of this was to promote his new book *Davy Jones: Daydream Believin'* which was finally released in February. His book signing tour took him around the country.

Davy remastered and reissued *Davy Jones Sings The Monkees and More* (same as *Live in Japan* from 1981) and self-released a "singles collection."

DAVY JONES SINGLES COLLECTION (DJ)

After Your Heart (Chuck Bianchi, Pat Taylor)
Daydream Believer (John Stewart) (1994 Video Version)
What a Night (Davy Jones)
Girl (Charles Fox, Norman Gimbel)
Look Inside Yourself (Davy Jones, Mark Clarke, Wreckless Eric)
Rainy Jane (Howard Greenfield, Neil Sedaka)
Hanging By A Thread (Davy Jones)
Dance Gypsy Dance (Davy Jones)
Baby Hold Out (Andy Sears, Davy Jones)
I'll Love You Forever (Davy Jones)
She Believes (Davy Jones, Mark Clarke, Wreckless Eric)
It's Not Too Late (Davy Jones)
Don't Go (Davy Jones)
Manchester Boy (Davy Jones)
It's Now (Davy Jones)
Sixteen Baby, You'll Soon Be Sixteen (live) (Alan Green)
Valleri (Tommy Boyce, Bobby Hart)

Who Was It? (Gilbert O'Sullivan)
(Hey Ra Ra Ra) Happy Birthday Mickey Mouse (Al Kasha, Joel Hirschorn)
You Don't Have to Be a Country Boy to Sing a Country Song (Tommy Boyce, Davy Jones)
Rubberene (Alan O'Day)
You're a Lady (Peter Skellern)

Micky hit the road in 2000 with a new version of The Teen Idols Tour, again with Peter Noone and Bobby Sherman. Dates performed were May 27-28, August 9 and October 7. Micky also performed over 20 solo concerts from April 8 through December 26. The October 19-20 concerts were performed before a full symphony orchestra in Fort Worth.

Micky was seen at the Sundance Film Festival in Salt Lake City in January, the Aspen Comedy Fest in Colorado and the 14th Annual Comedy Awards in Los Angeles on February 6, and the Academy Awards party thrown by BAFTA/LA on March 25, 2000, the night before the ceremony.

He was a guest on *The Roseanne Show* on April 14 and spent the summer visiting his daughters in England.

2001

Michael moved his Videoranch company from New Mexico to Monterey, California in January 2001.

Michael's 1992 live appearance at The Britt was finally released to video as *Nesmith Live* on March 13. *Live at the Palais* made its first CD appearance in January. Custom made Michael CDs called *Blossom Special* made their debut on Videoranch this year. This is a personal choice CD, so the content could be 12 tracks of anything in Michael's catalog of your choosing.

> **Author comment from Mark:** Here's my personal Blossom Special collection.

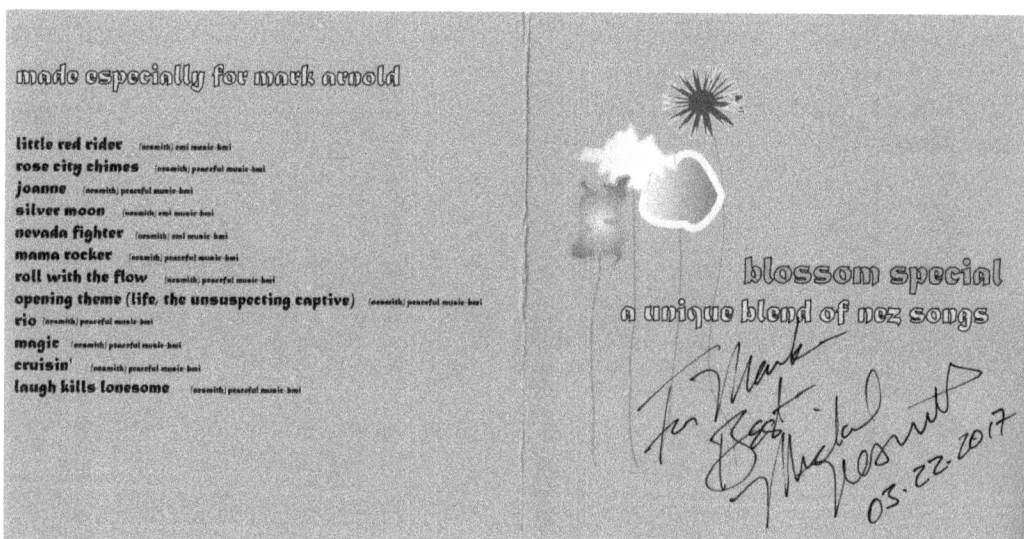

made especially for mark arnold

little red rider (nesmith/ rmi music box)
rose city chimes (nesmith/ peaceful music box)
joanne (nesmith/ peaceful music box)
silver moon (nesmith/ rmi music box)
nevada fighter (nesmith/ rmi music box)
mama rocker (nesmith/ peaceful music box)
roll with the flow (nesmith/ peaceful music box)
opening theme (life, the unsuspecting captive) (nesmith/ peaceful music box)
rio (nesmith/ peaceful music box)
magic (nesmith/ peaceful music box)
cruisin' (nesmith/ peaceful music box)
laugh kills lonesome (nesmith/ peaceful music box)

blossom special
a unique blend of nez songs

BLOSSOM SPECIAL (MN) (compilation)
Released: 2001

Despite Davy's insistence that his Monkees days were behind him, he cancelled part of a tour in 2001 to once again reunite with Micky and Peter. But first, he released another solo album with a title that is a play on The Monkees' album *Justus*.

JUST ME (DJ) Recorded from 1990-2001. *Released:* April 27, 2001

Hold Me Tight (Davy Jones, Johnny J. Blair)
When You Tell Me That You Love Me (Davy Jones, Johnny J. Blair)
Vivaldi Intro - I Wanna Be Me (Davy Jones, Johnny J. Blair)
My Love (She Means Everything) (Davy Jones)

Hurry Up Slow Down (Davy Jones, Johnny J. Blair)
Variations on Pachebel's Canon/It's Not Too Late (Davy Jones)
I'm Still in Love With You (Davy Jones)
If Only For One Moment in Time (Davy Jones)
What A Night (Davy Jones)
So Goes Love (Davy Jones)
I Ain't Gonna Love You No More (Davy Jones, Johnny J. Blair)
I'm Still in Love With You (Reprise) (Davy Jones) / Intro / Hold Me Tight (Davy Jones, Johnny J. Blair)

Hold Me Tight (Davy Jones, Johnny J. Blair) (DJ) (cassingle)
When You Tell Me That You Love Me (Davy Jones, Johnny J. Blair) (DJ) (cassingle)
It's Not Too Late (Davy Jones) (DJ) (cassingle)

Peter appeared in the short film *Mixed Signals* as a band manager. He promoted this appearance on *Total Access 24/7* which aired on October 14.

Peter performed ten shows with James Lee Stanley from January 12 through February 10, and 23 shows from April 7 through November 28 with Shoe Suede Blues. He was to perform SSB shows in January, February and March 2001, but those were canceled in favor of Monkees shows.

ONCE AGAIN (PT with James Lee Stanley)
Released: March 6, 2001

Easy Rider (Peter Tork)
Bulldozer (James Lee Stanley)
Another Side to This Life (Fred Neil)
Dirty Job (Tom Campbell, James Lee Stanley)
Little Girl (Peter Tork)
One Trick Pony (Paul Simon)
Some Say (James Lee Stanley)
Easy Rockin' (James Lee Stanley)
Hi Babe (Peter Tork)
Stolen Season (James Lee Stanley)
Daydream Believer (John Stewart)

Micky performed a number of solo shows as well as once more participating in the the Teen Idols Tour. However, the possibility and planning of a new Monkees tour took precedence.

While that was being planned, he appeared on the *100 Greatest Number One Singles* show airing on January 6 and the *I Love 1980's* documentary airing January 13. He recorded an appearance for the *Drew Carey Show* that aired in December, and directed the TV movie *Malpractice* that aired May 25. He sang the National Anthem at the New York Mets baseball game at Shea Stadium on July 17 and announced his engagement to Donna Quintner in October.

The Monkees sans Michael undertook another tour which featured not only the hits but some other more obscure songs as well. They even did an "unplugged" section where Micky and Peter played acoustic guitars. However, Peter left before the tour was over, while Micky and Davy continued on into 2002. Years later, Peter revealed that excessive drinking caused him to drop out.

2002

Michael's *Tapeheads* and *Square Dance* were released to DVD for the first time in 2002. Michael was still hard at work on the album that was to become *Rays*, would not see the light of day until 2006.

Micky was scheduled to perform solo on the Costa Victoria Cruise Ship from January 13-20, but it was canceled in favor of The Monkees shows with Davy which lasted until September. It would be the last time any of The Monkees worked together until 2011.

Micky appeared as The Vicar on the soap opera *As the World Turns*, which aired May 31 and June 3. He married his third wife, Donna Quinter, in the summer.

Davy did four solo shows in April and sang at the 2002 Flower Power Festival at the America Garden Theatre in Orlando, Florida in November. He took some time to do bookstore signings along the way, in Nashville, Lexington, and Chicago.

He also appeared on the March 13 edition of *Sally Jessy Raphael*; the *48 Hours* episode called "Idolmakers" which aired May 1; "The NBC All-Stars" edition of *The Weakest Link* on May 26; and on *The 1st 13th Annual Fancy Anvil Awards Show Program Special: Live in Stereo* on Cartoon Network, airing on March 23. He performed a voiceover for *Hey Arnold!* for the episode entitled "Gerald's Game" / "Fishing Trip" for Nickelodeon, which aired on April 27, and appeared in an infomercial for Time/Life Records.

Peter performed 27 shows with Shoe Suede Blues from January 3 through September 8, and two solo shows on March 14 and July 4. He appeared as himself in the TV movie *Bubblegum Babylon* which aired in November.

In sadder news, Peter's mother, Virginia Hope Straus Thorkelson, died at the age of 82 on April 25.

2003

Davy performed six solo shows from April 25 to July 19. He also appeared on the *TV Land Awards: A Celebration of Classic TV* on March 12, and hosted the 2003-2004 documentary series called *Meet the Royals* for A&E, debuting September 7.

Leaving It Up To You (Davy Jones, Johnny J. Blair) (DJ) (cassingle)

Micky appeared in the documentary *Easy Riders, Raging Bulls: How the Sex, Drugs and Rock 'N' Roll Generation Saved Hollywood*, released on March 9, and in the TV special *Rock Gardens* airing October 12.

Peter performed a show at The Cutting Room in New York on July 15. He also appeared as an evil acting teacher in the short film *Stella's Search for Sanity*, released on May 5.

In June, he released another Shoe Suede Blues collection featuring assorted rhythm and blues originals and classics.

SAVED BY THE BLUES (PT with Shoe Suede Blues)
Released: June 3, 2003

Saved by the Blues (Levine)
Cab Driver (Heinz Milkus, Tadg Galleran)
Help Me (Ralph Bass, Sonny Boy Williamson, Willie Dixon)
Hound Dog (Jerry Leiber, Mike Stoller)
Route 66 (Bobby Troup)
Kiss and Tell (James Armstrong, Tadg Galleran)
Dress Sexy for Me (Peter Tork, Tadg Galleran)
Treat Her Right (Gene Kurtz, Roy Head)
Big Boss Man (Al Smith, Luther Dixon)
Slender, Tender and Tall (Hughie Prince, Mike Jackson)
Wine-Texas BBQ (Williams)
Come On in My Kitchen (Robert Johnson)

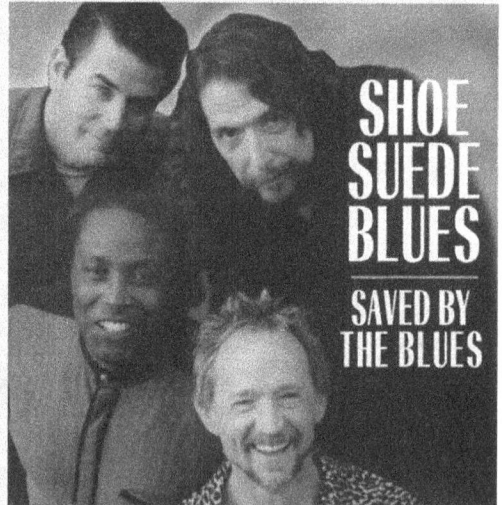

And yet another Nesmith compilation was released.

THE BEST OF MICHAEL NESMITH (MN) (compilation)
Released: July 12, 2003

Silver Moon (Michael Nesmith)
Listen to the Band (Michael Nesmith)
Little Red Rider (Michael Nesmith)
Smoke, Smoke, Smoke That Cigarette
(Merle Travis, Tex Williams)
The Upside of Goodbye (Michael
Nesmith)
Two Different Roads (Michael
Nesmith)
Harmony Constant (Michael Nesmith)
Calico Girlfriend (Michael Nesmith)
Tomorrow and Me (Michael Nesmith)
Some of Shelly's Blues (Michael
Nesmith)
The Crippled Lion (Michael Nesmith)
I Fall to Pieces (Harlan Howard, Hank
Cochran)
Tengo Amore (Michael Nesmith)
Rainmaker (Harry Nilsson, Bill Martin)
Grand Ennui (Michael Nesmith)
Mama Nantucket (Michael Nesmith)
She Thinks I Still Care (Dickey Lee, Steve Duffy)
Joanne (Michael Nesmith)

THE BEST OF **Michael Nesmith**

Michael's production of Lionel Richie's music video for "All Night Long" from 1983 appeared on *The Lionel Richie Collection*, released on November 18.

Peter and Shoe Suede Blues also contributed a few songs to a Christmas collection album. Even though "Angels We Have Heard on High" is the same song as Peter performed on *The Monkees Christmas Party* in 2019, here it is presented as a banjo instrumental.

A BEACHWOOD CHRISTMAS (PT with Tom Paxton, Pamala Stanley, James Lee Stanley) Three tracks only by Peter.
Released: 2003

PT's Noel (Masters in This Hall) (Peter Tork)
I Remember Christmas (Peter Tork)
Angels We Have Heard On High (traditional)

2004

As "the boys" grew older, their appearances and performances became more rare (with a few exceptions).

Peter performed a show at Jammin' Java in Vienna, Virginia on January 29, but otherwise not much was heard from him in 2004.

Davy performed five solo shows from April 16 to June 27. He also appeared in an episode of the TV Land series *Living in TV Land* called "Davy Jones" and appeared as himself in the comedy film *The J-K Conspiracy* which was released on November 18. You could also see him in *VH1: A Very Classic Thanksgiving*, airing on November 25, and in the UK documentary *The Kids from Coronation Street* on November 30.

Davy kept on releasing his own CDs for his fans, who apparently didn't complain much that many of these had already been released before. On *Just Me 2*, for instance, many of the songs are just remixes from *Just Me*.

JUST ME 2 (DJ) Recorded from 1990-2004.
Released: 2004

Hold Me Tight (Spoken Word Version) (Davy Jones, Johnny J. Blair)
When You Tell Me That You Love Me (Remix) (Davy Jones, Johnny J. Blair)
Run To Me (Davy Jones, Johnny J. Blair)
It's Just a Matter of Time (Davy Jones)
Hurry Up Slow Down (Remix) (Davy Jones, Johnny J. Blair)
I Ain't Gonna Love You No More (Remix) (Davy Jones, Johnny J. Blair)
You're in My Heart (Remix) (Davy Jones, Johnny J. Blair)
If Only For One Moment in Time (Remix) (Davy Jones)
Leaving It Up To You (Davy Jones, Johnny J. Blair)
It's Not Too Late (Remix) (Davy Jones)
Vivaldi Intro - I Wanna Be Me (Remix) (Davy Jones, Johnny J. Blair)
When All Else Fails (Davy Jones, Johnny J. Blair)
Hold Me Tight (Remix) (Davy Jones, Johnny J. Blair)

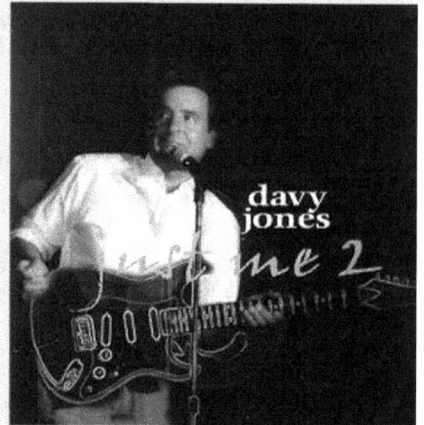

And Davy kept self-releasing more and more remixes and new compilations.

DAYDREAM BELIEVIN' (TIME TESTED HITS AND RARITIES) (DJ)
(compilation)
   Released: September 1, 2004

   Introduction by Mr. Harry Jones (Harry Jones) (1966)
   Daydream Believer (Video Soundtrack)
(John Stewart) (1994)
   Hold Me Tight (Davy Jones, Johnny J.
Blair) (2001)
   When You Tell Me That You Love Me
(Davy Jones, Johnny J. Blair) (2001)
   Valleri (*Incredible!* Version) (Tommy Boyce,
Bobby Hart) (1986)
   It's Not Too Late (Original Version) (Davy
Jones) (1994)
   Dance Gypsy Dance (Japanese Single)
(Davy Jones) (1982)
   You're in My Heart (Davy Jones, Johnny J.
Blair) (1994)
   After Your Heart (Chuck Bianchi, Pat Taylor)
(1986)
   Leaving It Up To You (Davy Jones, Johnny J. Blair) (2003)
   Don't Go (Single Mix) (Davy Jones) (1986)
   Girl (live) (Charles Fox, Norman Gimbel) (1992)
   I'll Love You Forever (*Incredible!* Version) (Davy Jones) (1986)
   Daydream Believer (Millennial Dance Mix) (John Stewart) (2001)

   Micky re-released his *I'm a Believer* book on May 4 with a new cover image but very little new material. The publisher changed from Hyperion to Cooper Square Press.
   Micky performed a solo show at Westbury Music Fair at Westbury, New York, on October 29, and appeared in the documentary *TV's Greatest Cars*, which aired on December 23. He continued to be seen around Hollywood, however, at various fundraisers and events.

   Michael, meanwhile, released an audio book of his novel *The Long Hair of Neftoon Zamora* and also released sheet music of his most popular tunes in a songbook entitled *The Best of Michael Nesmith.*

2005

Micky appeared on the "Trump-ed to Triumph: Danny K" episode of *Queer Eye for the Straight Guy*, which aired on August 16.

Micky also began his DJ stint on New York's WCBS 101.1 FM on January 10. His show lasted exactly 100 episodes before WCBS changed its format and fired all of the DJs. His final show aired June 3.

Peter performed a show with Shoe Suede Blues at The Mojo Room in New York on November 25.

Davy performed eleven solo shows from March 15 to October 16. He also appeared on the talk show *The Tony Danza Show* on November 18.

The *Dolenz, Jones, Boyce and Hart* album was finally released in the UK only on Cherry Red Records on September 26.

Michael finally released his album *Rays*. It was originally released in a limited edition but the unlimited edition came out in April of 2006.

A very hard to classify album musically, Michael called it "New Century Modern." Lots of synthesizers replace the standard steel guitar on the song "Rays," for instance, which later makes an appearance on his *Infinite Tuesday* collection.

The cover, drawn by Drew Friedman, shows Michael driving through his life with the Monkees, with the First National Band, as the host of "Elephant Parts" and as a rich writer in a Rolls Royce. In the middle, he's relaxing comfortably, saying "Suddenly, I'm not as hungry as I'd thought." Make of it what you will.

RAYS (MN)
Released: November 2005

Zip Ribbon (Michael Nesmith)
Dynaflow (Michael Nesmith)
Friedrider (Michael Nesmith)
Carhop (Michael Nesmith)
Boomcar (Michael Nesmith)
Best of It (Michael Nesmith)
Ed's October Café (Michael Nesmith)
Rays (Michael Nesmith)
Bells (Michael Nesmith)
Land o Pies (Michael Nesmith)
There It Is (Michael Nesmith)
Follows the Heart (Michael Nesmith)

2006

Davy performed five solo shows from May 12 to July 4, 2006.

Micky appeared in the episode "Pop and Easy Listening" in the UK documentary TV series *The Story of Light Entertainment*, which aired August 19, and then grew a beard and toured the country in a production of the play "Pippin," playing King Charlemagne. The tour ran into the early months of 2007.

Peter performed two shows at The Bamboo Room in Lake Worth, Florida on April 20, and Poor David's Pub in Dallas, Texas on July 12. He also appeared as Mr. Grady in the film *Cathedral Pines*, released in June.

The songs that appeared on this album are lively and sung with great harmonies and enhanced by the amusing repartee between Peter and James Lee Stanley. He even does his version of "Pleasant Valley Sunday" as well as a cover of Paul Simon's "One Trick Pony."

LIVE/BACKSTAGE AT THE COFFEE GALLERY (PT with James Lee Stanley)
Released: November 7, 2006

Easy Rider (Peter Tork)
Intro - James Lee Stanley
All I Ever Wanted (James Lee Stanley)
Peter and James Banter
One Trick Pony (Paul Simon)
James Whines and Complains
Daddy's Eyes (James Lee Stanley)
James Babbles and Then Introduces Peter
Peter Graciously Enters
Get What You Pay For (Peter Tork)
Get Out the Old Banjo - Peter Tork
Swing Banjo (Pete Seeger)
Folk Music - Peter Tork
Cuckoo (traditional)
Peter Hurts Himself for Crowd

145

Cripple Creek (traditional)
Peter and James - Cookie Monster Story
Racing the Moon (James Lee Stanley)
There (Mixmaster Michael Smith)
Come Home in My Kitchen (Robert Johnson)
Peter and James Banter 2 - The Crucifix
Hi Babe (Peter Tork)
Irony - James
Touch Like Magic (James Lee Stanley)
Peter and James Banter 3
Pleasant Valley Sunday (Gerry Goffin, Carole King)

2007

Peter performed six solo shows between August 1 and October 5. He also appeared in an unbilled cameo in the film *The Junior Defenders*, released on October 23, and appeared as himself in the documentary *The Holy Modal Rounders: Bound to Lose*, released on December 7.

Another Shoe Suede Blues album was released in February. With the exception of one new Tork-written song, they're all covers, including a laid back "Last Train to Clarksville" and a sitar-laden "For Pete's Sake." This is probably Peter's best solo album.

CAMBRIA HOTEL (PT with Shoe Suede Blues)
Released: February 27, 2007

I Know Love (Danny McBride)
One More Heartache (Marv Tarplin, Bobby Rogers, Ronnie White, Smokey Robinson, Pete Moore)
Bound to Lose (Richey Kevin Craig)
Last Train to Clarksville (Tommy Boyce, Bobby Hart)
The Mighty Are Falling (Alicia Morgan, Richard Mikuls)
Ain't Your Fault (Peter Tork)
Annie Had a Baby (Hank Ballard)
God Given Grant (Nick Thorkelson, Peter Tork)
For Pete's Sake (Joseph Richardson, Peter Tork)
Good Looker (Riley Cummings)
She Belongs to Me (Bob Dylan)
Sea Cruise (Frankie Ford, Huey "Piano" Smith)

PETER TORK AND SHOE SUEDE BLUES
CAMBRIA HOTEL

Davy performed 17 solo shows from February 17 to December 10. He also appeared as a singer in a movie called *Sexina*, released on November 6.

Author and artist Sandra Boynton ventured into book and song compilations featuring many guest stars. For this book, Davy gives a very lively performance.

BLUE MOO (one track by DJ) (compilation)
Released: November 8, 2007
Your Personal Penguin (Davy Jones, Sandra Boynton)

Micky and Davy appeared separately in the documentary series *TV Land Confidential* on the episode entitled "Finales", which aired July 18. They also appear separately on a later episode called "Music" which aired August 8.

Micky appeared in the UK TV documentary *The Truth About Boy Bands*, which aired on August 18, and as Derek Allen, the owner of a gun shop, in the Rob Zombie remake of *Halloween*, released on August 31.

Michael formed another company, Videoranch, LLC. "The virtual world moved me into another dimension and opened new possibilities," he said in *Infinite Tuesday*. "I set up an office / studio / warehouse in a small commercial district in Santa Fe, installed equipment and software, and went about building Videoranch, a website and virtual world." It was fairly successful, so he applied for a patent for his idea and told his wife Victoria about it, but she shied away and said he should not list her as one of the patent holders, which worried Michael. In March, he discovered that she had left him for a man she met—in Videoranch. The good news was that the patent was eventually granted. Michael had once more correctly predicted what the future of technology would hold.

2008

Micky performed three solo shows on February 1, July 10 and September 12. He also returned to WCBS 101.1 to do is 101st and final stint as a DJ on February 3 on a program entitled *New York Radio Greats*.

Davy performed fifteen solo shows from February 16 to December 6. He also appeared on the UK documentary series *Sex, Drugs and Rock 'n' Roll: The 60s Revealed*, airing on December 1. He then released another collection with a cover that has his head photoshopped over Jim Morrison's body for some reason. Incredible!

INCREDIBLE REVISITED (DJ) (Same as *Incredible!* (1988) with revised track listing.)
Released: 2008

Look Inside Yourself (Davy Jones, Mark Clarke, Wreckless Eric)
Make the Woman Love Me (Davy Jones, Mark Clarke, Wreckless Eric)
You're Only Dreaming (Davy Jones, Mark Clarke, Wreckless Eric)
Black and White (Davy Jones, Mark Clarke, Wreckless Eric)
Valleri (Tommy Boyce, Bobby Hart)
After Your Heart (Chuck Bianchi, Pat Taylor)
Incredible (Davy Jones, Mark Clarke, Wreckless Eric)
I'll Love You Forever (Davy Jones)
Hippy Hippy Shake (Chan Romero)
She Believes (Davy Jones, Mark Clarke, Wreckless Eric)
Secret Love (Davy Jones, John Stewart, Mark Clarke, Wreckless Eric)
The Greatest Story Ever Told (Alan Green, Davy Jones, Mark Clarke, Wreckless Eric)

Davy Jones

incredible revisited

Peter performed five solo shows between May 17 to December 13. He also appeared as himself on *The Bob Show* in an episode entitled "Super Mega Fest 2008," which aired on November 28.

Peter and Davy appeared together at the Egyptian Theatre in Hollywood, California, on November 12, to discuss the 40th anniversary of *Head*. The film was shown and both Monkees appeared in an engaging and funny interview. Michael and Micky would repeat this at the same venue almost exactly ten years later.

Michael had a very bad year. With a woman he loved finally leaving him instead of vice-versa, he felt alone and listless. His health deteriorated. His sight declined and he found it difficult to walk.

The sight was cured by an operation to remove cataracts, but the loss of flexibility took months to recover from. Many doctors tried to determine the cause of his loss of use of his left hand and his dragging of his right foot, both of which were extremely painful. All the doctors could offer were pain pills.

"I put together a little tour of my solo work to exercise this burgeoning health," Michael said in *Infinite Tuesday*. "It was time to move into the next phase of my life: more study, more prayer and meditation, more mathematics, more research and development, more performing, more playing."

Eventually, over time, the pain receded and went away, without any explanation.

Another huge compilation was then released, but many of the "best" songs are live versions.

RIO: THE BEST OF MICHAEL NESMITH (MN) (compilation)
Released: 2008

Rio (Michael Nesmith)
Casablanca Moonlight (Michael Nesmith)
More Than We Imagine (Michael Nesmith)
Navajo Trail (Majorie Elliot)
Magic (Michael Nesmith)
Tonight (Michael Nesmith)
Flying (Michael Nesmith)
Carioca (Michael Nesmith)
Cruisin' (Michael Nesmith)
Light (Michael Nesmith)
Yellow Butterfly (Michael Nesmith)
Laugh Kills Lonesome (Michael Nesmith)
Moon Over the Rio Grande (Michael Nesmith)
Juliana (Michael Nesmith)
In the Still of the Night (Cole Porter)
I Am Not That (Michael Nesmith)
...for the Island (Michael Nesmith)
Twilight on the Trail (Michael Nesmith)
Different Drum (live) (Michael Nesmith)
Two Different Roads (live) (Michael Nesmith)
Papa Gene's Blues (live) (Michael Nesmith)
Propinquity (live) (Michael Nesmith)

Some of Shelly's Blues (live) (Michael Nesmith)
Joanne (live) (Michael Nesmith)
Tomorrow and Me (live) (Michael Nesmith)
The Upside of Goodbye (live) (Michael Nesmith)
Harmony Constant (live) (Michael Nesmith)
Silver Moon (live) (Michael Nesmith)
5 Second Concerts (live) (Hobbs, Michael Nesmith)
Life, the Unsuspecting Captive (Michael Nesmith)
Nine Times Blue (Michael Nesmith)
Papa Gene's Blues (Michael Nesmith)
Sweet Young Thing (Michael Nesmith)
Dead Man's Duds (Michael Nesmith)
Escape to San Marcos (Michael Nesmith)
Capsule (Michael Nesmith, Al Perkins, David MacKay, Paul Leim, John Hobbs, Lenny Castro)

2009

Davy performed 21 solo shows from February 7 to December 14. His performance on December 7 was the basis for his *Billtown Bus Stop Radio Hour* album in 2011.

He also did a voiceover for the animated cartoon series *SpongeBob SquarePants* on an episode entitled "SpongeBob SquarePants vs. The Big One," which aired on April 17 on Nickelodeon, and appeared on the UK documentary *Stars on the Street*, airing December 19 on ITV. And he continued to pour out his own personal CDs for his fans.

Davy's final studio album released in his lifetime is among his best, heartfully covering many standards, and unlike Davy's other self-releases, this one even has a really nice cover. It is really a shame that Davy self-pressed these releases, whether by choice or by design—perhaps because of his history of arguing with his record labels over the years. As a result, much of Davy's finest material remains unheard except by his most loyal of fans. One wonders what could have happened if Davy would have been able to reconnect with a wider audience apart from The Monkees.

Note that "She" is not the same song that The Monkees performed, but instead an old song from the 70s which was later recorded by Elvis Costello for the film *Notting Hill*.

SHE (DJ)
Released: November 1, 2009

Fly Me to the Moon (Bart Howard)
She (Charles Aznavour and Herbert Kretzmer)
My Special Angel (Jimmy Duncan)
Are You Lonesome Tonight? (Roy Turk, Lou Handman)
Secret Love (Steve Porcaro, Bobby Kimball, David Paich)
Always On My Mind (Johnny Christopher, Mark James, Wayne Thompson)
Living Doll (Lionel Bart)
I'll Remember You (Kui Lee)
Singing the Blues (Melvin Endsley)
This Guy's in Love (Hal David, Burt Bacharach)
Cry (Churchill Kohlman)
What a Wonderful World (George Weiss, Robert Thiele)

Davy then released the finest Davy Jones in concert album. After years of touring with and without The Monkees, he had honed his craft so well to make a highly entertaining show that really encompasses all aspects of his career replete with some really good between song banter.

DAVY JONES LIVE!!! (DJ) Recorded live in 2004.
Released: November 11, 2009

Monkees Theme (Tommy Boyce, Bobby Hart)
A Little Bit Me, A Little Bit You (Neil Diamond)
Valleri (Tommy Boyce, Bobby Hart)
Look Out (Here Comes Tomorrow) (Neil Diamond)
Papa Gene's Blues (Michael Nesmith)
Girl (Charles Fox, Norman Gimbel)
She Hangs Out (Ellie Greenwich, Jeff Barry)
I'll Love You Forever (Davy Jones)
Bright Side Of The Road (Van Morrison)
On The Road With Archie And Edith
Wasted Days And Wasted Nights (Huey P. Meaux)
Meatloaf (?)
It's Nice To Be With You (Jerry Goldstein)
Band Introductions
Listen To The Band (Michael Nesmith)
(I'm Not Your) Steppin' Stone (Tommy Boyce, Bobby Hart)
About Mum...Is You Is Or Is You Ain't My Baby? (Billy Austin, Louis Jordan)
Daydream Believer (John Stewart)
No Time (Hank Cicalo)
I'm a Believer (Neil Diamond)
Monkees Theme (Tommy Boyce, Bobby Hart)

Michael released his second novel *The American Gene* in June.

Peter performed three solo shows between June 15 through November 28.

On March 3, Peter reported that he had been diagnosed with adenoid cystic carcinoma on his website. It is a rare, slow-growing form of head and neck cancer. A preliminary biopsy discovered that the cancer had not spread beyond the initial site. "It's a bad news / good news situation," explained Peter at the time. "It's so rare a combination (on the tongue) that there isn't a lot of experience among the medical community about this particular combination. On the other hand, the type of cancer it is, never mind the location, is somewhat well known, and the prognosis, I'm told, is good." Tork underwent radiation therapy to prevent the cancer from returning.

On March 4, Peter underwent successful surgery in New York City.

On June 11, a spokesman for Peter reported that his cancer had returned. Peter was reportedly "shaken but not stirred" by the news, and said that the doctors had given him an 80% chance of containing and shrinking the new tumor.

In July, while undergoing radiation therapy, he was interviewed by *The Washington Post*: "I recovered very quickly after my surgery, and I've been hoping that my better-than-average constitution will keep the worst effects of radiation at bay. My voice and energy still seem to be in decent shape, so maybe I can pull these gigs off after all."

He continued to tour and perform while receiving his treatments. Tork documented his cancer experience on Facebook and encouraged his fans to support research efforts of the Adenoid Cystic Carcinoma Research Foundation.

The cancer would ultimately claim Peter's life in 2019.

Micky appeared in seven episodes of the reality TV show *Gone Country* for some reason, which aired between January and March. He performed a solo show on Dundalk Heritage Fair in Maryland on July 5.

He also appeared in two documentaries: *The Boys: The Sherman Brothers' Story*, released on April 24; and *Hemispheres: A Documentary on Cerebral Palsy*, released in December.

2010

Davy performed sixteen solo shows in the US and Japan over the course of the year. While in Japan, he appeared on the show *The Best Hit USA* which aired on August 17.

Micky joined Howard Kaylan's "Happy Together 25th Anniversary Tour" from May 29 to September 26. He also appeared in the documentaries *Who Is Harry Nilsson (And Why Is Everybody Talkin' About Him?)*, released on September 10; and *Five Easy Pieces: BBStory*, released on November 23.

In the middle of all of this, his excellent tribute album to Carole King was released. It included a remake of The Monkees song "Sometime in the Morning" but not her other Monkees songs, such as "Pleasant Valley Sunday" and "Porpoise Song" (the later of which had previously appeared on *Micky Dolenz Puts You To Sleep*).

KING FOR A DAY (MD)
Released: August 31, 2010

Don't Let Me Down (Gerry Goffin, Carole King)
Sometime in the Morning (Gerry Goffin, Carole King)
Hey Girl (Gerry Goffin, Carole King)
Up On the Roof (Gerry Goffin, Carole King)
Take Good Care of My Baby (Gerry Goffin, Carole King)
Will You Love Me Tomorrow (Gerry Goffin, Carole King)
Sweet Seasons (Carole King, Toni Stern)
Crying in the Rain (Carole King, Howard Greenfield)
Go Away Little Girl (Gerry Goffin, Carole King)
Just Once in My Life (Gerry Goffin, Carole King, Phil Spector)
It Might as Well Rain Until September (Gerry Goffin, Carole King)
Point of No Return (Gerry Goffin, Carole King)
I Feel the Earth Move (Carole King)
Sometime in the Morning (Reprise) (Gerry Goffin, Carole King)

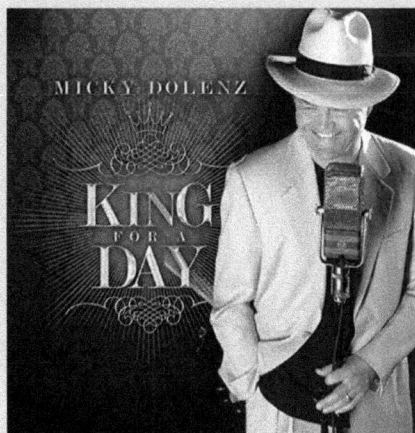

Davy continued to release his own songs on CD and cassettes.

Amore (Davy Jones) (DJ) (cassingle)

Michael remained silent during this year, but an old concert from 1974 was released as the fifth disc of a certain collection.

THE AMAZING ZIGZAG CONCERT (MN)
Recorded April 28, 1974. Disc five of a five disc set.
Released: October 11, 2010

Joanne (Michael Nesmith)
Some of Shelly's Blues (Michael Nesmith)
Silver Moon (Michael Nesmith)
Different Drum (Michael Nesmith)
Propinquity (Michael Nesmith)
Grand Ennui (Michael Nesmith)
Wax Minute (Richard Stekol)
Tomorrow and Me (Michael Nesmith)
The Upside of Goodbye (Michael Nesmith)
Roll with the Flow (Michael Nesmith)
Marie's Theme (Michael Nesmith)

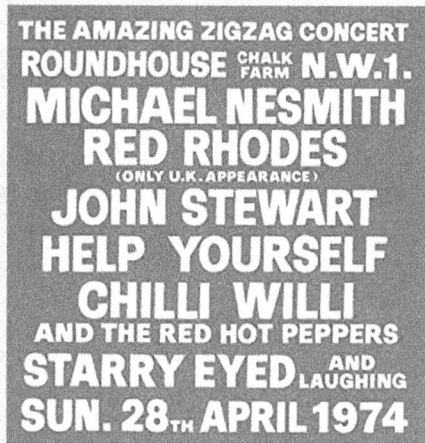

THE AMAZING ZIGZAG CONCERT
ROUNDHOUSE CHALK FARM N.W.1.
MICHAEL NESMITH
RED RHODES
(ONLY U.K. APPEARANCE)
JOHN STEWART
HELP YOURSELF
CHILLI WILLI
AND THE RED HOT PEPPERS
STARRY EYED AND LAUGHING
SUN. 28TH APRIL 1974

2011

Davy performed fifteen solo shows in 2011 and performed in the TV film *My Music: '60s Pop, Rock & Soul*, which aired on December 3, as well as playing himself in a TV movie called *The Dreamsters: Welcome to the Dreamery* as well as in *Goldberg, P.I.* He was a guest on *The Dr. Phil Show* on April 21, where the subject was "Reality TV Stars' Real Life Drama." He also provided the voice of a character named Nigel in the animated *Phineas and Ferb* episode "Bad Hair Day" / "Meatloaf Surprise", which aired on June 24 on The Disney Channel. On it, he performed a song called "Meatloaf." And, of course, he released more CDs for his fans, featuring many of the same songs again.

He then released three live CDs from various performances, the best of which is *Live in Tokyo*. It has a much different song selection but is not as exciting as the 2004 *Davy Jones Live*.

LIVE IN TOKYO (DJ) Recorded in March 1999.
Released: 2011

A Little Bit Me, A Little Bit You (Neil Diamond)
Look Out (Here Comes Tomorrow) (Neil Diamond)
Let Me Entertain You (Robbie Williams)
Valleri (Tommy Boyce, Bobby Hart)
She Hangs Out (Ellie Greenwich, Jeff Barry)
Is You or Is You Ain't My Baby? (Billy Austin, Louis Jordan)
Dance Gypsy Dance (Davy Jones)
Papa Gene's Blues (Michael Nesmith)
Sixteen Baby, You'll Soon Be Sixteen (Alan Green)
As Long as You Belong to Me (Holly Dunn, Chris Waters, Tom Shapiro)
It's Nice to Be With You (Jerry Goldstein)
I Wanna Be Free (Tommy Boyce, Bobby Hart)
I'll Love You Forever (Davy Jones)
Nobody Cares About the Railroads Anymore (Harry Nilsson)
Somebody Slap Me (Bob McDill, Roger Murrah)
It's Not Too Late (Davy Jones)
When All Else Fails (John Farnham)
It's Now (Davy Jones)
(I'm Not Your) Steppin' Stone (Tommy Boyce, Bobby Hart)
Daydream Believer (John Stewart)
No Time (Hank Cicalo)
Hippy Hippy Shake (Chan Romero)

The other two live Davy Jones albums appear to be download/streaming only from his web site.

BILLTOWN BUS STOP RADIO HOUR (DJ) Recorded on December 7, 2009. *Released:* 2011

Medley: Billtown Bus Stop Radio Hour Theme Song/Billtown Bus Stop Theme Song
A Little Bit Me, A Little Bit You (Neil Diamond)
Dialogue: On new music, Johnnie Ray
Cry (Churchill Kohlman)
Singin' the Blues (Melvin Endsley)
Dialogue: On Jimi Hendrix, left-handed musicians, Spanish lesson, Chip Douglas
God Rest Ye Merry Gentlemen (traditional)
Riu Chiu (traditional)
Smile (Charles Chaplin, John Turner, Geoffrey Parsons)
It's Just a Matter of Time (Davy Jones)
Dialogue: On Paul Williams, teen idols, Davy's TV resume, David Bowie, arts & entertainment
Someday Man (Paul Williams)
Dialogue: On Kenny Rogers, horses
Daydream Believer (Millennial Dance Version) (John Stewart)
Daydream Believer (John Stewart)
If I Knew (Bill Chadwick, Davy Jones)
Love Love Alone (John Hardy)
Dialogue: Good Night

UNPLUGGED IN THE MORNING (DJ) Radio broadcast from April 18, 1998. *Released:* February 22, 2011

Radio Interview Part 1 + Nobody Cares About The Railroads Anymore (Harry Nilsson)
Look Out (Here Comes Tomorrow) (Neil Diamond)
Radio Interview Part 2
Radio Interview Part 3: On Teen Idols, Monkees 30th Anniversary
Radio Interview Part 4: You and I (Micky Dolenz, Davy Jones), **Daydream Believer** (John Stewart)
It's Not Too Late (Teen Idols Remix) (Davy Jones)
Today's The Day (Thornally)

Micky appeared on the January 19 edition of the UK *Breakfast* TV series, and in the comedy horror movie *Mega Python vs. Gatoroid* (we are not making this up) which was released on January 29.

Next up is a Monkees cash-in EP of Micky's early singles tracks titled after the one track that has no Micky involvement.

PLASTIC SYMPHONY EP (MD) Micky's pre-Monkees recordings.
Released: July 12, 2011

Big Ben (?)
Don't Do It (Micky Dolenz)
Huff Puff (Gary Pipkin)
Plastic Symphony III (Romans, Fink, Richardson)

Peter performed two solo shows at Wolfgang's Vault in San Francisco on April 22, 2011, and The Towne Crier Cafe in Pawling, New York on November 18, 2011.

After being separated since 2008, Michael and Victoria filed for divorce in 2011.

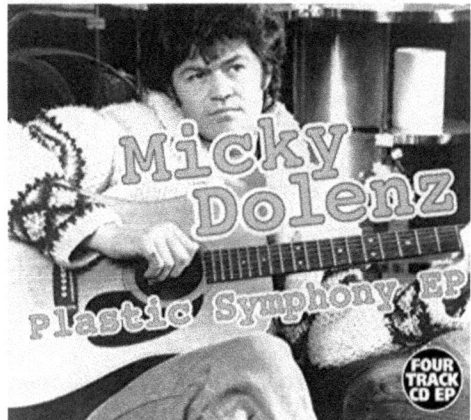

2012

Davy appeared at the Hollywood Autograph Show on February 11-12. He performed his final five solo shows from January 14 to February 19. He continued to re-record and re-release songs for his fans.

LET THEM BE LITTLE EP (DJ) Tracks 1-4 recorded live.
Released: January 30, 2012

Daydream Believer (John Stewart)
Let Them Be Little (Billie H. Dean, Richie McDonald)
It's Nice to Be With You (Jerry Goldstein)
"Oliver" Medley (Lionel Bart)
Here Comes My Baby (Cat Stevens)

A Little Bit Me, A Little Bit You (Neil Diamond) (DJ)

Girl (Charles Fox, Norman Gimbel) / **Rainy Jane** (Howard Greenfield, Neil Sedaka) (DJ) (Record Store Day reissue with picture sleeve)

Daydream Believer (John Stewart) / **I Wanna Be Free** (Tommy Boyce, Bobby Hart) (DJ)

Fans mourned the unexpected death of Davy at the age of 66 on February 29. Various articles appeared in the pages of various newspapers worldwide including *The New York Times, The Guardian, Los Angeles Times, Rolling Stone, Washington Post* and many others. His passing made the covers of *The Globe* and *People Weekly.*

"That David has stepped beyond my view causes me the sadness that it does many of you," Michael said upon hearing the news. "I will miss him, but I won't abandon him to mortality ... David's spirit and soul live well in my heart, among all the lovely people, who remember with me the good times, and the healing times, that were created for so many, including us."

"His talent will be much missed; his gifts will be with us always," said Peter. "My deepest sympathy to Jessica and the rest of his family."

"I am still in shock. I still have not digested it ... It's tough," Micky said. "This guy was in my life for 45 years ... I lost a member of my family."

Even Ringo Starr issued a short statement: "God bless Davy. Peace and love to his family."

The A&E series *Biography* devoted a show to Davy that aired on March 2 and many news reports appeared all over the TV and radio dials during the first week of March. Peter and Micky performed a memorial concert for Davy on April 3 in New York. He was saluted in memorials on *The 64th Primetime Emmy Awards* on September 23 and on *The 2012 Rock and Roll Hall of Fame Induction Ceremony* on May 5.

Davy had discussed how he wanted to be remembered in an interview with Peggy Lublin and Jill Smith for *Monkee Business Fanzine* #62 in September 1992. "Well, The Monkees, obviously, and the theatre that I've done. I'd just like to be remembered as somebody that had mixed emotions. Somebody who was predictable and unpredictable." He then added, "I'd like to personally find a way of staying alive forever."

In a way, he has.

Micky performed twenty eight solo shows across America from May 18 to December 15.

He also appeared in the episode "Go West: How the West Was Won" of the UK TV documentary series *How the Brits Rocked America*, which aired on January 27, the February 29 edition of *Piers Morgan Tonight*, the March 1 edition of *The Today Show*, and on the October 28 edition of *Kevin Pollak's Chat Show*.

Micky performed some of his favorite Beatles songs at a Beatles convention in New Jersey that spring, as well as sitting down and talking about the Beatles and music with Mark Hudson (of the Hudson Brothers).

> **Author comment from Michael:** I got Micky to autograph his book at the Beatles convention, and told him how much he had influenced my own musical career. He smiled broadly and held out his hand for me to shake it.

In the middle of all that, his excellent collection of some of the songs that meant the most to him over the years for various reasons was released. "Sugar, Sugar" was originally meant for The Monkees, but of course, The Archies had the hit. "Sometime in the Morning," "Randy Scouse Git" and "I'm a Believer" are re-recordings of The Monkees' hits. This is Micky's best solo album.

REMEMBER (MD)
Released: September 25, 2012

Good Morning, Good Morning (John Lennon, Paul McCartney)
An Old Fashioned Love Song (Paul Williams)
Diary (David Gates)
Many Years (Chris Eaton, David Harris, Joseph Williams)
Sometime in the Morning (Gerry Goffin, Carole King)

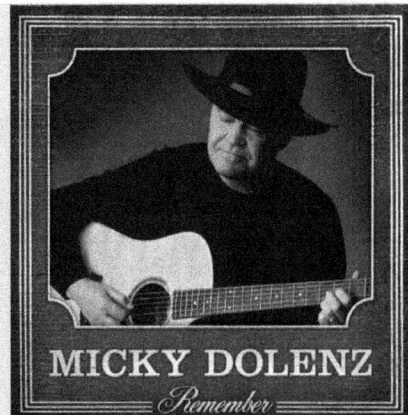

MICKY DOLENZ
Remember

Quiet Desperation (Micky Dolenz)
Randy Scouse Git (Micky Dolenz)
Johnny B. Goode (Chuck Berry)
Sugar, Sugar (Jeff Barry, Andy Kim)
Do Not Ask For Love (Michael James Murphey)
I'm a Believer (Neil Diamond)
Remember (Harry Nilsson)

Peter appeared on *Good Morning America* and *Inside Edition* on March 1, talking about Davy. He only performed three solo shows this year, between July 13 and September 13.

Michael reappeared after a long absence with two solo shows in England at The Royal Northern College of Music in Manchester on October 29, and at Union Chapel in London on October 30.

He also was finally awarded his Videoranch patent on Christmas Day. "I was wild with joy, so happy that the strength of my reaction surprised me," Michael said in *Infinite Tuesday*. He later gave the patent to the Gihon Foundation.

THE PACIFIC ARTS BOX (MN) (compilation) Five disc set comprised of *From a Radio Engine to the Photon Wing, Live at the Palais, Infinite Rider on the Big Dogma, Tropical Campfires* and four music videos from *Elephant Parts*.
    Released: October 22, 2012

2013

Peter performed fourteen solo shows from March 2 to November 29. He also appeared as himself in the documentary *Babe's and Ricky's Inn*, which was released on February 14, and made an appearance on *Good Day L.A.* on June 20.

Peter put out another quality collection of new and classic rhythm and blues standards for another go round with his group Shoe Suede Blues with remakes of Monkees tunes "She Hangs Out" and "Early Morning Blues and Greens." The recording quality is excellent and it's a shame these didn't get a better reception.

STEP BY STEP (PT with Shoe Suede Blues)
Released: April 25, 2013

Crash Course in the Blues (Cook, Jarvis, Wariner)
You Did What You Did (Thorkelson)
Step By Step (Winchester)
She Hangs Out (Ellie Greenwich, Jeff Barry)
Blue Light Boogie (Louis, Jordan, Jessie Mae Robinson)
I Still Believe in the Blues (Evans, Aschmann)
Hoochie Coochie Man (Willie Dixon)
Sally Go Round the Roses (Abner Spector, Lona Stevens, Zell Sanders)
Your Molecular Structure (Mose Allison)
Early Morning Blues and Greens (Diane Hilderbrand, Jack Keller)
Don't Let Go (Stone)
Glory to the Name of the Lord (Peter Tork)

Micky performed eighteen solo shows from March 8 to November 16. Six of the shows were part of the Teen Idols Tour.

He also appeared in the documentary *Glen Campbell: The Rhinestone Cowboy*, released January 18; on the February 25 edition of *Good Day L.A.*; and on the July 18 TV special *From Broadway with Love: A Benefit Concert for Sandy Hook*.

A performance at B.B. King's in Times Square was saved and turned into another live CD from Micky, but it's pretty much his standard show of crowd pleasures and commentary.

LIVE AT B.B. KING'S (MD)
Released: 2013

(I'm Not Your) Steppin' Stone (Tommy Boyce, Bobby Hart)
That Was Then, This is Now (Vance Brescia)
She (Tommy Boyce, Bobby Hart)
Words (Tommy Boyce, Bobby Hart)
Sometime in the Morning (Gerry Goffin, Carole King)
D.W. Washburn (Jerry Leiber, Mike Stoller)
Last Train to Clarksville (Tommy Boyce, Bobby Hart)
Johnny B. Goode (Chuck Berry)
Purple Haze (Jimi Hendrix)
Blackbird (John Lennon, Paul McCartney)
Crying in the Rain (Carole King, Howard Greenfield)
Different Drum (Michael Nesmith)
Sugar, Sugar (Jeff Barry, Andy Kim)
Randy Scouse Git (Micky Dolenz)
Daydream Believer (John Stewart)
A Little Bit Me, A Little Bit You (Neil Diamond)
Oh! Darling (John Lennon, Paul McCartney)
White Rabbit (Grace Slick)
Goin' Down (Micky Dolenz, Diane Hildebrand, Davy Jones, Michael Nesmith, Peter Tork)
Pleasant Valley Sunday (Gerry Goffin, Carole King)
Listen to the Band (Michael Nesmith)
I'm a Believer (Neil Diamond)

Michael went on a major tour, delighting his fans, and performed 33 solo shows from March 21 to November 24.

He appeared in a mini-documentary *The Making of Timerider*, released on March 19.

Davy posthumously appeared on *My Music Archives: The Best of the 60s*, a TV movie music documentary that aired on November 30, wherein he sings "Daydream Believer" from a performance shot sometime in the 2000s.

For some reason, a CD Christmas single from his Christmas album was released in the middle of February of that year.

Rockin' Around the Christmas Tree (Johnny Marks) (DJ) (CD single)
Released: February 11, 2013

2014

Micky had an active 2014, performing 24 shows from January 30 to December 14.

He also appeared in the July 10 edition of The Sixties documentary series called "The British Invasion" as well as on *Oprah: Where Are They Now?*, airing on November 9, and in the documentary short *Lennon or McCartney*, released on December 12. He also made an appearance on the December 7 edition of *Gilbert Gottfried's Amazing Colossal Podcast*. Then he found time for another Beatles convention in Chicago.

He spent a few months in Connecticut in the fall acting in a play called "Comedy is Hard!" from *The Simpsons'* producer and writer Mike Reiss. Micky played an ex-Catskills comic, with Joyce DeWitt as a former Broadway dramatic actress. The odd couple meet at a home for retired performers and hilarity ensued.

Micky's first wife, Samantha Juste (born Sandra Slater), passed away on February 5, at the age of 69, and Micky and his daughter Ami made very public announcements expressing their sadness.

Michael performed fifteen shows from March 15 through September 28. He also appeared in the *Portlandia* episode entitled "3D Printer" that aired on April 24 on IFC.

MOVIES OF THE MIND (MN) Live album recorded during Michael's 2013 solo tour. *Released:* February 2014

Welcome and Band Introductions
Calico Girlfriend (Michael Nesmith)
Nine Times Blue (Michael Nesmith)
Little Red Rider (Michael Nesmith)
Propinquity (I've Just Begun to Care) (Michael Nesmith)
Tomorrow and Me (Michael Nesmith)
Different Drum (Michael Nesmith)
Some of Shelly's Blues (Michael Nesmith)
Joanne (Michael Nesmith)

Silver Moon (Michael Nesmith)
Rio (Michael Nesmith)
Casablanca Moon (Michael Nesmith)
Yellow Butterfly (Michael Nesmith)
Light (Michael Nesmith)
Rays (Michael Nesmith)
Cruisin' (Michael Nesmith)
Dance (Michael Nesmith)
Tonight (Michael Nesmith)
Grand Ennui (Michael Nesmith)
Rising in Love (Michael Nesmith)
Listen to the Band (Michael Nesmith)

Peter performed a solo show at The Open Arts Stage Theatre in Bordentown, New Jersey on November 29.

2015

Peter, Michael and Micky appeared separately in the documentary of *The Wrecking Crew!* released March 13.

Micky performed in the comedy short *Bag Boy*, released on February 21, and performed eight concerts between September 18 and December 4. He also appeared on the September 24 episode of *The Tonight Show Starring Jimmy Fallon* on NBC, sitting in with house band The Roots, where he promoted his latest album, a live recording with lots of interesting comments between the songs.

A LITTLE BIT BROADWAY, A LITTLE BIT ROCK AND ROLL (MD)
Released: September 25, 2015

Hey Micky (Intro) (Nicholas Barry, Michael Donald Chapman, Maria Da Graca, Meneghel Xuxa)
D.W. Washburn (Jerry Leiber, Mike Stoller)
A Little Bit Broadway, A Little Bit Rock and Roll
Last Train to Clarksville (Tommy Boyce, Bobby Hart)
My Party Piece
Don't Be the Bunny (Mark Hollmann, Greg Kotis)
To See or Not to See
Mister Cellophane (Fred Ebb, John Kander)
Russian Clouds
But Not For Me (George Gershwin, Ira Gershwin)
Brilliant Brill Building
As We Go Along (Carole King, Toni Stern)
Hey Monkee Man...
Oh! Darling (John Lennon, Paul McCartney)
I'm Told I Had a Great Time
Randy Scouse Git (Micky Dolenz)
You Should Be So Lucky...
Some Enchanted Evening (Oscar Hammerstein II, Richard Rodgers)
Shrek Schmeck
I'm a Believer (Neil Diamond)
Run Silent, Run Monkee

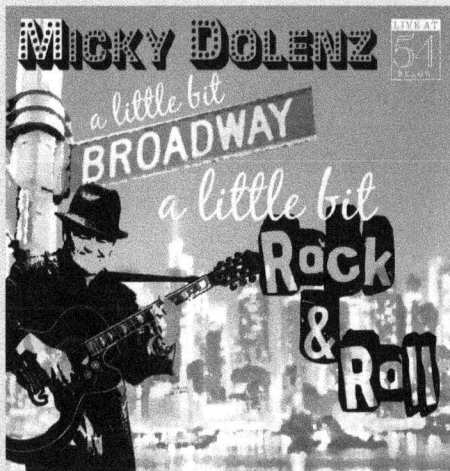

Pleasant Valley Sunday (Gerry Goffin, Carole King)
Don't Sing Along; It Puts Me Off
Daydream Believer (John Stewart)
One Foot On the Dock, One On the Boat...
One of the Good Guys (Richard Maltby, Jr., David Shire)
These Guys Are Really Good, Too
Goin' Down (Micky Dolenz, Diane Hildebrand, Davy Jones, Michael Nesmith, Peter Tork)
Pure Imagination (Leslie Bricusse, Anthony Newley)

Micky has been asked many times if he ever gets tired of singing the same songs for so many years, but he replies that he loves it. "I'm giving the audience what they want," the consummate showman usually replies.

To confirm this, he released a single of some of his favorite songs to sing, done with Circe Link and Christian Nesmith (Yes, that's Michael's son). It was released on the new "7a" label, named after the banter at the start of the album version of "Daydream Believer." ("What number is this, Chip?")

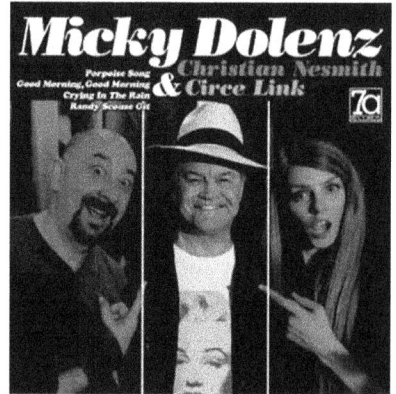

The Porpoise Song (Gerry Goffin, Carole King) / **Good Morning, Good Morning** (John Lennon, Paul McCartney) // **Crying in the Rain** (Carole King, Howard Greenfield) / **Randy Scouse Git** (Micky Dolenz) (MD with Christian Nesmith and Circe Link)

Michael appeared on the May 11 edition of *Gilbert Gottfried's Amazing Colossal Podcast*. His appearance was recorded at the recent Chiller convention.

ORIGINAL ALBUM CLASSICS (MN) (compilation) Five disc set comprised of *Magnetic South*, *Loose Salute*, *Nevada Fighter*, *Tantamount to Treason* and *And The Hits Just Keep On Comin'*.
Released: September 18, 2015

Michael then released his final "new age" album.

THE OCEAN (MN) Sequel to *The Prison* and *The Garden*.
Released: 2015

The Ocean (Michael Nesmith)
The Ocean Without Vocal (Michael Nesmith)

INFINITIA (MN) (compilation) Set comprised of *The Prison*, *The Garden*, and *The Ocean*. The first edition was numbered, signed and dated.
Released: October 17, 2015

Peter performed a one off solo concert at the Sellersville Theater in Sellersville, Pennsylvania on October 2.

2016

Micky performed ten solo shows between January 16 to September 12, and in the middle of all this, 7a released a spoken word album with Peter Noone.

AN EVENING WITH PETER NOONE & MICKY DOLENZ (MD) (spoken word)
Released: March 11, 2016

Three Minutes to Tell Our Life Stories
My Mom Was a Huge Fan of Yours
The Bee Gees' Dad
Don't Get Me Drunk, Pissed Off and Armed
Ah! Mr. Sinatra!
A Herrin' on the Griddle-O
The Greatest Bull in All of Mexico!
It Was the Beginning of Weed
Micky and the One Nighters
Weeing My Pants
There Was a War
Randy Scouse Git (Micky Dolenz)
Tell Me About Brian Jones
I Met Elvis, Who Did You Meet?
I Have So Many Regrets
Not Many People Have Been Beaten Up By John Lennon
Deja Voodoo
Little Richard, Chuck Berry and Johnny Mathis
That Sounds Rude!
I'd Never Been... to a Brothel
Let's Go and Meet Those Monkee Guys
The Beatles Came Second
Walla Walla Bing Bang
The Cavern Didn't Have Booze
I Was the Total Freak
Pleasant Valley Sunday (Gerry Goffin, Carole King)
Monkee Meets Beatle
I Met Johnny Cash
Brian Wilson Is Coming Over
I Got to Hang with John Lennon
The Odd Couple
I've Forgotten the Lyrics to Clarksville
Second Verse, Same As the First

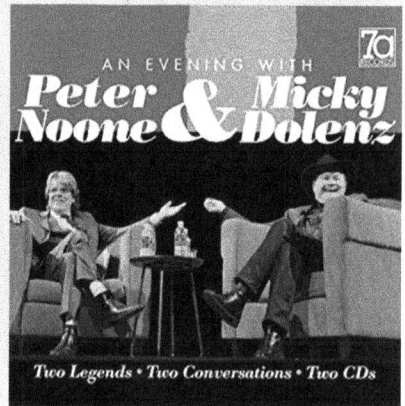

7a had spent quite some time organizing, obtaining, and remixing Micky's recordings from the 70s that he had done for MGM, and the collection makes for a wonderful and eclectic listen.

THE MGM SINGLES COLLECTION (MD) (compilation)
Released: October 7, 2016

Easy on You (Micky Dolenz)
Oh Someone (David Price)
Unattended in the Dungeon (Bobby Jones)
A Lover's Prayer (Randy Newman)
Johnny B. Goode (Chuck Berry)
It's Amazing to Me (Micky Dolenz)
Daybreak (Mono Version) (Harry Nilsson)
Love War (Micky Dolenz)
Buddy Holly Tribute (Norman Petty, Jerry Allison, Buddy Holly)
Ooh She's Young (Micky Dolenz)
Daybreak (Stereo Version) (Harry Nilsson)
Love Light (John Brown, Gerald Brown)
Alicia (Micky Dolenz)
To Be or Not to Be (Britten, Robertson)
Beverly Hills (Micky Dolenz)
Chance of a Lifetime (Micky Dolenz, Mike Slamer, Tom De Luca)
Chance of a Lifetime (Alternate Version) (Micky Dolenz, Mike Slamer, Tom De Luca)
Living on Lies (Micky Dolenz, Mike Slamer, Tom De Luca)
Porpoise Song (Gerry Goffin, Carole King) / **Good Morning, Good Morning** (John Lennon, Paul McCartney)
Crying in the Rain (Carole King, Howard Greenfield)
Randy Scouse Git (Micky Dolenz)
Iain Lee Interviews Micky Dolenz

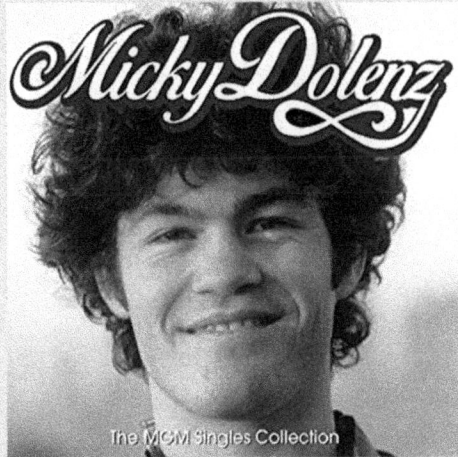

Chance of a Lifetime (Micky Dolenz, Mike Slamer, Tom De Luca) / **Livin' On Lies** (Micky Dolenz, Mike Slamer, Tom De Luca) (MD)

A strange little single came out around now, from an old Japanese Micky concert.

Sunny Girlfriend (Michael Nesmith) / **Zor and Zam (Live in Japan 1982)** (Bill Chadwick, John Chadwick) (MD)

Peter performed two solo shows at Chiller Theatre in Parsippany, New Jersey on April 23, and ay Club 66 in Edgewood, Maryland on October 14.

Michael performed a solo show at the Fire Relief Mega-Benefit in Monterey, California on August 12.

2017

Davy's estate continued to release material, which included a 1994 concert with Micky.

Daydream Believer (live) (John Stewart) / **I Want to Be Free (live)** (DJ)
Released: March 3, 2017

PITTSBURGH AUGUST '94 (DJ & MD)
Released: July 28, 2017

Davy Interview
Station ID Introduction
Theme From The Monkees (Tommy Boyce, Bobby Hart)
That Was Then, This Is Now (Vance Brescia)
Chat
A Little Bit Me, A Little Bit You (Neil Diamond)
She Hangs Out (Ellie Greenwich, Jeff Barry)
Every Step Of The Way (Mark Clarke, Ian Hunter)
Chat
D.W. Washburn (Jerry Leiber, Mike Stoller)
Look Out (Here Comes Tomorrow) (Neil Diamond)
Chat
Sometime In The Morning (Gerry Goffin, Carole King)
Last Train To Clarksville (Tommy Boyce, Bobby Hart)
It's Nice To Be With You (Jerry Goldstein)
Pleasant Valley Sunday (Gerry Goffin, Carole King)
I Wanna Be Free (Tommy Boyce, Bobby Hart)
Band Introductions
Brady Bunch Theme (Sherwood Schwartz, Frank De Vol)
Girl (Charles Fox, Norman Gimbel)
I'll Love You Forever (Davy Jones)
Chat
Too Much Monkey Business (Chuck Berry)
Chat

Purple Haze (Jimi Hendrix)
Since I Fell For You (Buddy Johnson)
Valleri (Tommy Boyce, Bobby Hart)
Chat
Goin' Down (Micky Dolenz, Diane Hildebrand, Davy Jones, Michael Nesmith, Peter Tork)
(I'm Not Your) Steppin' Stone (Tommy Boyce, Bobby Hart)
I'm A Believer (Neil Diamond)
Daydream Believer (John Stewart)
Station Outro
Fireworks Laser soundtrack

Michael's autobiography *Infinite Tuesday: An Autobiographical Riff* was released, and he appeared at the Ann and Jerry Moss Theatre on April 27, discussing his memoir and signing copies. The cover showed a number of monkeys in various colors. A later paperback reprint wisely replaced this with a picture of Michael, along with glowing reviews the book received.

An album was then released containing some of the songs talked about in the book.

INFINITE TUESDAY: AUTOBIOGRAPHICAL RIFFS THE MUSIC (MN) (compilation)
Released: April 14, 2017

The New Recruit (Bob Krasnow, Sam Ashe)
Papa Gene's Blues (Michael Nesmith)
Different Drum (Michael Nesmith)
The Girl I Knew Somewhere (First Recorded Version/Stereo Remix) (Michael Nesmith)
Listen to the Band (Michael Nesmith)
Joanne (Michael Nesmith)
Silver Moon (Michael Nesmith)
Some of Shelly's Blues (Michael Nesmith)
Opening Theme - Life, the Unsuspecting Captive (Michael Nesmith)
Rio (Michael Nesmith)
Cruisin' (Michael Nesmith)
Light (Michael Nesmith)
Laugh Kills Lonesome (Michael Nesmith)
Rays (Michael Nesmith)

Infinite Tuesday: Autobiographical Riffs The Music — Michael Nesmith

7a then released another live album. It's fairly short, containing three classic songs and then Michael discusses "The Prison" and plays some songs from that album. 7a's packaging, which a large booklet inside, makes up for the short programming.

AT THE BBC PARIS THEATRE (MN) Recorded live on November 27, 1975 in London.
Released: September 22, 2017

Silver Moon (Michael Nesmith)
Some of Shelly's Blues (Michael Nesmith)
Joanne (Michael Nesmith)
Dance Between the Raindrops (Michael Nesmith)
Marie's Theme (Michael Nesmith)
Closing Theme (Lampost) (Michael Nesmith)

Micky did some more voice overs in 2017, including a character named Wendell the Love Grub on "The Saga of Robopiggeh!" episode of *Mighty Magiswords* airing on July 23. He appeared as himself in the September 5 episode called "Fuzz Buddies" on the Hulu series *Difficult People*, in which he answers Billy's childhood fan letter, and on the *WGN Morning News* on June 13.

But mostly he spent the year performing 47 shows from January 20 through December 16, 2017. The April 15 show at Western Oregon University in Monmouth, Oregon was performed with a full orchestra and released on CD as *Out of Nowhere*.

OUT OF NOWHERE (MD and The American Metropole Orchestra) Recorded live April 15, 2017
Released: November 24, 2017

Lip Sinker (Intro)
Last Train to Clarksville (Tommy Boyce, Bobby Hart)
Sometime in the Morning (Gerry Goffin, Carole King)
D.W. Washburn (Jerry Leiber, Mike Stoller)
A Little Bit Me, A Little Bit You (Neil Diamond)
(I'm Not Your) Steppin' Stone (Tommy Boyce, Bobby Hart)
Hey Bulldog (Instrumental) (John Lennon, Paul McCartney)
Porpoise Song (Gerry Goffin, Carole King)
Randy Scouse Git (Micky Dolenz)
Since I Fell for You (Buddy Johnson)

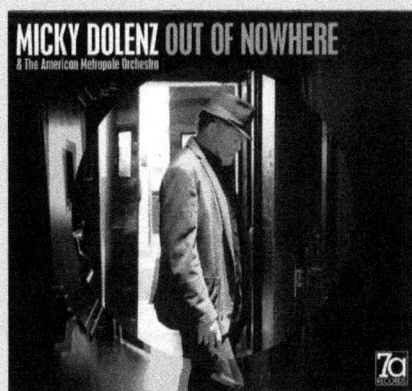

Pleasant Valley Sunday (Gerry Goffin, Carole King)
I'm a Believer (Neil Diamond)

Author Comment from Mark: This one is kind of exciting for me as I was in the audience for the concert. I was hoping that it would be recorded since it was kind of a special thing for Micky to perform his songs in front of a full orchestra; something many pop singers don't get an opportunity to do nowadays. Thanks to 7a Records being such fans. They record such opportunities, as they sense the same uniqueness that I did.

Author Comment from Michael: I saw this tour when he played in Pennsylvania, without an orchestra but with a great backing band.

Micky and Peter toured together, but not as a performing duo, but just making personal appearances at three Wizard World Comic Cons from March 17 to May 7. They were supposed to make a concert appearance together on July 4 in Greece, New York, but the date was canceled.

Micky appeared alone at the Wizard World Comic Con in Des Moines, Iowa from May 19-21 and at the Northeast Comic Con and Collectibles Extravaganza in Hanover, Massachusetts on July 22-23.

Peter performed a solo show at NYCB Theatre in Westbury, New York on October 21. He also portrayed David Lyndale in the movie *I Filmed Your Death*, but as of this printing, it has not yet been released. This would turn out to be Peter's final acting appearance.

2018

Peter released his last album in January. This album focuses on the works of the legendary Huddie William Leadbetter a.k.a. Lead Belly. Peter's brother, Nick, also appears.

RELAX YOUR MIND (PT with Shoe Suede Blues and Nick Thorkelson)
Released: January 15, 2018

Hello, Central (Lead Belly)
Bottle Up and Go (Lead Belly)
Fannon St. (Mr. Tom Hughes' Town)
(Lead Belly)
On a Monday (Lead Belly)
Black Betty (Lead Belly)
Relax Your Mind (Lead Belly)
Irene (Goodnight, Irene) (Lead Belly)
Good Morning, Blues (Lead Belly)
How Come You Do Me Like You Do?
(Lead Belly)
Easy Rider (Lead Belly)
He Never Said a Mumblin' Word (Lead
Belly)
Duncan and Brady (Lead Belly)
Come and Sit Down Beside Me (Lead Belly)
Jean Harlow (Lead Belly)

With the care they had shown with their other releases, 7a then began releasing some of Davy's material, and with a good cover for once.

Rainbows (Chip Douglas) / You Don't Have to Be a Country Boy to Sing a Country Song (Tommy Boyce, Davy Jones) (DJ)
Released: June 15, 2018

"Rainbows" had originally been recorded in 1981 but had never been released. It was written by Monkees producer Chip Douglas (*Headquarters* and *Pisces, Aquarius, Capricorn and Jones, Ltd.*). The B-side had appeared previously in various collections.

There was also a posthumous book release on May 23 called *When the World and I Were Young: Snapshots from the Collection of Davy Jones: Along Came Jones.*

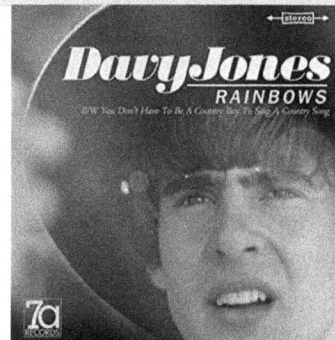

Michael delighted fans by performing five shows with a revamped First National Band from January 21 to 28. The show at the Troubadour was recorded and was a historic return to the same venue where Michael first appeared with the original First National Band almost 50 years ago.

LIVE AT THE TROUBADOUR (MN)
Released: August 3, 2018

Intro
Nevada Fighter (Michael Nesmith)
Calico Girlfriend (Michael Nesmith)
Nine Times Blue (Michael Nesmith)
Little Red Rider (Michael Nesmith)
The Crippled Lion (Michael Nesmith)
Joanne (Michael Nesmith)
Dedicated Friend (Michael Nesmith)
Grand Ennui (Michael Nesmith)
Lady of the Valley (Michael Nesmith)
50 Years Ago
Propinquity (I've Just Begun to Care) (Michael Nesmith)
Different Drum (Michael Nesmith)
Papa Gene's Blues (Michael Nesmith)
Tengo Amore (Michael Nesmith)
Keys to the Car (Michael Nesmith)
Mama Nantucket (Michael Nesmith)
Bye Bye Bye (Michael Nesmith)
Some of Shelly's Blues (Michael Nesmith)
Silver Moon (Michael Nesmith)
Thanx for the Ride (Michael Nesmith)

Micky performed four solo shows from February 17 to March 16. He also appeared in the following documentaries: *Rerun It: Some Things Are Worth Repeating* on April 11; and *Great Performances: Grammy Salute to Music Legends* on October 5.

Michael made a documentary appearance utilizing 1969 stock footage of him riding his Triumph motorcycle in the 1969 Mexican Baja 1000 Off-Road race. The documentary was released on May 10.

Micky and Michael then announced a tour as "The Monkees Present: The Mike Nesmith and Micky Dolenz Show." Peter did not join Micky and Michael on this tour as his cancer had returned, even though this was not publicized at the time. The tour was scheduled for 17 dates from June 1-28; however, the final four shows after the 19th had to be canceled due to Michael's congestive heart failure. He underwent a quadruple bypass surgery.

Author Michael comments: I was there at the concert near Philadelphia, waiting in the lobby for the show to begin when Andrew Sandoval, their manager, appeared and explained to the thirty or so of us gathered there early that the show had to be cancelled because of Michael's illness. I am proud to announce that not one person there complained, as they were all more concerned for Michael than upset that the concert was not going on. They said they would honor my ticket for when it would be rescheduled but unfortunately I was unable to attend.

Michael recovered magnificently and started making personal appearances again. A significant one was at Grauman's Egyptian Theatre in Hollywood, California, on November 1, where Michael appeared alongside Micky and Andrew Sandoval, as well as Henry Diltz, Rodney Bingenheimer, and Victor Mature's daughter in attendance to celebrate the 50th anniversary of *Head*. A short film by Diltz was shown beforehand featuring numerous black and white photos he shot in 1968. Afterwards, Michael and Micky were interviewed by Sandoval and answered various questions about the film. Michael was in great spirits as was Micky (who seemed to be slightly tipsy) but they answered all the questions posed to them. This is the same venue where Davy and Peter were interviewed almost exactly ten years earlier for *Head*'s 40th anniversary.

Author Mark comments: I was there alongside Jerry Beck who wrote the introduction to our last Monkees book, *Long Title: Looking For the Good Times.*

The Monkees ended 2018 with what may be their final album of original material, a studio Christmas album called *Christmas Party*. It was released on October 12. It features two Davy Jones Christmas songs dating from 1991 that originally appeared in slightly different form on Davy's *It's Christmas Time Again*, plus the final new song recorded by Peter Tork.

The album peaked at #66 on the *Billboard* Top Album Chart, and #2 on the Billboard Holiday Album Sales chart.

2019

After struggling with cancer of the tongue and throat off and on since 2009, Peter Tork finally succumbed to the disease on February 21, eight days after his 77th birthday.

Newspaper coverage was even more sparse than with the death of Davy seven years prior with obituaries appearing in *The Guardian*, *Rolling Stone*, *Washington Post*, *The New York Times*, *Variety*, and *People Weekly*, with no magazine covers. Most of the coverage was on TV, radio and over the internet. MeTV paid tribute to Peter by playing special episodes of *The Monkees*.

Micky admitted in *Billboard* magazine that their emotions were a bit different than their fans. "We went through that last year," Dolenz told *Billboard*, noting that Tork told him and Nesmith that he could not be part of shows with them during 2018. Tork's death "did not come as a surprise, not like David's (Jones) did. Peter acknowledged a few years ago, in fact, that he had some health issues. So Mike and I sorta went through (the mourning) last year, 'cause we had an idea what was coming."

Micky and Michael resumed their "The Monkees Present: The Mike Nesmith and Micky Dolenz Show" honoring the shows that had been canceled due to Michael's bypass surgery and adding new ones. In the wake of Peter's passing, the tour served as a tribute to the late Monkee.

Dolenz and Nesmith pay tribute to their fallen Monkees with specific songs: "Daydream Believer" for Jones, and Tork's "For Pete's Sake," as well as an intermission video of Tork, playing guitar along to a recording of the Mills Brothers' "Till Then."

These new shows began with a private show on February 28, with a US tour from March 1-16, followed by a New Zealand-Australia tour from June 8-18.

While in Australia, Micky and Michael did some very insightful interviews including one for *Studio10* on June 5, which included Michael's admission that he "never liked Peter and he never liked me" but then goes on to say "I got the call that Peter had died—and I broke into tears." And then he did again, live on television.

Michael also admitted again to his false 35 million Monkees record sales claim and Micky admitted to his false claim that Charles Manson auditioned for The Monkees.

Finally, Michael confirmed that he would be retiring again from The Monkees at the end of 2019, but then changed his mind.

Michael appeared in the documentary *Biography: I Want My MTV,* on May 1. He also introduced his Mike Hat Collection clothing line on his VideoRanch website in July, and made his only convention appearances at the Fanboy Expo on July 12-14 in Knoxville, Tennessee. He later made solo concert appearance with The First National Band in the Southern California area for three shows in October.

Micky continued to perform solo songs live, and in June, announced a tour with Todd Rundgren, Christopher Cross, Joey Molland (Badfinger) and Jason Scheff (Chicago) that would pay tribute to the Beatles' White Album while also highlighting their own hits. The tour ran from September through October.

> Author Michael comments: This was a great concert. Each guest did two of their own hits and the rest was spent on Beatles covers. Micky did "I'm a Believer" and "Pleasant Valley Sunday." A funny scene happened when Todd Rundgren sang "Everybody's Got Something to Hide Except for Me and My Monkey" and Micky walked to him and stared at him as if to say "You talkin' to me?" Honestly, I would have preferred hearing all these guys play more of their own songs, because there are plenty of Beatles cover bands out there.

7a Records continued its new and archival Monkees solo releases with a reissue and remastering of Davy's 1981 album *Live in Japan* and his 1982 laserdisc as a CD and DVD of *Hello Davy*, in a new two CD / one DVD combo package called (what else?) *Live in Japan*, plus two triple-disc vinyl sets. It's the first US release for both, released on August 9. The track listings are the same as the original releases, but with 22 bonus tracks. The bonus tracks are as follows:

LIVE IN JAPAN (DJ)
Released: August 9, 2019

CD 1: *Live In Japan* Bonus Tracks
(Theme From) The Monkees (Tommy Boyce, Bobby Hart)
(Theme From) The Monkees (Alt. Mix) (Tommy Boyce, Bobby Hart)
Daydream Believer (Alt. Mix) (John Stewart)
A Little Bit Me, A Little Bit You (Alt. Mix) (Neil Diamond)
I Wanna Be Free (Alt. Mix) (Tommy Boyce, Bobby Hart)
Star Collector (Alt. Mix) (Tommy Boyce, Bobby Hart)
How Do You Know (Alt. Mix) (Tommy Boyce, Bobby Hart)
I'm A Believer (Alt. Mix) (Tommy Boyce, Bobby Hart)
Cuddly Toy (Alt. Mix) (Tommy Boyce, Bobby Hart)

Last Train To Clarksville (Alt. Mix) (Tommy Boyce, Bobby Hart)
Valleri (Alt. Mix) (Tommy Boyce, Bobby Hart)
(I'm Not Your) Steppin' Stone (Alt. Mix) (Tommy Boyce, Bobby Hart)
It's Now (Alt. Mix) (Davy Jones)
(Theme From) The Monkees (Outro) (Tommy Boyce, Bobby Hart)

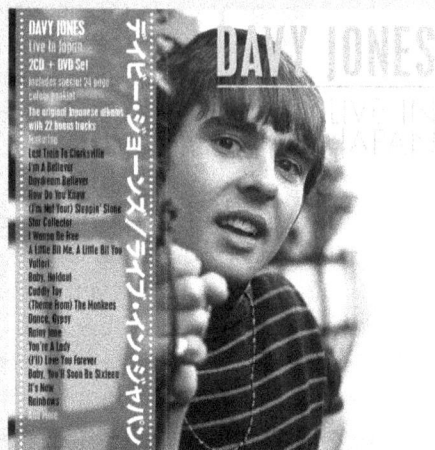

CD 2: *Hello Davy* Bonus Tracks
It's Now (Davy Jones)
How Do You Know (Davy Jones)
Dance Gypsy Dance (Davy Jones)
Can She Do it Like She Dances (Gerry Robinson, Steven Duboff)
Sixteen Baby, You'll Soon Be Sixteen (Alan Green)
Baby, Holdout (Andy Sears, Davy Jones)
(Hey Ra Ra Ra) Happy Birthday Mickey Mouse (Al Kasha, Joel Hirschorn)
You Don't Have to Be a Country Boy to Sing a Country Song (Tommy Boyce, Davy Jones)
Rainbows (Chip Douglas)

THANK YOU, MISTER ROGERS: MUSIC AND MEMORIES (one track by MD) (compilation)
Released: October 25, 2019
It's a Perfectly Beautiful Day (Fred Rogers)

Micky contributed the song "It's a Perfectly Beautiful Day" for the album of Mister Rogers songs called *Thank You, Mister Rogers—Music and Memories*, released on October 18. The album is a companion piece to the movie about the life of Mister Rogers called *A Beautiful Day in the Neighborhood*, starring Tom Hanks as Fred Rogers.

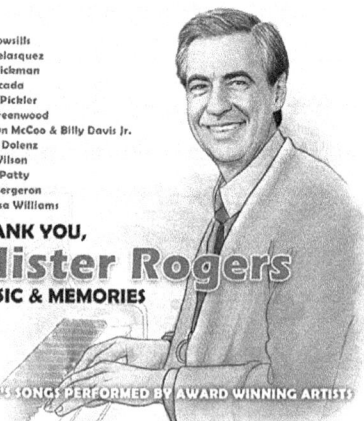

Following this, Micky joined Sammy Hagar, Queen's Brian May, Paul Shaefer and Joe Walsh onstage on November 12-13 in Nashville, Tennessee, for James Burton and Friends: Rock and Roll Meets Country. Other artists on the bill included Jason Scheff, Matthew and Gunnar Nelson, Albert Lee, Roy Orbison, Jr. with Wesley and Alex Orbison, Steve Cropper, John Carter Cash, Marty Haggard and Johnny Owens.

In December, Rolling Stone magazine produced its list of the best songs of the decade, and "Me and Magdelena" (from the *Good Times!* album) came in at #76. "The voices of Michael Nesmith and Micky Dolenz blend together as perfectly as they did in the Sixties," said Rolling Stone. "And now with decades of wisdom and tough loss underneath their glossy exterior (beloved members Peter Tork and Davy Jones are no longer with us), they somehow mean more than ever."

Michael ended the year issuing an album with the cooperation of 7a Records called *Cosmic Partners* by Michael Nesmith and Red Rhodes. This was a concert recorded at McCabe's in Santa Monica, California, on August 18, 1973, and unreleased until now. The recording was made available on CD and LP, and picture disc. Some of the tracks are just stage banter.

COSMIC PARTNERS: THE McCABE'S TAPES
Released: November 22, 2019
Welcome to McCabe's
Tomorrow and Me (Michael Nesmith)
The Upside of Goodbye (Michael Nesmith)
The Sock Cymbal Scared Me
Grand Ennui (Michael Nesmith)
Some of Shelly's Blues (Michael Nesmith)
Cosmic Partners
Rose City Chimes (J. Robert Garrett)
A Dog Wrote It
Poinciana (Nat Simon, Buddy Bernier)
The Crippled Lion (Michael Nesmith)
Alice Nesmith
The One Rose (Jimmie Rogers)
Propinquity (I've Just Begun to Care) (Michael Nesmith)
The Great Escape
Joanne (Michael Nesmith)
Silver Moon (Michael Nesmith)

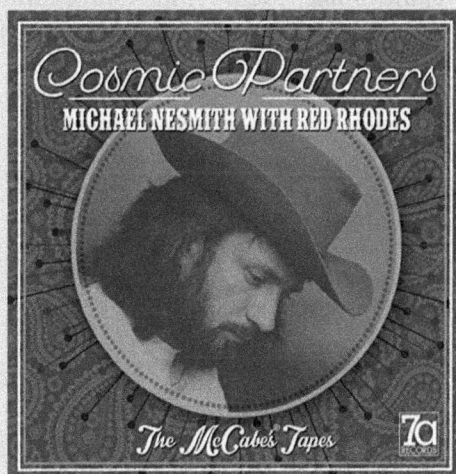

2020

As this book was finished in December of 2019, we admit that we do not have 2020 vision. However, the following have been announced:

Micky is set to appear in the documentary *Let There Be Drums!*, which is scheduled for release sometime in 2020.

Micky and Michael will do another tour starting in April, promising "all the hits and deep cuts" and a new album called *The Mike and Micky Show Live*. Anyone purchasing a ticket for the concert will get their choice of a CD or a digital copy. The album will be produced by Andrew Sandoval and mixed by Christian Nesmith and is from the 2019 concert tour. Beside the standard hits, it will also include cuts from *Good Times!*

Most assuredly there will be new Monkees compilations, and new releases by Micky and/or Mike, and posthumous releases by Davy and Peter.

No matter what, their place in history is assured.

Monkees U.S. Discography

Some dates are approximate, and are only listed by month. If a record made the Billboard charts, the highest position is indicated.

1963
?:   Wanderin' / Well Well (MN)

1965
2:   DAVID JONES (DJ)
     Dream Girl / Take Me to Paradise (DJ)
?:   How Can You Kiss Me / Just a Little Love (MN)
7:   What Are We Going to Do? / This Bouquet (DJ) #93
9:   The New Recruit / A Journey with Michael Blessing (MN)
11: The Girl From Chelsea / Theme for a New Love (DJ)
     Until It's Time for You to Go / What Seems to be the Trouble Officer (MN)

1966
9:   Last Train to Clarksville / Take a Giant Step #1
10: THE MONKEES #1
12: I'm a Believer / (I'm Not Your) Steppin' Stone #1

1967
2:   MORE OF THE MONKEES #1
3:   Don't Do It / Plastic Symphony III (MD) #75
     A Little Bit Me A Little Bit You / The Girl I Knew Somewhere #2
4:   Just a Little Love / Curson Terrace (MN)
5:   HEADQUARTERS #1
7:   Pleasant Valley Sunday / Words #3
8:   Huff Puff / Fate (MD)
11: PISCES, AQUARIUS, CAPRICORN & JONES, LTD. #1
     Daydream Believer / Goin' Down #1

1968
3:   Valleri / Tapioca Tundra #3
4:   THE BIRDS THE BEES AND THE MONKEES #3
5:   D.W. Washburn / It's Nice to Be With You #19
6:   THE WICHITA TRAIN WHISTLE SINGS (MN) #144
7:   Don't Cry Now / Tapioca Tundra (MN)
10: Porpoise Song / As We Go Along #62
12: HEAD #45

1969
2:   INSTANT REPLAY #32
     Tear Drop City / A Man Without A Dream #56
5:   Listen to the Band / Someday Man #63
6:   THE MONKEES GREATEST HITS #89
9:   Good Clean Fun / Mommy and Daddy #82
10: PRESENT #100

1970

6: MAGNETIC SOUTH (MN) **#143**
CHANGES **#152**
Oh My My / I Love You Better **#98**
7: Little Red Rider / Rose City Chimes (MN)
8: Joanne / One Rose (MN) **#21**
11: LOOSE SALUTE (MN) **#159**
Silver Moon / Lady of the Valley (MN) **#42**

1971

1: BARREL FULL OF MONKEES **#207**
5: NEVADA FIGHTER (MN) **#218**
Nevada Fighter / Here I Am (MN) **#159**
DAVY JONES (DJ) **#205**
Rainy Jane / Road to Love (DJ) **#52**
6: Texas Morning / Tumbling Tumbleweeds (MN)
9: I Really Love You / Sitting in the Apple Tree (DJ)
10: I've Just Begun to Care (Propinquity) / Only Bound (MN)
Easy on You / Oh Someone (MD)
12: Girl / Take My Love (DJ)

1972

1: Mama Rocker / Lazy Lady (MN)
2: TANTAMOUNT TO TREASON VOL. 1 (MN) **#211**
I'll Believe in You / Road to Love (DJ)
6: Unattended in the Jungle / A Lover's Prayer (MD)
8: AND THE HITS JUST KEEP ON COMIN' (MN) **#208**
Roll With the Flow / Keep On (MN)
9: REFOCUS (reissued in 1976 as MONKEES GREATEST HITS) **#58**
10: Johnny B. Goode / It's Amazing to Me (MD)
11: You're a Lady / Who Was It? (DJ)

1973

1: Rubberene (DJ)
5: Daybreak / Love War (MD)
9: PRETTY MUCH YOUR STANDARD RANCH STASH (MN)

1974

?: THE PRISON (MN)
4: Buddy Holly Tribute / Ooh She's Young (MD)

1975

12: I Remember the Feeling / You and I (DJBH)

1976

5: DOLENZ, JONES, BOYCE & HART (DJBH)
I Love You (and I'm Glad I Said It) / Saving My Love (DJBH)

1977

5: FROM A RADIO ENGINE TO A PHOTON WING (MN) **#209**
Rio / Life, The Unsuspecting Captive (MN)
12: CHRISTMAS JONES (DJ)
Christmas is My Time of Year / White Christmas (DJ)

?:   COMPILATION (MN)

1978
5:   Happy Birthday Mickey Mouse / You Don't Have to be a Country Boy (DJ)
8:   LIVE AT THE PALAIS (MN)
     Roll With The Flow / I've Just Begun to Care (Propinquity) (MN)

1979
5:   INFINITE RIDER ON THE BIG DOGMA (MN) **#151**
6:   Magic (The Night is Magic) / Dance (Dance and Have a Good Time) (MN)
8:   Cruisin' (Lucy and Ramona and Sunset Sam) / Horserace (MN)

1981
2:   (I'm Not Your) Steppin' Stone / Higher and Higher (PT)

1982
10:   MORE GREATEST HITS OF THE MONKEES

1986
6:   THEN AND NOW ... THE BEST OF THE MONKEES **#21**
7:   That Was Then, This is Now / (Theme from) The Monkees **#20**
11:   Daydream Believer (remix) / Randy Scouse Git **#79**

1987
7:   LIVE 1967
     MISSING LINKS
8:   POOL IT! **#72**
9:   Heart and Soul / MGBGT (live) **#89**
11:   Every Step of the Way / (I'll) Love You Forever (live)

1988
1:   INCREDIBLE (DJ)

1989
3:   THE NEWER STUFF (MN)

1990
1:   MISSING LINKS VOLUME 2

1991
10:   LISTEN TO THE BAND
     MICKY DOLENZ PUTS YOU TO SLEEP (MD)
11:   THE OLDER STUFF (MN)
12:   IT'S CHRISTMAS TIME AGAIN (DJ)

1992
9:   TROPICAL CAMPFIRES (MN)

1993
9:   THE COMPLETE FIRST NATIONAL BAND RECORDINGS (MN)

1994
4:   BROADWAY MICKY (MD)

6:   STRANGER THINGS HAVE HAPPENED (PT)
8:   THE GARDEN (MN)

1995
6:   JUST FOR THE RECORD VOL. 2 (DJ)

1996
3:   MISSING LINKS VOLUME 3
6:   JUST FOR THE RECORD VOL. 4 (DJ)
10: JUSTUS
12: TWO MAN BAND (PT)

1998
3:   THE MASTERS (MN)
6:   TEEN IDOLS 1998 TOUR (DJ)
     DON'T GO (DJ)
10: DEMOISELLE (MD)
11: JUST FOR THE RECORD VOL. 1 (DJ)
     JUST FOR THE RECORD VOL. 3 (DJ)

1999
5:   SIXTEEN ORIGINAL CLASSICS (MN)
7:   LIVE AT THE BRITT FESTIVAL (MN)
?:   MICKY DOLENZ LIVE (MD)

2000
2:   SHOE SUEDE BLUES LIVE (PT)
8:   TIMERIDER (MN)

2001
2:   MUSIC BOX
3:   ONCE AGAIN (PT)
4:   JUST ME (DJ)

2003
4:   THE BEST OF THE MONKEES #20
6:   SAVED BY THE BLUES (PT)
9:   THE HEADQUARTERS SESSIONS
11: THE BEST OF MICHAEL NESMITH (MN)

2004
?:   JUST ME 2 (DJ)
9:   DAYDREAM BELIEVIN' (DJ)
11: RAYS (MN)

2006
11: LIVE/BACKSTAGE AT THE COFFEE GALLERY (PT)

2007
2:   CAMBRIA HOTEL (PT)

2008
?:   INCREDIBLE REVISITED (DJ)

?:   RIO: THE BEST OF MICHAEL NESMITH (MN)

2009
11:   SHE (DJ)
      DAVY JONES LIVE (DJ)

2010
8:    KING FOR A DAY (MD)

2011
?:   LIVE IN TOKYO (DJ)
      BILLTOWN BUS STOP RADIO HOUR (DJ)
2:    UNPLUGGED IN THE MORNING (DJ)

2012
9:    REMEMBER (MD)
10:   THE PACIFIC ARTS BOX (MN)

2013
4:    STEP BY STEP (PT)
?:   LIVE AT B.B. KING'S (MD)

2014
2:    MOVIES ON THE MIND (MN)

2015
9:    A LITTLE BIT BROADWAY, A LITTLE BIT ROCK AND ROLL (MD)
      ORIGINAL ALBUM CLASSICS (MN)
?:   THE OCEAN (MN)

2016
3:    AN EVENING WITH PETER NOONE AND MICKY DOLENZ (MD)
5:    GOOD TIMES! #14
7:    THE POINT! (MD & DJ)
10:   THE MGM SINGLES COLLECTION (MD)
      Chance of a Lifetime / Livin' On Lies (MD)

2017
3:    Daydream Believer (live) / I Want to Be Free (live) (DJ)
4:    INFINITE TUESDAY (MN)
      OUT OF NOWHERE (MD)
7:    PITTSBURGH AUGUST '94 (DJ & MD)
9:    AT THE BBC PARIS THEATER (MN)

2018
1:    RELAX YOUR MIND (PT)
6:    Rainbows / You Don't Have to Be a Country Boy to Sing a Country Song (DJ)
8:    LIVE AT THE TROUBADOUR (MN)
10:   CHRISTMAS PARTY #66

2019
8:    LIVE IN JAPAN (DJ)
12:   COSMIC PARTNERS: THE McCABE'S TAPES (MN)

Solo TV and Movie Appearances

Micky Dolenz as actor or self:
The Steve Allen Plymouth Show - 9/16/56
Today - 9/17/56
Circus Boy - Corky - 1956-1958
Episodes:
 Meet Circus Boy - 9/23/56
 The Fabulous Colonel Jack - 9/30/56
 The Great Gambino - 10/7/56
 The Amazing Mr. Sinbad - 10/14/56
 Corky and the Circus - 10/21/56
 Casey Rides Again - 11/4/56
 The Little Fugitive - 11/11/56
 The Proud Pagliacci - 11/18/56
 White Eagle - 11/25/56
 The Little Gypsy - 12/2/56
 The Masked Marvel - 12/9/56
 The Good Samaritans - 12/23/56
 Daring Young Man - 12/30/56
 Farewell to the Circus - 1/6/57
 Elmer the Aeronaut - 1/13/57
 The Remarkable Ricardo - 1/20/57
 Big Top Angel - 1/27/57
 The Return of Colonel Jack - 2/10/57
 The Knife Thrower - 2/17/57
 Joey's Wedding Day - 2/24/57
 Man From Cimarron - 3/3/57
 The Great Gambino's Son - 3/10/57
 Corky's Big Parade - 3/24/57
 The Lady and the Circus - 3/31/57
 Counterfeit Clown - 4/7/57
 The Pawnee Strip - 4/14/57
 The Cub Reporter - 4/21/57
 General Pete - 4/28/57
 The Tumbling Clown - 5/5/57
 Death-Defying Dozetti - 5/12/57
 Colonel Jack's Brother - 5/19/57
 The Swamp Man - 5/26/57
 Hortense the Hippo - 6/2/57
 The Fortune Teller - 6/9/57
 The Gentle Giant - 6/16/57
 Little Vagabond - 6/23/57
 Elmer the Rainmaker - 9/19/57
 Royal Roustabout - 9/26/57
 Bimbo, Jr. - 10/3/57
 Alex the Great - 10/10/57
 The Return of Casey Perkins - 10/17/57
 Major Buffington - 10/24/57
 The Clemen Boys - 10/31/57

The Magic Lantern - 11/7/57
The Dancing Bear - 11/14/57
The Marvelous Manellis - 11/21/57
Uncle Cyrus - 11/28/57
The Judge's Boy - 12/5/57
The Return of Buffalo Bill - 12/12/57
Zane Grey Theater: The Vaunted - Ted Matson - 11/27/58
Playhouse 90: The Velvet Alley - Melvin - 1/22/59
The Steve Allen Playhouse - 10/10/62
Mr. Novak: Born of Kings and Angels - Ed - 12/1/64
Peyton Place: Episode #1.52 - Kitch Brunner - 3/16/65
Peyton Place: Episode #1.53 - Kitch Brunner - 3/18/65
Peyton Place: Episode #1.55 - Kitch Brunner - 3/25/65
American Bandstand: Episode #10.14 - 12/17/66
Good Times - Jungle Gino - 5/67
Top of the Pops: Episode #4.26 - 6/29/67
Top of the Pops: Episode #5.21 - 5/23/68
Monterey Pop - 12/26/68
The Funky Phantom - Skip Gilroy - 1971-1972
Episodes:
    Don't Fool With a Phantom - 9/11/71
    Heir Scare - 9/18/71
    I'll Haunt You Later - 9/25/71
    Who's Chicken - 10/2/71
    The Headless Horseman - 10/9/71
    Spirit Spooked - 10/16/71
    Ghost Town Ghost - 10/23/71
    We Saw a Sea Serpent - 10/30/71
    Haunt in Inn - 11/6/71
    Mudsy Joins the Circus - 11/13/71
    Pigskin Predicament - 11/20/71
    The Liberty Bell Caper - 11/27/71
    April's Foolish Day - 12/4/71
    The Forest's Prime-Evil - 12/11/71
    The Hairy Scary Houndman - 12/18/71
    Mudsy and Muddlemore Manor - 12/25/71
    Ghost Grabbers - 1/1/72
My Three Sons: Barbara Lost - John Simpson and Brian Lipsker - 4/6/72
Adam-12: Dirt Duel - Oiler - 9/13/72
Cannon: Bitter Legion - Cappy - 9/27/72
The Night of the Strangler - Vance - 10/1/72
Butch Cassidy and the Sundance Kids - Harvey or Wally - 1973-1974
Episodes:
    The Scientist - 9/8/73
    The Counterfeiters - 9/15/73
    One of Our Ships is Missing - 9/22/73
    Double Trouble - 9/29/73
    The Pearl Caper - 10/6/73
    The Gold Caper - 10/13/73
    Road Racers - 10/20/73
    Hong Kong Story - 10/27/73
    Operation G-Minus - 11/3/73
    Orient Express - 11/10/73

    The Parrot Caper - 11/17/73
    The Super Sub - 11/24/73
    The Haunted Castle - 12/1/73
Owen Marshall, Counselor at Law: The Camerons are a Special Clan - Rick Schenk - 10/24/73
Top of the Pops: 10 Years of Pop Music: 1964-1974 - 12/27/73
Devlin - Todd Devlin - 1974-1975
Episodes:
    Victory Over Fear - 9/7/74
    Hero Worshiper - 9/14/74
    Save That Lion - 9/21/74
    Tod's Triumph - 9/28/74
    Up, Up and Away - 10/5/74
    The Challenge - 10/12/74
    Sandy's Choice - 10/19/74
    Sandy's Idol - 10/26/74
    The Big Blast - 11/2/74
    Innocent or Guilty - 11/9/74
    Like Father, Like Son - 11/16/74
    Jester's Secret - 11/23/74
    The Stowaway - 11/30/74
    Sandy's Turn - 12/7/74
    Sandy's Decision - 12/14/74
    The Storyteller - 12/21/74
These Are the Days - various voices - 1974-1976
Episodes:
    Sensible Ben - 9/7/74
    The Fire Brigade - 9/14/75
    Danny's Musical Dilemma - 9/21/75
    Danny Runs Away - 9/28/75
    Ben for President - 10/5/74
    The Good Luck Charm - 10/12/74
    Kathy's Job - 10/19/74
    The Runaway Horse - 10/26/74
    How Ben Was Cowed - 11/2/74
    Grandpa and the Great Cyclic Harmonium Swindle - 11/9/74
    The Visitor - 11/16/74
    The Most Precious Gift of All - 11/23/74
    The Spa - 9/6/75
    Hello, Mrs. McGivern, Goodbye - 9/13/75
    The Balloon - 9/20/75
    The Feud - 9/27/75
Partridge Family 2200 A.D. - various voices - 1974-1975
Episodes:
    Danny, the Invisible Man - 9/7/74
    If This is Texas - It Must Be Doomsday - 9/14/74
    The Incredible Shrinking Keith - 9/21/74
    Cousin Sunspot - 9/28/74
    The Wax Museum - 10/5/74
    The Dog Catcher - 10/12/74
    Cupcake Capere - 10/19/74
    Laurie's Computer Date - 10/26/74
    Movie Madness - 11/2/74
    The Pink Letter - 11/9/74

Orbit the Genius - 11/16/74
The Switch - 11/23/74
My Son, the Spaceball Star - 11/30/74
Car Trouble - 12/7/74
The Roobits - 12/14/74
Let's All Stick Together - 12/21/74
Keep Off My Grass! - You Know - 3/75
The Hoyt Axton Country Western Boogie Woogie Gospel Rock and Roll Show - 3/22/75
Linda Lovelace for President - Lt. Fenwick - 4/75
Dinah!: Episode #2.88 - 1/21/76
Rock Concert: Episode #3.20 - 2/14/76
The Mike Douglas Show: Episode #15.120 - 2/27/76
American Bandstand: Episode #19.24 - 3/13/76
Break the Bank: Episode #1.28 - 5/19/76
Tomorrow Coast to Coast - 9/1/77
Wonder Wheels segment of The Skatebirds - Willy Sheeler - 1977-1978
Episodes:
    Wonder Wheels in The County Fair - 9/10/77
    Wonder Wheels and The Rustlers - 9/17/77
    Wonder Wheels and The Skyscraper - 9/24/77
    Wonder Wheels and The Gold Train Robbery - 10/1/77
    Wonder Wheels and The Snowmen - 10/8/77
    Wonder Wheels and The Vanishing Prince - 10/15/77
    Wonder Wheels and The Ghost Town - 10/22/77
    Wonder Wheels and His Double Trouble - 10/29/77
    Wonder Wheels and The U.F.O. - 11/5/77
    Wonder Wheels and The Hermits' Horde - 11/12/77
    Wonder Wheels and The Air Race - 11/9/77
    Wonder Wheels and The Animals - 11/26/77
    Wonder Wheels and The Idol's Eye - 12/3/77
    Wonder Wheels and The Race Horse - 12/10/77
    Wonder Wheels and The Studio Steal - 12/17/77
    Wonder Wheels and The Golden Globe - 12/24/77
Captain Caveman and the Teen Angels - various voices - 1977-1980
Episodes:
    The Kooky Case of the Cryptic Keys - 9/10/77
    The Mixed Up Mystery of Deadman's Reef - 9/17/77
    What a Flight for Fright - 9/24/77
    The Creepy Case of the Creaky Charter Boat - 10/1/77
    Big Scare in the Big Top - 10/8/77
    Double Dribble Riddle - 10/15/77
    The Crazy Case of the Tell-Tale Tape - 10/22/77
    The Creepy Claw Caper - 10/29/77
    Cavey and the Kabuta Clue - 11/5/77
    Cavey and the Weirdo Wolfman - 11/12/77
    The Disappearing Elephant Mystery - 11/19/77
    The Fur Freight Fight - 11/26/77
    Ride 'em Caveman - 12/3/77
    The Strange Case of the Creature from Space - 12/10/77
    The Mystery Mansion Mix-Up - 12/17/77
    Playing Footsie with Bigfoot - 12/24/77
    Disco Cavey - 9/9/78
    Muscle-Bound Cavey - 9/16/78

    Cavey's Crazy Car Caper - 9/23/78
    Cavey's Mexicali 500 - 9/30/78
    Wild West Cavey - 10/7/78
    Cavey's Winter Carnival Caper - 10/14/78
    Cavey's Fashion Fiasco - 10/21/78
    Cavey's Missing Missile Miss-tery - 10/28/78
    The Scarifying Seaweed Secret - 3/8/80
    The Dummy - 3/15/80
    Cavey and the Volcanic Villain - 3/22/80
    Prehistoric Panic -3/29/80
    Cavey and the Baffling Buffalo Man - 4/5/80
    Dragonhead - 4/12/80
    Cavey and the Murky Mississippi Mystery - 4/19/80
    Old Cavey in New York -4/26/80
    The Albino Rhino - 5/3/80
    Kentucky Cavey - 5/10/80
    Cavey Goes to College - 5/17/80
    The Haunting of Dog's Hollow - 5/24/80
    The Legend of Devil's Run - 5/31/80
    The Mystery of the Meandering Mummy - 6/7/80
    The Old Caveman and the Sea - 6/14/80
    Lights, Camera, Cavey! - 6/21/80
Our Show - 12/17/77
Tiswas: Episode #4.21 - 1/28/78
Celebrity Squares: Episode #3.26 - 7/1/78
The Scooby-Doo/Dynomutt Hour: The Diabolical Disc Demon - 11/18/78
Top of the Pops - 2/8/79
Wings Over the World - 3/16/79
Get it Together: Episode #4.6 - 5/15/79
Celebrity Squares: Episode #4.22 - 5/26/79
Star Games - 12/4/79
Star Games - 12/25/79
An Audience with Dame Edna Everage - 12/26/80
An Audience with Dudley Moore - 12/26/81
Pop Quiz: Episode #3.9 - 6/11/83
The New Mike Hammer: Deadly Collection - Scott Warren - 2/25/87
Nightlife: Episode #1.138 - 3/18/87
Your Alcohol I.Q. - 1988
MTV Music Video Awards - 9/6/89
A.M. Los Angeles - 6/29/89
Nashville Now - 8/15/89
Nashville Now - 10/16/89
A.M. Los Angeles - 3/9/90
Inside Edition - 5/1/90
Pick of the Pilots - 8/11/90
Voices That Care - 2/28/91
A.M. Los Angeles - 9/17/91
MTV News: The Week in Rock - 10/11/91
Totally Hidden Video - 11/2/91
Crook and Chase - 11/22/91
Country Kitchen - 11/30/91
Nightlife - 1991
Breakfast Television - 4/3/92

Batman: The Animated Series: Two-Face Part II - Min and Max - 9/28/92
The Ben Stiller Show: With Rob Morrow - Josh Goldsilver - 11/15/92
Vicki! - 6/18/93
Today - 9/6/93
CBS News Up to the Minute - 9/27/93
Deadfall - Bart - 10/8/93
Larry King Live - 10/18/93
Showbiz Today - 11/23/93
Late Night with Conan O'Brien - 12/16/93
Marilu - 2/14/94
Monty: My Dad Could Beat Up Your Dad - Eli Campbell - 1994
The Tonight Show with Jay Leno: Episode #3.145 - 8/10/94
The Tick - Arthur and Captain Lemming - 1994-1995
Episodes:
    The Tick vs. The Idea Man - 9/10/94
    The Tick vs. Chairface Chippendale - 9/17/94
    The Tick vs. Dinosaur Neil - 9/24/94
    The Tick vs. Mr. Mental - 10/1/94
    The Tick vs. The Breadmaster - 10/8/94
    The Tick vs. El Seed - 10/15/94
    The Tick vs. The Tick - 10/22/94
    The Tick vs. The Uncommon Cold - 10/29/94
    The Tick vs. Brainchild - 11/5/94
    The Tick vs. Pineapple Pokopo - 11/12/94
    The Tick vs. The Mole-Men (a.k.a. The Mole-Men Step Out) - 11/19/94
    The Tick vs. The Proto-Clown (a.k.a. Day of the Clown) - 2/4/95
    The Tick vs. Arthur's Bank Account - 2/11/95
Boy Meets World: Band on the Run - 11/11/94
Aaahh!!! Real Monsters: Simon Strikes Back/The Ickis Box - Jed and Kilowog - 1/21/95
Boy Meets World: Rave On - Gordy - 11/17/95
You Can't Do That! The Making of A Hard Day's Night - 1995
Politically Incorrect - 2/14/96
George and Alana - 2/20/96
Showbiz Today - 2/29/96
Good Day L.A. - 3/1/96
Pacific Blue: Pilot - Mayor Micky - 3/2/96
Pacific Blue: No Man's Land - Mayor Micky - 3/16/96
Muppets Tonight: Cindy Crawford - 4/4/96
Midday - 10/11/96
Politically Incorrect - 10/23/96
Breakfast News - 1/10/97
The National Lottery - 1/11/97
Noel's House Party: Episode #6.11 - 1/11/97
Access Hollywood - 7/11/97
The Tonight Show with Jay Leno: Episode #5.73 - 4/23/97
The Tonight Show with Jay Leno: Episode #5.177 - 10/8/97
Arthel and Fred - 10/20/97
The Wonderful World of Disney: The Love Bug - Donny Shotz - 11/30/97
Debt - 12/1/97
Politically Incorrect - 12/19/97
Pictionary - 1/7/98
Pictionary - 1/8/98
Pictionary - 1/9/98

The Secret Files of the Spydogs - Ralph and Scribble - 1998-1999
Episodes:

 K-9 / Postal - 9/12/98
 Hair / Homework - 9/19/98
 Bone / Time - 9/26/98
 Earnest / Spin - 10/3/98
 Twilight / Fetch - 10/10/98
 Small / Water - 11/7/98
 I.H.R.F. / Oatz - 11/14/98
 D'Cell / Halfday - 11/28/98
 Zero / Pups - 1/30/99
 Obedience / DoggyLand - 2/6/99
 Lunch / Iditarod - 2/13/99
 Porkzilla / Money - 2/20/99
 Mange / Scribble - 2/27/99
 Tusk / Install - 1999
 Charlie / Automutt - 1999
 Granny / Founders - 1999
 Tail / Tomorrow - 1999
 Howl / Thirteen - 1999
 Escape / Exposed - 1999
 Virgil / Bunny - 1999
 DNA / Santa - 1999
 B.A.R.K. / Being - 1999

Politically Incorrect - 12/15/98
Invisible Mom II - 8/31/99
The Roseanne Show - 4/14/00
Hollywood Rocks the Movies: The Early Years (1955-1970) - 7/2/00
Entertainment Tonight - 9/20/00
Extra - 9/21/00
Access Hollywood - 9/21/00
Behind the Music: Anniversary Show - 9/24/00
Men Are From Mars, Women Are From Venus - 10/4/00
100 Greatest Number One Singles - 1/6/01
I Love 1980's: I Love 1980 - 1/13/01
Walk on By: The Story of Popular Song: Pure Pop - 5/5/01
The Drew Carey Show: Drew and the King - Mr. Metcalf - 12/19/01
Entertainment Tonight - 1/10/02
Breakfast - 1/21/02
Richard and Judy - 1/22/02
This is Your Life: Bill Oddie - 1/31/02
As the World Turns: Episode #1.11769 - The Vicar - 5/1/02
Easy Riders, Raging Bulls: How the Sex, Drugs and Rock 'n' Roll Generation Saved Hollywood - 3/9/03
Rock Gardens - 12/12/03
TV's Greatest Cars - 12/23/04
Queer Eye: Trumped to Triumph: Danny K - 8/16/05
The Story of Light Entertainment: Pop and Easy Listening - 8/19/06
TV Land Confidential: Finales - 7/18/07
TV Land Confidential: Music- 8/8/07
The Truth About Boybands - 8/18/07
Halloween - Derek Allen - 8/31/07
Gone Country: Lights on Broadway - 1/24/09
The Bonnie Hunt Show - 1/26/09

Gone Country: Learning the Ropes - 1/31/09
Gone Country: Playing Your Cards Right - 2/7/09
Gone Country: Bustin' Loose - 2/14/09
Gone Country: Stars and Stripes - 2/21/09
Gone Country: Artistic Expression - 2/28/09
Gone Country: Showtime - 3/7/09
The Boys: The Sherman Brothers' Story - 4/26/09
Hemispheres: A Documentary on Cerebral Palsy - 12/09
Angela and Friends: Episode #1.62 - 2/16/10
Who is Harry Nisson (and Why is Everybody Talkin' About Him?) - 9/10/10
Five Easy Pieces: BBStory - 11/23/10
What The - 1/1/11
Breakfast - 1/19/11
Mega Python vs. Gatoroid - 1/29/11
Iron Core Talk - 7/14/11
Jimi Hendrix: The Guitar Hero - 2011
How the Brits Rocked America: Go West: How the West Was Won - 1/27/12
Piers Morgan Tonight - 2/29/12
Today - 3/1/12
Good Morning America - 3/1/12
The 2012 Rock and Roll Hall of Fame Induction Ceremony - 5/5/12
Kevin Pollack's Chat Show - 10/28/12
Glen Campbell: The Rhinestone Cowboy - 1/18/13
Good Day L.A. - 2/25/13
From Broadway with Love: A Benefit Concert for Sandy Hook - 7/18/13
The Guys Who Wrote 'Em - 2/12/14
The Sixties: The British Invasion - 7/10/14
Oprah: Where Are They Now? - 11/9/14
Lennon or McCartney - 12/12/14
The Wrecking Crew - 3/13/15
Bagboy - 2/21/15
The Tonight Show Starring Jimmy Fallon - 9/24/15
WGN Morning News - 6/13/17
Mighty Magiswords: The Saga of Robopiggeh! - Wendell the Love Grub - 7/23/17
Difficult People: Fuzz Buddies - 9/5/17
Rerun It: Some Things Are Worth Repeating: - Micky Dolenz - Monkee Business - 4/11/18
Great Performances: Grammy Salute to Music Legends - 10/5/18
Studio 10 - 6/5/19
Let There Be Drums! - 2020

Micky Dolenz as director:
The Monkees: Mijacogeo - 3/25/68
Pop Gospel: Episode #1.1 - 2/13/79
Pop Gospel: Episode #1.2 - 2/20/79
Pop Gospel: Episode #1.3 - 2/27/79
Pop Gospel: Episode #1.4 - 3/6/79
Pop Gospel: Episode #1.5 - 3/13/79
Pop Gospel: Episode #1.6 - 3/20/79
Pop Gospel: Episode #1.7 - 3/27/79
Premiere: Story Without a Hero - 12/13/79
Metal Mickey: Metal Mickey Lives - 9/6/80
Metal Mickey: School Master Mickey - 9/13/80
Metal Mickey: Mickey Takes Money - 9/20/80

Metal Mickey: Taking the Mickey - 9/27/80
Metal Mickey: Hiccy Mickey - 10/4/80
Metal Mickey: Top Secret Mickey - 10/11/80
Metal Mickey: Mickey in Love - 10/18/80
Metal Mickey: Music Man Mickey - 10/25/80
The Box - 4/12/81
Metal Mickey: It Came From Outer Mickey - 9/5/81
Metal Mickey: A Girlfriend for Mickey - 9/12/81
Metal Mickey: Goodbye Mickey - 9/19/81
Metal Mickey: Football Crazy Mickey - 10/3/81
Metal Mickey: Marshal Mickey - 10/24/81
Gateway to the South - 11/81
Metal Mickey: Merry Christmas Mickey - 12/19/81
Metal Mickey: Panto Mickey - 12/26/81
Murphy's Mob - 1982
Metal Mickey: Maturity Mickey - 9/18/82
Metal Mickey: A Night Out with Mickey - 9/25/82
Metal Mickey: Go Away Mickey - 10/2/82
Metal Mickey: Fancy Mickey - 10/30/82
Metal Mickey: The Incredible Shrinking Mickey - 11/20/82
Metal Mickey: Mickey to the Rescue - 1/1/83
No Problem!: Chicken Toshiba - 1/14/83
No Problem!: Radio Runnings - 1/21/83
Luna: Habivron Sweet Habivron - 1/22/83
No Problem!: The Dub - 1/28/83
Luna: The Clunkman Cometh - 1/29/83
No Problem!: Noah, Noah - 2/11/83
No Problem!: Hot Chocolate - 2/18/83
No Problem!: The Willesden One - 2/25/83
Luna: When Did You See Your Peter Batch Mix Donor? - 2/26/83
For 4 Tonight: Episode #1.1 - 10/1/83
For 4 Tonight: Episode #1.2 - 10/8/83
For 4 Tonight: Episode #1.3 - 10/15/83
For 4 Tonight: Episode #1.4 - 10/22/83
For 4 Tonight: Episode #1.5 - 10/29/83
For 4 Tonight: Episode #1.6 - 11/5/83
Television Parts - 1985
From the Top: Episode #1.1 - 9/23/85
From the Top: Episode #1.2 - 9/30/85
From the Top: Episode #1.3 - 10/7/85
From the Top: Episode #1.4 - 10/14/85
From the Top: Episode #1.5 - 10/21/85
From the Top: Episode #1.6 - 10/28/85
Aladdin (TV Movie) - 1990
Boy Meets World: Turnaround - 12/16/94
Pacific Blue: Moving Target - 4/27/96
Boy Meets World: "Bee True - 4/9/99
Malpractice - 5/25/01

Davy Jones:
BBC Sunday-Night Play: Summer Theatre: June Evening - Benny Whittle - 7/10/60
Coronation Street: Episode #1.25 - Colin Lomax - 3/6/61
Magnolia Street: Episode #1.2 - Tommy Wright - 6/23/61

Z Cars: Four of a Kind - Willie Thatcher - 1/2/62
Z Cars: The Best Days - Frankie Sale - 4/10/62
Z Cars: On Watch - Newtown - Boy Footballer - 9/19/62
The Ed Sullivan Show: Episode #17.19 - The Artful Dodger - 2/9/64
Ben Casey: If You Play Your Cards Right, You Too Can Be a Loser - Gregg Carter - 12/27/65
The Farmer's Daughter: Moe Hill and the Mountains - Roland - 1/7/66
Rowan and Martin's Laugh-In: Episode #2.19 - 2/10/69
This is Tom Jones: Episode #1.2 - 2/14/69
The Andy Williams Show: Episode #1.6 - 10/25/69
The Peapicker in Piccadilly - 11/24/69
Letters to Laugh-In - 12/8-12/12/69
Love, American Style: Love and the Elopement - Ronald - 10/23/70
Make Room for Granddaddy: The Teen Idol - 11/30/70
Lollipops, Roses and Talangka - 6/5/71
The Brady Bunch: Getting Davy Jones - 12/10/71
The New Scooby-Doo Movies: The Haunted Horseman in Hagglethorn Hall - 12/2/72
Treasure Island - Jim Hawkins - 7/11/73 (theatrical); 4/29/80 (TV)
Love, American Style: Love and the Model Apartment - Ray - 11/30/73
Oliver Twist - The Artful Dodger - 7/10/74 (theatrical); 4/14/81 (TV)
The Wonderful World of Disney: The Bluegrass Special - Davey Sanders - 5/22/77
Our Show - 12/17/77
Tiswas: Episode #4.21 - 1/28/78
Horse in the House: Stable Girl, Part 1 - Frank Tyson - 3/12/79
Horse in the House: Stable Girl, Part 2 - Frank Tyson - 3/19/79
The Little and Large Show: Episode #4.5 - 1/14/84
Blue Peter - 1/6/86
New Love, American Style: Love-a-Gram; Love and the Apartment - 1/10/86
Sledge Hammer!: Sledge, Rattle and Roll - Jerry Vicuna - 1/15/88
My Two Dads: The Wedge - Malcolm O'Dell - 2/7/88
My Two Dads: Fallen Idol - Malcolm O'Dell - 2/15/89
ABC Afterschool Special: It's Only Rock and Roll - Albert Lynch - 3/22/91
Trainer: No Way to Treat a Lady - Steve Moorcroft - 11/24/91
Herman's Head: The One Where They Go on the Love Boat - 11/22/92
Boy Meets World: Rave On - Reginald Fairfield - 11/17/95
Lush Life: The Not So Lush Rock Star - Johnny James - 10/14/96
The Single Guy: Davy Jones - 11/21/96
Hitz: It Ain't Over Till... - 9/2/97
Sabrina, the Teenage Witch: Dante's Inferno - 10/10/97
Hey Arnold!: Gerald's Game/Fishing Trip - 4/27/02
Sexina: Popstar, P.I. - 11/6/07
Spongebob Squarepants: Spongebob Squarepants vs. The Big One - 4/17/09
The Dreamsters: Welcome to the Dreamery - 2011
Goldberg, P.I. - 2011
Beatles Stories - 4/11
Phineas and Ferb: Bad Hair Day/Meatloaf Surprise - Nigel - 6/24/11

Michael Nesmith:
The Lloyd Thaxton Show - 11/12/65
American Bandstand - 12/17/66
The Beatles: A Day in the Life - 1967
The David Frost Show - 10/14/71
The David Frost Show - 12/16/71
American Bandstand – 5/8/71

Top of the Pops - 3/31/77
Rio - 1977
Rock Concert - 8/11/77
Rock Concert - 6/20/80
Elephant Parts - various - 7/1/81
Late Night with David Letterman - 1/13/83
Saturday Night Live - Man in Black Hat - 1/10/81
Saturday Night Live - Man in Foreign Film - 1/24/81
An Evening with Sir William Martin - Foyer the Butler - 1981
Today - 12/2/82
Timerider: The Adventure of Lyle Swann - Race Official (uncredited) - 12/11/82
An All Consuming Passion - Academy Award Presenter - 11/14/84
Entertainment Tonight - 3/6/85
Today - 3/7/85
Michael Nesmith in Television Parts - Host, various - 1985
Episodes:
        March 7, 1985
        June 14, 1985
        June 21, 1985
        June 28, 1985
        July 5, 1985
Burglar - Cabby - 3/20/87
Showbiz Today - 6/22/87
Tapeheads - Water Man - 10/21/88
Headline News - 3/21/89
Crook and Chase - 3/21/89
Showbiz Today - 3/21/89
Crook and Chase - 3/8/90
Austin City Limits - 1/16/93
Showbiz Today - 1/27/93
AFI Life Achievement Award: A Tribute to Elizabeth Taylor - 5/6/93
Later - 12/1/94
KTLA Morning News - 1/25/99
Today - 1/30/99
Nesmith Live (1992) - 3/13/01
Making of Timerider - 3/19/13
Portlandia: 3D Printer - 4/20/14
Legends of Baja - 5/10/18
Biography: I Want My MTV - 5/1/19
Studio 10 - 6/5/19

Countryside Record releases (all 1973):
LPs:
Garland Frady: Pure Country - CS-101
Red Rhodes: Velvet Hammer in a Cowboy Band - CS-102

45s:
Garland Frady: A Good Love is a Good Song (promo only) - CS-45101
J.G. O'Rafferty: Cause I Have You / Sweet Heart - CS-45102
Tom Holbrook: Welfare Hero (promo only) - CS-45103
Garland Frady: The Barrooms Have Found You / Silver Moon - CS-45104
J.G. O'Rafferty: Sweet Heart / Cause I Have You - CS-45838

Pacific Arts Records releases (non-Nesmith):
LPs:
Kaleidoscope: When Scopes Collide - ILPA-9462 - 1976
Swami Nadabrahmananda: Swamiji - PACR7-105 - 1978
Biff Rose: Roast Beef - PAC7-108 - 1978
Joyce Yarrow: Jumping Mouse - PAC7-109 - 1977
Henry Wolff and Nancy Hennings: Tibetan Bells II - PACR-110 - 1979
Bhagavan Das: Ah - PACR7-111 - 1979
Rank Strangers - PAC7-112 - 1977
Hamza El Din: Eclipse - PACR7-119 - 1978
Zytron: New Moon in Zytron - PACB7-120 - 1978
Pacific Steel Company - PAC7-121 - 1978
Celebration - PAC7-122 - 1978
Charles Lloyd: Weavings - PAC7-123 - 1978
Biff Rose: Thee Messiah Album Live at Gatsby's - PAC7-127 - 1979
Ennio Morricone: Days of Heaven Soundtrack - PAC7-128 - 1979
Jet - PAC7-129 - 1979
Chris Darrow: Fretless - PAC7-132 - 1979
Kenneth Jenkins: DBA:Success - PAC7-133 - 1979
Deadly Ernest and The Honky Tonk Heroes: Michael Sheeler - PAC7-134 - 1979
Susan Muscarella: Rainflowers - PACB7-135 - 1980
Trefethen: Am I Stupid or Am I Great? - PAC7-136 - 1980
Mike Cohen: Moments - PACB7-137 - 1979
Michael Chapman: Life on the Ceiling - PAC7-138 - 1979
Charles Lloyd: Big Sur Tapestry - PAC7-139 - 1979
The Pirates: Hard Ride - PAC7-140 - 1980
The Mark-Almond Band: Best of Live - PAC7-142 - 1980
John Morris: The Elephant Man Soundtrack - PAC8-133 - 1981
Randy Morriss: Circle of Stone - PA-2001 - 1988
The Hellecasters: The Return of the Hellecasters - PAAC-5055 - 1993

45s:
Corky Carroll and the Cool Water Casuals: Tan Punks On Board / From Pizza Towers to Defeat - PAC45-103 -1979
Celebration: Starbaby / Getting Hungry - PAC45-105 - 1979
Tom Trefethen: Moving Blunders (March of the Marble People) (promo only) - PAC45-109 - 1980
Pacific Steel Company: Fat 'n Sassy / Rio - PAC45-111 - 1980

Peter Tork:
Wild in the Streets - ticket buyer - 5/29/68
California Dreams: Romancing the Tube - The Surf Guru - 11/14/92
Boy Meets World: Career Day - Jedediah Lawrence - 5/12/95
Boy Meets World: Rave On - Jedediah Lawrence - 11/17/95
Wings: She's Gotta Have it - 11/14/95
7th Heaven: No Sex, Some Drugs and a Little Rock 'n' Roll - Chris - 11/16/98
The King of Queens: Best Man - Band Leader - 11/11/99
7th Heaven: One Hundred - Chris - 1/29/01
Mixed Signals - Band Manager - 2001
Stella's Search for Sanity - Evil Acting Teacher - 5/5/03
Cathedral Pines - Mr. Geary - 6/06
The Junior Defenders - 10/23/07
I Filmed Your Death - David Lyndale - 2017 (unreleased)

Index

About the Authors

Mark Arnold is an animation, comic book and pop music historian with books on Harvey Comics, TTV (Underdog), Cracked Magazine, The Beatles, Disney, DFE (Pink Panther), Dennis the Menace, The Monkees to his credit. He is currently working on a TTV Scrapbook and eventually a book on Mad Magazine. He lives in Springfield, Oregon.

Michael A. Ventrella writes witty adventure novels and edits story anthologies, including the new "Across the Universe" which features fantasy stories about the Beatles. His short stories have appeared in various anthologies as well. He lives in the beautiful Pocono Mountains with his award-winning artist wife Heidi Hooper. In his spare time, he is a lawyer. His web page is www.MichaelAVentrella.com

About the Artist

For almost fifty years, **Scott Shaw!** has written and drawn underground comix (*Fear and Laughter, Gory Stories Quarterly*), mainstream comic books (*Captain Carrot and his Amazing Zoo Crew!, Sonic the Hedgehog, Simpsons Comics*), children's books (*Marooned Lagoon, Marooned Lagoon, Too!*) syndicated comic strips (Bugs Bunny, Woodsy Owl), graphic novels (*Shrek, Annoying Orange*), TV cartoons (*Jim Henson's Muppet Babies, The Completely Mental Misadventures of Ed Grimley, Camp Candy*), toys (McFarlane Toys' line of Hanna-Barbera and Simpsons action figures), trading cards (Garbage Pail Kids, Oddball Comics), video games (also GPK), advertising (Pebbles Cereal commercials and print ads starring the Flintstones), and music package art (The Monkees' *A Barrel Full of Monkees* and *Justus*). His work has garnered him has four Emmy Awards, an Eisner Award, and a Humanitas Award. Scott also is known for his presentations of "the craziest comic books ever published", Oddball Comics Live! (with a long-awaited Oddball Comics book coming from TwoMorrows) and his regular participation in Quick Draw! with Mark Evanier and Sergio Aragonés. Scott was also one of the kids who created what is currently known as Comic-Con International: San Diego. https://www.shaw-cartoons.com/